22 Keys
to Creating
a Meaningful
Workplace

Tom Terez

Adams Media Corporation
Holbrook, Massachusetts

DEDICATION
To Angela, with love

✦ ✦ ✦

Published by
Adams Media Corporation
260 Center Street, Holbrook, MA 02343. U.S.A.

ISBN: 1-58062-266-6

Printed in the United States of America.

J I H G F E D C B A

Library of Congress Cataloging-in-Publication Data
Terez, Tom.
22 keys to creating a meaningful workplace / by Tom Terez.
p.   cm.
Includes index.
ISBN 1-58062-266-6
1. Job satisfaction. 2. Psychology, Industrial. 3. Work environment.
4. Industrial management—Psychological aspects.
I. Title: Twenty-two keys to creating a meaningful workplace. II. Title.
HF5549.5.J63 T47   2000
650.1--dc21   00-028872
CIP

This publication is designed to provide accurate and authoritative information with regard to
the subject matter covered. It is sold with the understanding that the publisher is not engaged
in rendering legal, accounting, or other professional advice. If legal advice or other expert assistance is required, the services of a competent professional person should be sought.
—From a *Declaration of Principles* jointly adopted by a Committee of the American Bar
Association and a Committee of Publishers and Associations

This book is available at quantity discounts for bulk purchases.
For information, call 1-800-872-5627.

Visit our exciting small business Web site: www.businesstown.com

TABLE OF CONTENTS

FOREWORD

I am on an extended sabbatical, basking in a new state which I describe as being a "harmless, amusing eccentric." I am still trying to define what an extended sabbatical is. And I find it a challenge, becoming "harmless and amusing," to say nothing of "eccentric." But I like the phrase and I'm sticking with it.

One way I have used my semi-retirement is to read a little and comment on what I have read. Among my readings is Tom Terez's book 22 *Keys to Creating a Meaningful Workplace*.

22 *Keys* is a lively and easy-to-read compendium of what-to-dos, how-to-do-its, and how-to-think-about-its. It's filled with stories and examples gleaned from Tom's numberless interviews and experiences. These stories have points—good old-fashioned morals—that teach helpful things to do and things that should be avoided.

Tom's book is an obvious recommendation for CEOs and middle-managers, but I can see an additional readership: the ordinary workers. They will see in this book stories about people like themselves, and one of the first things they will conclude is, "See! We aren't crazy! These same things have been experienced by others!" Ordinary employees working for ordinary companies will thus feel reassured.

This book also contains examples of companies with benevolent policies, delightful workplaces. And there are the opposite—onerous workplaces with malignant policies—and many in between. All of these stories can be discussed by ordinary workers, perhaps in small brown-bag dialogue groups, and the brief "reality checks" that conclude each chapter can be used to enrich the conversation. This will allow employees to do with this book whatever they are ready to do. Individually each worker will change, and there is likely to be a dramatic collective transformation as well. It is critical that thought-provoking leaders such as Tom Terez provide the impetus for this transformation.

I am troubled by what might be called the "re-dehumanization" of the workplace. During the mid-1980s there appeared to be a rethinking of the American workplace. Fostered by W. Edwards Deming's philosophy and other contributors, we rediscovered such values as honesty and integrity. There seemed to be a return to workplace civility and decency. And then it seemed to go away. The quality movement has been reduced to a fad, or so it appears. Many reprehensible practices of American management—such things as quotas, MBO, performance appraisals, creating competition among workers—have crept back into practice. (Indeed, many had never stopped doing these things, but it was commonplace to at least question their usefulness.) In fact, the worst of American practices have been exported to Japan.

Buoyed by the optimism of the U.S. economy and the lackluster performance of the previously unstoppable Japanese economy, there has been a troubling trend (with some wonderful exceptions) in which American management has grown complacent once again. With this complacency has developed an almost smug reassurance in the rightness of American management. Thus what I call the re-dehumanization of our workplaces.

Tom Terez's book will help us look at what we are doing—and what we should be doing differently. His voice needs to be joined with hundreds of thousands of others. *22 Keys to Creating a Meaningful Workplace* is a welcome addition to the literature. Those who read it will be armed with new inspiration and tools. We should all be grateful for this worthy contribution.

Peter R. Scholtes
Bestselling author of *The Team Handbook* and *The Leader's Handbook*

From 1987 to 1993, Peter Scholtes shared the platform with W. Edwards Deming, helping to educate corporations about the new philosophy of the Quality movement. He was one of the first to synthesize the principles of the organizational development field with the teachings of Dr. Deming.

ACKNOWLEDGMENTS

In my research for this book, I conducted interviews and focus groups with people from all walks of life. There are too many people to list here, and some of them want to remain anonymous, but you know who you are! Thanks so much for generously sharing your work-related experiences, hopes, and aspirations. You've given this book a firm grounding in reality.

Hundreds of others provided input through e-mails and informal conversations. Many of these people contacted me after learning about my work from an article, Web site, or conference presentation. In other cases, I approached them—in fact, just about everyone who came within 10 feet of me during the past few years got asked a question or two about their vision of a meaningful workplace. This wasn't research in the formal sense, but it certainly informed the book.

As I gathered all of this input, my network of colleagues helped in many different ways. Some of them served as sounding boards. Others invited me to their workplaces for learning-filled visits. Still others sent me articles, books, Web-site addresses, and other leads—all to enrich my research. Included are my friends in the All States Quality Forum, the Association for Quality and Participation, and the American Society for Quality. A special thanks to Linda Leto (Iowa), Bev Zylstra (Iowa), Jim Carlson (Oregon), Nathan Strong (South Carolina), Chuck Grubb (North Carolina), Barry Crook (Washington), Joe Sensenbrenner (Wisconsin), Todd Raphael (California), Anita Jennings (Ohio), Tamera Bryant (Ohio), and Laralyn Sasaki (Ohio).

My agent, Sheree Bykofsky, and her associate, Janet Rosen, saw the glimmer of a book in my original proposal. Both of you are a joy to work with, and I consider it an honor to be a part of your literary family.

Jere Calmes, Dawn Thompson, and their colleagues at Adams Media shepherded this book from the proposal to the finished form you're now holding. Jere and I had our first conversation by phone while I was in Las Vegas—an appropriate location because I consider myself so lucky to be working with him.

Then there's Angela, my wife. I don't know where to begin in describing Angela's contribution to these pages. An accomplished editor with a master's degree in journalism, she went through two versions of the manuscript with a very sharp red pencil. (This puts interesting strains on a marriage!) She helped me think through the concepts and structure of the book. And whenever I felt overwhelmed by the sheer enormity of the project, she gently reminded me that this book *would* get done and that it *would* make a difference. Thanks, Ang, for helping to make this project so meaningful.

INTRODUCTION

It is not enough to be busy; so are the ants.
The question is: what are we busy about?
—HENRY DAVID THOREAU

Eager to live a simple life, Thoreau moved away from "modern" society. He built a cabin by Walden Pond and immersed himself in nature. And he wrote, leaving a legacy of reflection that seems even more relevant some 140 years later.

If Thoreau could see us today, he would surely rush back to the pond. Cell phones, pagers, e-mail, and computers keep us hopping. The average time spent at a full-time job per year has climbed by 180 hours in the past two decades. Even the newest, most popular magazine about organizations is aptly titled *Fast Company*.

Ironically, we spend a lot of our time trying to make better use of our time. Many organizations have gone through the rational, but ultimately futile, exercise of moving around the "manageable" pieces of divisions and work units. Others have opted for feel-good slogans and cheerleading. Still others have focused exclusively on teams or measurement or something else, only to find that the richness of most workplaces defies one-track anything.

What *are* we busy about? Is it just motion, or does it make a difference? Is it just work, or is it something more? Does it keep only our hands occupied, or does it engage our hearts and minds as well?

What You Can Expect

Throughout this book, you'll develop your own answers as you learn all about the keys to a meaningful workplace. You'll make important discoveries about yourself, your colleagues, and your organization. You'll explore a wide range of action ideas, and in the process, you'll figure out better ways to bring out the best in yourself and the people around you.

The first two chapters lay the groundwork, describing why a meaningful workplace is so important and providing an overview of the 22 "meaning keys." Then it's on to an in-depth look at the keys. Each is covered in a complete chapter that's more like an intensive workshop. They're grouped into five sets: mission keys, people keys, development keys, community keys, and me keys.

The last two chapters are all about workplace transformation. You'll get practical guidance on creating an action plan, achieving early progress, and maintaining forward momentum. You'll also receive an invitation to join a growing community of people who want to keep learning together as they create meaningful workplaces. In that sense, the end of this book can be a beginning.

The content and format are guided by three fundamental beliefs:

THERE ARE NO QUICK ANSWERS

> Complex problems have simple, easy-to-understand wrong answers.

Being so busy, we all like shortcuts: the five easy steps, the simple formula, the quick fix. But when it comes to creating a meaningful workplace, there *are* no shortcuts. The material on these pages is presented in a simple, straightforward fashion—but it's by no means simplistic.

ENRICHING THE WORKPLACE IS EVERYONE'S BUSINESS

Specialization can lead to division. Yet there are books just for supervisors, just for CEOs, just for mid-level managers, just for front-line employees, just for senior executives, just for people who work in human resources, and so on. This book is written for *all* these people because they all play an important role in the overall workplace system. Whoever you are, wherever you are, expect to find rich ideas in the pages ahead. Use them to open a dialogue with your colleagues, whatever their titles or positions, so you can create a meaningful workplace together.

WISE ACTION BEGINS WITH REFLECTION

Our hurried world has a bias toward action. *Just do it.* We try one thing, then another, then another, creating the illusion of progress from all of our motion but never quite getting the results we had hoped for. This book urges you to take your time. Reflect on the 22 meaning keys, analyze what's going on in your workplace, then uncover those several significant actions that will make a difference. *Just do it, but think deeply first.*

How This Book Came to Be

Work and workplaces have been on my mind for several decades, ever since my first paying job delivering the *Cleveland Press* to 40 homes in a northern Ohio suburb. I should have checked my *Farmer's Almanac* before joining the workforce because that long ago November proved to be colder than normal, and December was colder still. But nothing compared to January, which marked the beginning of the coldest and snowiest Cleveland winter in years.

I spent my earliest work months hauling newspapers through knee-deep snow, during which I had way too much time to reflect on this concept of employment. I learned the fine art of complaining and acquired the ability to put those papers in milk chutes and mailboxes without devoting a single point of IQ to the task. As far as emotions were concerned, those were stirred primarily when Boscoe, the demonic collie, broke free of his chain and "greeted" me curbside. To say the least, this was an inauspicious way to begin a lifetime of work. I wasn't reading Thoreau at the time, but I sure did wonder: What *am* I busy about?

I'll spare you the details of my job at McDonald's (major burn on the fish fryer), or my job at a discount department store (first male cashier), or my job as a daily newspaper reporter (never got used to the deadlines), or my job as a starving college student preparing afternoon teas for the math professors (I'd eat half of the coffeecake while setting up). I took a path (or the path took me) that's followed by millions of people. Then I helped launch a magazine, and when my entrepreneurial energy ran seriously low, I decided to go back to school for more business skills.

> Happiness comes only when we push our brains and hearts to the farthest reaches of which we are capable.
> —LEO ROSTEN

My growing interest in workplaces led me to a management-consulting firm, where my projects focused on organizational change. That's when I began to obsess over this notion of the meaningful workplace. Why? Because my consulting work and research uncovered so few of them—and so many people seemed to want them. I went on to lead the Meaning at Work Project, an extensive series of interviews and focus groups with people from all walks of life. This book shares the many lessons and discoveries that emerged.

Thoreau set out to "live deliberately." It's a powerful vision, and it's what creating a meaningful workplace is all about. Welcome to the journey.

Tom

Tom Terez
Columbus, Ohio
On the Web: www.22Keys.com
E-mail: TomTerez@aol.com

PART ONE

THE MEANINGFUL WORKPLACE

Chapter 1

A Meaningful Workplace Starts with You

You're going to spend about ninety thousand hours of your life at work. This assumes an average life span and full-time employment, but cut it in half and you still have a staggering number. And there's more. Add in time getting ready for work, commuting, and doing work at home, and the figure climbs to well over one hundred thousand hours. *That's more than one third of your waking adult life.*

It's amazing how work can creep into all the other hours. Do you ever find yourself in a wonderfully scenic location— say, on an outcropping that overlooks the Grand Canyon— when it suddenly pops into your head? "That report, that damn report! When are we going to get those figures from the finance office?" Or you're desperate to park in front of the TV for a half hour of mindless decompression when the briefcase suddenly seems to get a voice: "Open me," it says. "I have work for you that must be done by tomorrow morning!"

If we're going to spend all that time in the workplace, along with time virtually at the workplace, it better be meaningful. It is *not* asking too much to stand up and declare: I want a workplace that engages not only my hands, but also my heart and mind!

So there's the personal imperative. But what is the benefit to the organization as a whole? Why should *we* pursue this?

> Any mention of weekend seems to comfort people. "Good weekend?" "Have a good weekend?" People like anything with weekend in it. Thursday's good for "One more day," which usually prompts the easy "You said it" rejoinder.
>
> —JERRY SEINFELD, from *SeinLanguage*

The short answer has several parts:

Recruitment: A meaningful workplace attracts great people.

Retention: It fosters a deep sense of loyalty among the people who work there.

Performance Excellence: It brings out the best in these people . . .

Quality: . . . so they can deliver the best stuff (products and services) in the best ways (processes and systems) to their customers.

Customer Loyalty, Market Share, Revenue: And it results in thrilled customers who can't wait to come back.

Yes, a truly meaningful workplace does all that. What's good for the heart and mind is also good for the bottom line.

> This isn't just a nudge toward a more meaningful workplace—it's a full body slam.

The Search for Talent

For proof, look at McKinsey & Co.'s major study of 77 companies and 6,000 managers and executives. Their concluding report affirmed that people are now the prime source of competitive advantage. (That's right, not capital, not technology, not strategy—*people*.) It emphasized that the demand for talented people will continue to soar while the supply steadily dwindles, all of which will stoke a war for talent. This isn't just a nudge toward a more meaningful workplace—it's a full body slam.

According to Ed Michaels, a McKinsey director who helped lead the study, "Only 60 percent of the corporate officers . . . said they were able to pursue most of their growth opportunities. They have good ideas, they have money—they just don't have enough talented people to pursue those ideas." Another shocker: "Of the executives we surveyed, 75 percent said that their companies either don't have enough talent sometimes or are chronically short of talent."

What can companies do to get those talented people? Provide "a great company and a great job," Michaels says. "When they talk about a great company, they mean one that's well-managed, that has terrific values, and has a great culture." In other words, a meaningful workplace. (For more on the McKinsey study, where these and other comments from Michaels appear, check out the August 1998 issue of *Fast Company*.)

"You Don't Want to Leave"

Of course, after you get great people, there's the challenge of keeping them. My research into the cost of turnover turned up wide-ranging figures, in part because there are so many factors that feed into the equation. The U.S. Labor Department estimates that it costs about 33 percent of a new recruit's annual salary to replace a lost employee. Another common formula pegs it at 25 percent of an employee's annual salary plus 25 percent of the benefits cost.

In a study of 206 medium- to large-size companies, conducted by consulting firm William M. Mercer, nearly half the respondents said that turnover costs them more than $10,000 per employee—and one in five companies put the cost at more like $30,000. There are many more studies, all concluding that the cost of turnover has lots of zeros behind it.

The huge hedge against turnover—perhaps the only hedge against it—is a great place to work. That's the message coming loud and clear from *Fortune* magazine's annual collection of "100 Best Companies to Work for in America." Ken Alvares, Human Resource (HR) chief at Sun Microsystems, said in the 1998 *Fortune* report: "Our goal is to keep people so busy having fun every day that they don't even listen when the headhunters call." And Floyd Williams, a senior production manager at sports-equipment maker K2, had this to say in *Fortune*'s 1999 article: "When you get used to a certain level of freedom and excitement, you don't want to leave." By the way, close to half of the organizations on the 2000 list had turnover rates in the single digits.

> **Focusing on the Best**
> For some great examples of meaningful workplaces, turn to *Fortune* magazine's yearly report on the "100 Best Companies to Work for in America." The special issue comes out each January—just in time for people who want to establish some New Year's resolutions for positive workplace change.

The Value of a Meaningful Workplace

What about the very bottom of the bottom line? Does a meaningful workplace help with something like revenue growth?

Sears knows the answer. Back in 1992, the retail giant was on the ropes, with net losses of $3.9 billion on sales of $52.3 billion. Desperation prompted an all-out push to reinvent the organization, and as outsiders (many of them from Wall Street) watched, the company radically changed its strategies.

On the inside, however, something even more fundamental was under way. The entire organization began to adopt a new employee–customer–profit

> If we can find meaning in work, we can keep ourselves recharged, and the organizations we work for stand a chance of staying renewed themselves.
> —Robert H. Waterman

model aimed at turning Sears into a "compelling place to work, shop, and invest." Just another well-turned slogan? Not in this case. The Sears team went far beyond words, launching a massive effort to understand the causal link between employee attitudes, employee retention, customer service, customer satisfaction, customer retention, and financials like revenue growth.

And did they ever find a link! An 800-store analysis determined that a five-point improvement in employee attitudes regarding their jobs and the company drives an improvement of 1.3 points in customer satisfaction, which in turn *drives a 0.5 percent improvement in revenue growth.* "If we knew nothing about a local store except that employee attitudes had improved by five points on our survey scale, we could predict with confidence that if revenue growth in the district as a whole were 5 percent, revenue growth at this particular store would be 5.5 percent." That's according to three Sears executives who tell the full story in the January/February 1998 issue of the *Harvard Business Review.* This is must reading for anyone who doubts the bottom-line impact of an enriched workplace.

If you're a hardened Wall Street veteran, you still might be skeptical. Well, the folks from *Fortune* took their 1999 "best" list, pulled out the 55 companies whose stocks had been publicly traded for at least five years, and compared their results to those of the Russell 3000, whose stocks are comparable. Wouldn't you know, over the same five-year period, *Fortune's* 55 best companies had an average annual appreciation of 25 percent—well ahead of the 19 percent gain by the Russell index.

And note this: A study by Ernst & Young's Center for Business Innovation found that "people factors" are getting more attention from investment portfolio managers. In a list of 39 nonfinancial criteria investors use to pick stocks, the "ability to attract and retain" talented employees is right up there in the top five.

Time for a Reality Check

Here's a common retort: "Sure, we need to attract and hold onto great employees, and we need to crank out great quality. But our workplace is just fine."

Maybe it is, and maybe it isn't.

According to a major study by Hewitt Associates, 66 percent of employees are satisfied with their workplace culture. It sounds pretty good until you pull out your calculator. Let's see, 34 percent are less than satisfied . . . and there are about 131 million people age 16 and over working in America . . . which means that we could be talking about 45 million people who are at least somewhat dissatisfied with their workplace culture.

Then there's the Hay Employee Attitude Survey, in which 28 percent of the respondents said their companies "take employees' interests into account." That's 28 percent as in *only* 28 percent. Go back to the calculator for a reality check: 94 million working Americans just might feel that they're getting second-class treatment on the job.

What about fairness? Data from the Towers Perrin Workplace Index show that the glass is more than half full, with 56 percent of respondents agreeing that "in general, workplace policies are administered fairly." Of course, if you're one of the 44 percent who disagree, the glass is bone dry.

And look at findings from the Watson Wyatt WorkUSA survey: 61 percent of respondents are satisfied with their jobs, half of them are satisfied with the company as a whole, yet only 36 percent say their opinions and suggestions are heard. The numbers speak for themselves.

You hear a lot about job satisfaction. In fact, some surveys show that most people are "satisfied" with their "jobs." But think about the language. "Satisfied" is a lot like your minimum daily requirement—it keeps you going, but that's about it. Some surveys have a narrow focus, zeroing in on people's immediate work—as opposed to their workplace. In effect, they ignore the context in which the jobs are occurring. There's a world of difference between "I'm satisfied with my job" and "my workplace is deeply fulfilling." And a world of difference in the bottom-line impact.

> ### Honk If You Agree
> These four bumper stickers pretty much sum up how many people feel about work:
>
> *Monday is an awful way to spend one-seventh of your life.*
>
> *Monday is the root of all evil.*
>
> *Hard work has a future. Laziness pays off now.*
>
> *Relax. Only dread one day at a time.*

The Meaning at Work Project

In the 1980s, as the total-quality movement got under way, I thought that TQM (and its various spin-offs) would be the salvation for people who wanted more than just "job satisfaction." And in fact, with its core principle of employee

A Daily Dose of Dilbert

For some people, the cartoon character Dilbert puts in pictures exactly what's on their minds—and it ain't pretty. If you need proof that our workplaces are crying out for renewal, check out the latest Dilbert strip.

Book Group

Wondering how to get your colleagues thinking and talking about meaningful workplaces? Here's something you can do right now: Create a book discussion group. Participants can read a chapter or two of this book each week, and then come together to talk about things.

If it's difficult to find the time, get together over lunch. As for what to talk about, don't worry—you'll find plenty of dialogue-starting questions in the upcoming pages.

involvement, the quality movement has given many people a fuller work life. Yet nearly two decades after Dr. Deming's pioneering work with Ford, a remarkable number of employees still report that their work and workplaces leave them unfulfilled. Their hands are still in motion, but their hearts and minds remain unengaged—despite all sorts of new concepts, tools, techniques, and so-called best practices.

I searched libraries, bookstores, and the Internet for anything and everything even remotely related to meaningful workplaces. Much of what's out there is based on a first-person perspective ("My 40-year career has convinced me that . . . "). There also is plenty of theory ("Based on Maslow's Hierarchy of Needs . . . ") and a fair number of pump-you-up books ("Wake up and tell yourself: This is going to be a great day!"). What I had in mind was something more down to earth and practical. And when I couldn't find it on the shelf, I decided to find it in the field. Thus began the Meaning at Work Project.

Through fifteen focus groups and an extensive series of one-on-one interviews, I heard from people from all walks of life—and all walks of work. All told, they accounted for 3,000 years of work experience. Our research conversations explored every facet of the meaningful workplace issue. I asked participants: How do you define "meaningful workplace"? How does "fulfillment" differ from "satisfaction"? What was your most meaningful work experience and why? Your least meaningful? How can people find more meaning in their work lives?

These and other questions always stirred an engaging and revealing conversation. People were eager—in some cases almost desperate—to talk. A typical comment: "I wish we'd have conversations like this back where I work."

Following the research phase, I spent months poring over my notes, listening to audiotapes of the focus groups and interviews, going back to the notes, pondering, and analyzing. There seemed to be so much information—and no pat answers, easy formulas, or cookbook approaches to creating a meaningful workplace. But I *did* find something of tremendous value: the 22 keys. The next chapter provides a complete overview, along with an immediate opportunity to put the keys to work.

Time to Make Some Promises . . . to Yourself

To set the stage for reading this book and turning its words into action, give the following statements some serious thought.

1. *Within my area of influence, I would like to see the workplace transform from an environment in which:*

   _____
   _____
   _____
   _____

   . . . into an environment in which:

   _____
   _____
   _____
   _____

   Once you put your thoughts in writing, you'll feel an immediate tension between what is and what could be. Hold onto it. This same tension will be an important source of energy once you start taking action.

2. Of course, most visions tend to be on the hazy side. That's why this next prompt is so important—it's a chance to bring your vision into clearer focus.

   Thinking in very practical terms, here is what would be happening in my work-place if this transformation took place:

   _____
   _____
   _____

3. It's only natural to think of other people as the barriers to our great plans. Well, deep down, we all know that a fair share of obstructionism can be found within ourselves. That's the bad news. The good news is that you can control you! Use the next fill-in statement to do some honest self-analysis, then develop a goal for nipping any self-defeating tendencies in the bud.

When it comes to workplace change, I myself might be an obstacle because I tend to:

_____

_____

_____

_____

I plan to address this by:

_____

_____

_____

_____

4. A great way to learn is by teaching. And the surest way to achieve positive workplace change is by making it a collective effort. You can use both of these principles to your advantage by sharing the information from this book with your colleagues. List the names of at least three people, and plan to start a conversation with them about meaningful workplaces the first chance you get.

I will talk about the insights from this book with:

_____

_____

_____

Chapter 2

A Quick Course on the 22 Meaning Keys

At first, Dwayne thought it was just a crazy rumor. No way would management do that! Then some construction people started walking around . . . looking . . . taking notes . . . blueprints in hand. And within two months, there it was: a second-story platform circling the plant floor, so management could keep an eye on operations. "The managers would stand up there on the walkway, leaning on the railing, just watching us," Dwayne said. "We'd be on the floor working our tails off, and they'd be up there in their ties staring down."

My field research had brought the two of us together. Dwayne was one of the first people I interviewed, and as he told his story, his hands trembled. He was sick and tired of being watched all day by management. Sick and tired of the work and the company and the whole damn system. His story put a grim face on the concept of top-down management.

> I heard about hundreds of workplaces and workplace situations. They ran the full range, from depressing to downright inspiring.

As the research unfolded, I heard about hundreds of workplaces and workplace situations. They ran the full range, from depressing to downright inspiring. Each conversation provided clues into the essential elements of a truly fulfilling workplace. Here are more samples straight from my files.

For years, many of the clerical employees at Joan's government agency ended up in limiting jobs with low pay scales. Joan and her colleagues teamed up and worked to change things, redesigning the system to create paths to other administrative positions within the civil-service system. Inspired by a committed leader, a clear vision, and an open field for creativity, the team pursued its work with passion. Then the results began to come in, and that's when team members found the deepest meaning in their work. "We saw people grow from this," Joan said. Today, 20 years later, she often encounters people who went through the program and are now leaders in government. "It's so rewarding."

True Stories about Real People

The pages ahead are filled with anecdotes—you'll find them sprinkled in the margins of Chapters 3–24. These stories were gathered during the interviews and focus groups for this book. They're a powerful reminder that the workplace is fundamentally about people.

As the systems chief at a graphic-design firm, John has plenty to keep him busy. So he had to bite his tongue—and keep biting it for a full hour—during an unforgettable manager's meeting. A couple of employees had recently shown up late for work, and top management wanted a solid rule. So the meeting had been set up to define "late." One supervisor kept insisting it was 20 minutes, while others thought 10 minutes. Then a coalition started building around five minutes, and the debate raged on. They eventually settled on a time and ordered up a new written policy. "It was ridiculous," John said. "My only goal during that conversation was to make sure the new policy included the words 'to be applied at the manager's discretion.'"

The 20-person insurance company where Amy works has a policy manual, and she can quote from it chapter and verse. But that manual is hardly the organizational be all and end all. "We are obsessed with our customers," Amy said. "We're totally mission-driven. The rules are sort of there in the background." After one of Amy's colleagues got married and bought a house, he asked for a change in his salary-commission mix. A written policy stated a recommended balance, but it was just that— a recommendation. "He was able to get a larger base and a smaller commission because he wanted the extra income security," Amy said. "It was no big deal. We talk about valuing employees, and that's what this was all about."

The Meaning Keys

With a scientist's rigor, I analyzed the major ideas from two years' worth of interviews and focus groups. Then I pulled these together, careful to preserve the nuanced differences. A mix of tools, including results mapping and affinity diagrams, helped along the way. Themes began to emerge, and the more I analyzed, the clearer things became.

The analysis ultimately uncovered 22 key ingredients to a meaningful workplace—referred to throughout this book as the meaning keys. They divide into five sets of related keys: mission keys, people keys, development keys, community keys, and me keys. Each set speaks to a different workplace priority.

THE MISSION KEYS
Purpose, Direction, Relevance, Validation

Throughout the interviews and focus groups, people talked about the importance of making a difference in their work lives. I had pretty much expected this—the narrow definition of "meaning" relates to purpose. But they took the idea of "mission" much further. They cited the need to create the future, pursue meaningful milestones, and spend time on mission-critical activities. And they stressed the value of seeing the fruits of their labor. As one person remarked, "The only thing better than having a mission is accomplishing a mission."

> Whereas the mission keys focus on what the organization does, the people keys are about valuing who does it.

THE PEOPLE KEYS
Respect, Equality, Informality, Flexibility, Ownership

Whereas the mission keys focus on what the organization does, the people keys are about valuing who does it. Throughout the research, respect and equality came up time and again from just about everyone as core principles of the meaningful workplace. (Dwayne's watchtower workplace comes to mind.) And with surprising frequency, so did informality and flexibility. A meaningful workplace puts people ahead of rules, policies, protocol, traditions, habits, organization charts, and other artificial constructs. It sees people as true partners who have freedom to collaborate, access information, make decisions, and improve how things are done.

THE DEVELOPMENT KEYS
Challenge, Invention, Support, Personal Development

This third set of keys is about valuing growth—the thoughtful growth of the business and the ongoing development of the people who make it happen. It acknowledges that development is not just a competitive requirement, but also a deep human need. People spoke passionately about wanting activities that call on their knowledge, skills, interests, imagination, and power to invent—and a workplace that makes improvement and innovation everyone's business. They also made clear that a meaningful workplace provides an open field for building active support networks and ensuring ongoing personal development.

The Community Keys
Dialogue, Relationship Building, Service, Acknowledgment, Oneness

The community keys affirm the importance of togetherness and collective effort. A meaningful workplace is a lot like a healthy social system, people said. It's filled with opportunities to engage in open dialogue, to nurture relationships, and to serve. There's also plenty of acknowledgment—not extrinsic rewards, but sincere appreciation. When this kind of social system is thriving, there's a profound sense of oneness. People see the parts, but they think and act in ways designed to benefit the whole.

The Me Keys
Self-Identity, Fit, Balance, Worth

Complementing the community keys, the me keys are all about valuing the individual. Again and again in the research, people talked about the importance of being able to be themselves, use their skills, express their unique styles, and follow their deep interests. They spoke of their need to fit—not to "fit in" in the conformist sense, but to understand and feel good about their fit in the bigger picture of the workplace. Balance also came up, confirming that a meaningful workplace doesn't require impossible tradeoffs between work and the rest of a person's life. All this leads to self-worth . . . bringing us full circle back to the very first meaning key, purpose.

On pages 17–19, you'll find brief descriptions of all 22 meaning keys. Think of this three-pager as an executive summary. You'll get much more information as the book unfolds. In fact, an entire chapter is devoted to each of the keys.

Key Connections

Some of the keys are "drivers" that cause or heavily influence other keys. For instance, dialogue can lead to relationship building, service, invention, direction, support, service, and other meaning keys. Respect feeds into service, support, balance, equality, self-identity, and worth.

By comparison, a key like worth is more like an outcome. It is largely shaped by activities related to many other keys, including purpose, validation, respect, equality, ownership, and acknowledgment.

There's a Reason for "Keys"

It's no accident that keys have been chosen as the metaphor for the essential ingredients of a meaningful workplace. Many conversations about fulfillment in the workplace start and end on a hazy, theoretical note. The meaning keys provide an essential measure of tangibility. People can literally get their hands on them.

> Many conversations about fulfillment in the workplace start and end on a hazy, theoretical note. The meaning keys provide an essential measure of tangibility.

They can also choose which keys are the most important to them. Everyone has a unique set of three or four top priorities when it comes to a meaningful workplace.

For John, the most important meaning keys might be respect, equality, dialogue, and balance. If all these keys exist in the workplace, he'll find it to be deeply fulfilling. His colleague, Karen, might share the equality key, yet have three others among her top priorities: challenge, personal development, and acknowledgment. For her, these are the most important factors that define a meaningful workplace.

Of course, a person's top keys are likely to change as the years go by. For an employee who becomes a brand-new parent, balance (the ability to strike the right blend between your work life and the rest of your life) is likely to become a crucial meaning key. For the person who moves to a new town where everyone's a stranger, the relationship building key might take on added importance.

Using the Keys to Understand

Because they're so tangible, the meaning keys can be used to understand what's happening in a workplace—and what's important to the people who are involved. This deep understanding is vital to anyone who wants to take wise action and truly make things better.

Remember Dwayne? I interviewed him as part of my research, and his story started this chapter. He's the person who worked in a manufacturing plant that had been encircled by a management watchtower. When you think about his story in terms of the meaning keys, you realize it's all about respect, equality, and oneness—or the lack thereof.

Then there was Joan, who helped start a program to give clerical employees more career opportunities in the civil-service system. She and her colleagues were truly mission-driven, and they ended up seeing the results of

Learning Together
Want to interact with
people from other
organizations who are
reading this book and
enriching their work-
places? A special Web
site (www.22Keys.com)
has been set up so you
can pose questions,
share ideas, gain
insights, and engage in
some virtual networking.

all of their work—two concepts that are captured in the meaning keys of purpose and validation.

John told about the management meeting to define "late." He couldn't believe that so many people would spend so much time grappling with this issue, and for him, the story sent a message (not a very good one) about issues of flexibility and relevance.

And last but not least, Amy told that wonderful anecdote about an insurance company where mission and people are most important, and the rules take a back seat. It's a story that combines all sorts of meaning keys: purpose, relevance, respect, flexibility, and support.

You don't know much about Dwayne, Joan, John, and Amy. But I'll bet you can tell from their stories, and from your new knowledge about the meaning keys, what is important to them when it comes to creating a meaningful workplace.

Your Most Important Keys

What about *you*? Which five or so meaning keys are *your* most important ingredients of a meaningful workplace? Go to the three-page summary on pages 17–19, and checkmark five or so of your top keys. You'll gain a deeper understanding of yourself, and you'll set the stage for the rest of this book.

The 22 Meaning Keys

MISSION KEYS

Purpose
+ The organization's underlying purpose involves more than just producing goods or services, making money, or even being the best in a given business.
+ There's a feeling widely shared among people that daily activities, even individual tasks, fit the theme of that larger purpose.

Direction
+ A compelling vision of the future draws people in a common direction.
+ People understand and are invested in goals and objectives that serve as a meaningful, down-to-earth complement to the vision.

Relevance
+ People spend their time on activities that are relevant to the mission.
+ Rules and red tape are kept to an absolute minimum.

Validation
+ Individuals can see the impact of their work.
+ Even when people produce intangibles, they have opportunities to see how their work benefits others.

PEOPLE KEYS

Respect
+ People show respect for one another regardless of rank and title.
+ The golden rule is an implicit working principle throughout the organization.

Equality
+ People throughout the workplace genuinely feel that they're on the same level, regardless of titles and positions.
+ All individuals are considered to be equally important, and actions back this up.

Informality
+ An open-door policy is practiced by everyone, not because the business books encourage it, but because it simply seems like the right thing to do.
+ It's not unusual for a major project to turn into a major pizza party—with the work still getting done.

Flexibility
+ Good judgment is used in applying rules. People accept the subjectivity that goes along with this.
+ If a rule, policy, or procedure stands in the way of awesome service to a customer, people do what's best for the customer.

Ownership
+ People view themselves as owners of their work and act accordingly.
+ Change is done *by* people instead of *to* people. Co-creation is the method of choice for setting direction, developing ideas, and seizing opportunities.

DEVELOPMENT KEYS
Challenge
+ The workplace offers a wealth of challenges to employees who want them.
+ People understand what is meant by a *positive* challenge. It is not seen as piling on more work in order to get more done with less.

Invention
+ Risk-taking in the name of improvement and innovation is strongly encouraged.
+ Improvement and innovation are seen as everyone's business—and not the restricted domain of people with certain credentials or titles.

Support
+ People have access to all the resources they need to be successful in their work, such as information, time, funding, learning opportunities, and equipment.
+ Managers know when to get involved and when to stay out of the way. They offer help instead of imposing it.

Personal Development
+ The workplace provides people with all sorts of opportunities to learn and grow.
+ People take responsibility for their own personal development.

COMMUNITY KEYS
Dialogue
+ People widely recognize the benefits of engaging in constructive conversation.
+ People at all levels and in all areas of the organization have freedom and opportunities to talk among themselves about work-related problems, issues, and opportunities.

Relationship Building
+ People in the workplace understand the need to build strong relationships with each other.
+ Workdays are filled with opportunities to build relationships.

Service
+ People create all sorts of opportunities to help one another.
+ There's an organizational obsession with helping others to be successful. "Others" is broadly defined: colleagues, customers, the community.

Acknowledgment
+ Genuine appreciation is at the heart of all acknowledgment in the workplace.
+ Everyone helps bring acknowledgment to the workplace. It is not seen as something periodically "given" to people by management.

Oneness
+ There's a prevailing sense that "we're all in this together."
+ Working relationships are best described as collaborative, not competitive.

ME KEYS

Self-Identity
+ Differences are viewed as something that people can learn and benefit from, rather than something that must be "dealt with."
+ The workplace makes the most of people's unique know-how and skills.

Fit
+ Individual employees see how they and their work fit into the bigger mission of the organization.
+ People feel a good fit between their own values and the values of the workplace.

Balance
+ People can take work home if they want to—but they don't feel guilty if they choose otherwise.
+ There's an understanding and acceptance of the fact that employees will sometimes bring family concerns and other preoccupations to the workplace.

Worth
+ A belief is widely held that each and every employee is important to the organization.
+ People believe that the work they do is important and valued.

PART TWO

THE MISSION KEYS

We value what we do.

The Mission Keys

- Purpose
- Direction
- Relevance
- Validation

Purpose

Andy used to work in the printing plant of a big-city newspaper. It was dirty work— "literally the dirtiest I ever had," he says. The job was tough, the pay was average, and the press operators had to keep working through holidays. At the end of each shift, he'd spend the better part of 15 minutes trying to scrub the ink and grime off his hands. Yet today, 20 years and several jobs later, Andy's eyes light up as he recalls his years at the newspaper. "The way we saw it, we weren't just working a press or printing a newspaper, we were providing a service to the community," he says. "Sure, we complained about the conditions and all that, but we were on a mission." Ever since, Andy has been trying to find a workplace with the same deep sense of purpose. He now works as the marketing chief for a regional magazine, where his hands stay clean but his heart remains unengaged. "My colleagues and I are making the numbers, but shouldn't there be more to it than that?"

Andy makes a lot more money these days. His mortgage is paid off, he can go on a couple of vacations each year, and he just bought a boat. But as far as work is concerned, that's all it is for him—work. He sees it strictly as a series of tasks. His compensation arrives every other week in a No. 10 envelope, it's promptly deposited in the bank, and the cycle starts all over again. In some respects, Andy has become a machine, dutifully cranking out his "work units" but feeling completely dehumanized by it all.

> "My colleagues and I are making the numbers, but shouldn't there be more to it than that?"

Maybe he's ungrateful. After all, he's pulling down a hefty paycheck and cruising around in a brand-new 25-foot boat.

If you view fulfillment in monetary terms, sure he's ungrateful. But if you recognize that people want to feel some deep-down purpose in what they do—that money is not enough—it's easy to see where he's coming from. The desire to make a difference runs deep in the human spirit. Nearly everyone wants to feel that his or her work contributes to some greater good. That's what converts "work" into something bigger and better and more fulfilling.

In a meaningful workplace, this sense of making a difference is alive and well, and it's felt by everyone. Andy's long-ago dirty work at the newspaper plant certainly fit this bill. He and his colleagues weren't task-driven or rule-driven or efficiency-driven. More than anything, they were mission-driven.

> True happiness . . . is not attained through self-gratification, but through fidelity to a worthy purpose.
> —Helen Keller

As for his current situation, Andy needs to stop wringing his hands and start taking action. And if his story sounds even remotely familiar, you need to do the same. If you wait for purpose to pop up one day in the form of some flashing revelation, you'll be waiting a very long time. And purpose sure won't come along like a dental plan or annual bonus or some other new benefit. It needs to be nurtured. There are practical things you can do, on your own and with your colleagues, to transform work into more than just work.

Pose Some Purposeful Questions

First of all, climb off that hamster wheel of endless tasks and ponder whether you're making a difference. We're not talking about a few minutes of fleeting thought while waiting for the light to turn green. The idea is to spend some significant time evaluating this notion of purpose and how it factors into your work. Your discoveries might surprise you.

Here are several questions to jumpstart your thinking. Answer them in order, since they build on each other. Feel free to take mental notes, but it might be more eye-opening to jot down your answers on paper because the writing process will force you to get specific.

What do you do on a week-to-week basis? In other words, what is your "work"? List the activities that fill your typical week. You might even want to do a quick breakdown to show the approximate percentage of time spent on each task.

Who's on the receiving end of this work you do? In other words, who are your customers? Be sure to include the internal folks who count on you as the workweek unfolds. They're very much your customers. And if you start to get the feeling that you don't have any customers, try this: Imagine that an emergency calls you away from work for a full week. Who would miss your contribution while you're gone?

How do your customers benefit from your work? Don't sell yourself short here. You have customers because you're providing something that adds value. Even if what you do at work seems mundane, it's a fair bet that someone's counting on you. Again, if you're skeptical, imagine that you suddenly have to take the week off. What would happen?

How does all this fit into the big picture? Take things to the next level: Who are your customers' customers? In what ways does your work ultimately reach *them*? As you think about this, you'll begin to see just how interdependent we all are—and how those seemingly trivial tasks might actually be important in the bigger scheme of things.

It takes a fair amount of discipline to explore these questions. You almost have to suspend your skepticism and open yourself up to the possibility that what you do really does have some purpose. Your big challenge is to figure out how the work you do contributes to something greater than the tasks themselves.

Starting a Conversation on Purpose

Most folks want to pose these questions in the comfort and privacy of their own space. That's fine as a starting point, but if you're seriously lacking a sense of purpose, chances are you're not alone. Right there alongside you, some of your

---

"Show me the money!"
That was the catchphrase of *Jerry Maguire*, but as the movie unfolds, you learn that money is far less important than a deep sense of mission.

In the title role, Tom Cruise spends a highly caffeinated night coming to terms with his own purpose—or the lack thereof—as a sports agent. He ends up spilling his guts and spelling out his mission in a report titled "The Things We Think and Do Not Say," and he rushes off before sunrise to get copies for his 110 colleagues.

"What I was writing was a bit touchy-feely. I didn't care. I had lost the ability to bullshit. It was the me I always wanted to be."

Jerry spends the rest of the movie trying to live up to his written words. It's an exciting struggle that ends up transforming his life.

There's no need to be excessively formal here— no three-hour meetings around a solid-oak conference table, please.

colleagues probably feel the same way. Consider getting them in on a conversation about this notion of making a difference.

There's no need to be excessively formal here—no three-hour meetings around a solid-oak conference table, please. Make it as casual as possible so people will be comfortable opening up. The aim is not to conjure up a literary masterpiece of a purpose statement. Nor is it to coerce someone into seeing once and for all that there's merit to what they do. This conversation is intended simply to get people thinking and exchanging ideas.

The same questions you might ask on your own can be used with a group. Here they are again with a few minor adjustments. Just be sure to clarify the scope before things get rolling. In other words, determine ahead of time whether you're exploring the purpose of a job, a team, or a work unit— or something bigger, like a functional area, a region, or even the organization as a whole.

What do we do on a week-to-week basis? In other words, what is our "work"?

Who's on the receiving end? Who are our customers?

How do our customers benefit from our work?

How does all this fit into the big picture?

If you and your colleagues are pressed for time, you might want to cut to the chase with a single question. The bad news with this approach is that it can keep the conversation at the surface level. The good news is that you're at least talking and starting to put purpose on the collective radar screen. Make this the first in a series of conversations. And whatever you do, don't try to crunch all of your thoughts into a fast-food-equivalent mission statement. There's no need to write; just talk, listen, think, and explore.

Here's a simple prompt that's likely to open up the dialogue:

Why are we in business? What is our core reason for being?

Decide from the start whether "we" means a team, a work unit, a functional area, or something else. As far as responses are concerned, some people might say a work unit's purpose is "to make money" or, in the case of a public-sector organization, "to fill a statutory requirement." Urge people to reach beyond and identify a deeper explanation for why they're in business.

The Pitfalls of Statement Writing

While Andy was talking about his mission-filled days at the newspaper plant, and his more recent workplace with its seeming lack of purpose, he ruefully mentioned that he had been involved in writing a mission statement. Just two months earlier, he and about 20 of his colleagues had gone to a retreat site for a day's worth of facilitated conversation. They methodically went about the task of producing a vision statement, mission statement, goals, and objectives—all of which were efficiently typed up and circulated to the many employees who hadn't been included in the conversation.

The two hours spent developing a mission statement may have started with good intentions. But according to Andy, it quickly turned into a headache-inducing round of group writing. The conversation moved away from purpose and began to focus on the difference between commas and semicolons. Never again, he vows.

Andy experienced what has become epidemic across the country: a factory-like approach to purpose in which the primary aim is to crank out a mission statement. You've seen them hanging on office walls, you've read them in company brochures, you've noticed them in glossy ads. Perhaps you even have a laminated-card version tucked away in your wallet. They make for nice PR, but what do these paragraphs do for our sense of purpose? Hardly anything. In fact, by compacting the conversation into an hour or two of group writing, then mentally disposing of our output by hanging it on a wall, we risk seriously diminishing the sense of purpose. It trivializes the whole concept of making a difference.

So what to do? For starters, forget about doing like the Joneses. Not everyone needs a mission *statement*. Instead, think in terms of mission *conversations*. With a statement, you crank it out, tack it up, and it's done—and people go back to their tasks. With ongoing conversation, people are always exploring and reaching deeper levels of understanding. The ideas stay fresh. And perhaps most important, those who do the work get to renew their sense that all the tasks and activities really do contribute to some greater good.

Workplaces all over the country devote hours each week to meaningless reviews of numbers, schedules, rules, policies, and so on. A portion of

BELIEVE IT OR NOT

Get Us a Big Eraser

A team was formed to evaluate an organization's mission statement. As instructed in the team charter, the members were required to report their results in measurable terms.

The team worked and worked, wanting to do the right thing. They submitted a revised mission statement, along with a crisp declaration of their results: "We have reduced the statement from 35 words to seven words—an 80 percent improvement."

> Each of our acts makes a statement as to our purpose.
> —Leo Buscaglia

conversation time devoted entirely to purpose seems well worth it. If you're in a position to shape the agenda, start trimming down those one-way information dumps that can easily be plopped onto paper and provided as a handout. Use the time you save for something that defies easy crunching into a paragraph—namely, purpose.

If you can't set the agenda, perhaps you can influence it. Start an informal conversation away from the formal get-togethers as a way of stirring interest. Also consider proposing a one-time, one-hour conversation on purpose at an upcoming session—enough to get things started, but not enough to turn off the agenda-keeper. As that precious one hour winds down, ask your colleagues whether they'd like to keep the dialogue going. Have the group figure out how, and you're on your way.

Some Tough Love Regarding Purpose

Let's assume you try all the aforementioned and still find yourself coming up empty. Your work remains a series of tasks; you simply can't connect with a larger purpose. This is when you need to pose a question that's even more fundamental than the ones already provided:

Why do I feel that there's no real sense of purpose to my work?

Here are some possible responses, along with comments to stir your thinking. As you read, you'll realize why the title of this section refers to "tough love."

I don't have any customers.

If you don't, you're in a tiny minority. Just about everyone has a customer. It's simply a matter of thinking systemically and identifying the people who count on you to provide whatever it is you create as the workday unfolds. Perhaps you provide something like knowledge—it's not a product in a boxable sense, but it definitely adds value. Maybe you deliver a service—again, not as tangible as a product, but something that's just as important. If your best systemic thinking still turns up no customers, you'd better find some soon. They're essential for a deep sense of purpose—not to mention job security.

I might have customers, but I don't know who they are.

Imagine yourself being suddenly away from the workplace for an entire month. Who would be the first to notice? And what if you invoiced people directly for what you do at work? Who would get the bill? Start figuring out who these precious people are, and as soon as you do, engage them in dialogue to make sure what you're doing for them truly adds value.

My work simply isn't important. I could disappear from the workplace and no one would miss me.

Are you sure about that? Again, apply the one-month-away test and imagine how things would be. If you remain firmly convinced that your work is completely unimportant, you need to take on new challenges, and if they're not nearby in your current workplace, you might need to move on. The operative word here is "you." It's not up to your boss, or a significant other, or a mentor, or a neighborhood palm reader. You can get their opinions, to be sure, but you're the one who needs to make the decisions and take the action.

My work used to be important, but technology has made it irrelevant.

This one's relatively simple: Become an obsessive learner. Instead of letting yourself get blindsided by all this new technology, start reading and talking about it. Surf the Web. Start a discussion group. Take a college course. Attend a workshop. Ask a colleague for informal coaching. There are all sorts of possibilities. We'll talk more about this in the chapter on personal development.

I feel like a drone. My work has me doing the same thing over and over and over.

Plenty of people feel this way, but few of them do anything about it. You'll be the exception, right? Try to take on new activities, even if you have to do it one small step at a time, and even if it bumps up your

---

BELIEVE IT OR NOT

Mission: Invisible

In its reception area, a mortgage company had a framed wall-hanging that trumpeted its mission. "Our most important customer is the home-buyer," it said. "All our efforts are aimed at putting the home-buyer first."

This was good news indeed to the new customer who was waiting for his first meeting with a mortgage consultant. But when he mentioned the wall-hanging once inside the consultant's office, a silence filled the room.

"What mission statement?" the consultant asked. The one on the wall. "Which wall?" The consultant stood up and asked to see for herself. The customer happily led the way.

> Just because others seem to be money-driven doesn't mean you have to be as well.

workload. Balance it out by dumping those age-old tasks that no longer add value. If you're in a group where everyone does the same things, get folks talking about the current situation—and how things can be better. If you feel like a drone, they probably do, too. And they're probably just as eager to change things for the better.

Everyone here is so focused on making money; I can't see any other purpose.
First of all, you're making the blanket assumption that everyone is dollar obsessive. That might very well be the case, but unless you've engaged in open conversation about purpose with your colleagues, you really don't know. And just because others seem to be money-driven doesn't mean you have to be as well. You have a clear choice to make. Don't blame it on everyone else.

The people around me don't care about purpose or mission or making a difference or whatever you want to call it.
Again, it sounds like you're making a pretty big assumption. The truth is, most people want to have a positive impact. It's just that the system in which they work can make it difficult for them to do so. My suggestion is that you start talking with them about this notion of purpose. If it seems too daunting to assemble a group, make it a lunchtime topic with one of your workplace friends.

Are You Obsessed with Your Customers?

You may have noticed a certain word coming up time and again in this chapter: customer. That's because they're central to the purpose of most groups, teams, work units, whole organizations—and individuals. There's always someone at the receiving end of what we do. Even if you produce enormous castings that are shipped off to a factory, they're really going to the people who work in that factory and will be using that casting. Whatever service or product you help create, it follows that to deepen your sense of purpose, you need to get and stay in contact with your customers. Hearing from them on a regular basis keeps the mission alive and immediate.

One approach is to call at least one customer a day, ask how he or she is enjoying the product or service, then open your ears and mind to their feedback. If you're one of those fortunate people who have customers on-site—

yes, fortunate!—consider taking some time to engage them in a five-minute, face-to-face chat.

You're bound to get an occasional chewing-out from a disgruntled customer, and others may think you're being nosey. But most will supply you with useful feedback, and they'll appreciate the opportunity to give it. Even more important is that these conversations will steadily deepen your own sense of purpose. Skeptical? Try it for two weeks—at least one customer contact per day—and see for yourself.

If your workplace uses customer surveys, take them seriously and try to act on the input. But only after you've made sure the survey is worthwhile. Often they're simply public-relations gimmicks masking as serious data-collection tools, or they've been slapped together by folks who didn't do the necessary homework. If you think that's the case in *your* workplace, either set a process in motion to make the survey effective, or dump it entirely, or (if you can do nothing else) ignore the data.

Dare People to Make More of a Difference

You'll also want to make customers a regular focus of your conversations with colleagues. Here's an excellent question to add to the ones that were spelled out earlier in this chapter:

What can we as a group do to help our customers be more successful?

When this question is posed to people who are connected by a similar mission—say, everyone who works in the shipping department—the answers will be slow in surfacing. But once they start, expect a flood of ideas as everyone gets loosened up and starts thinking in terms of purpose. Also possible is a sort of backtracking in which other questions get raised: Who really are our customers? How can we do a better job of staying in touch with them? What have we heard from them lately? These are pivotal questions that call for

CAROLYN'S STORY

Listening to Carolyn talk, you quickly get the feeling that she cuts little slack in her work as a police officer. This is one cop who gives out tickets and not warnings.

Dig deeper, though, and you'll find a person who sees her real role as being a facilitator of positive change. "I have the power to become involved in others' lives," she says.

When responding to domestic disputes, for instance, Carolyn doesn't simply slap on the handcuffs and write a report. She also talks with the family and does her best to improve the long-term situation, even if it involves non-emergency visits back to the home.

"I have the power to assist them in creating change, no matter how difficult their lives are." This, she says, is the real source of meaning in her work.

thoughtful conversation. Explore them fully, but make a point of coming back to the action question: What can we do?

As this conversation winds down, it's important that people commit to at least one action—something new or different that will heighten the sense of purpose throughout the workplace. In all likelihood, several action ideas will emerge, with some calling for collective effort while others involve just one or two people. Put these action ideas—perhaps "action commitments" is a better term—in writing. Then agree on a future day and time when all of you can get together again to review your progress and pose the "What can we do?" question all over again.

Reality Check: PURPOSE

1 = very strongly disagree
2 = strongly disagree
3 = disagree
4 = neutral; neither disagree nor agree

5 = agree
6 = strongly agree
7 = very strongly agree

_____ The organization has a larger purpose—something beyond producing goods and services, making money, or even being the best in a given business.

_____ There's a feeling widely shared among people that daily activities, even individual tasks, fit the theme of that larger purpose.

_____ Customers figure prominently in people's understanding of why their workplace exists.

_____ Individuals feel that their work contributes to the greater good. It may be in small ways, but it still has a positive impact.

_____ The organization is truly mission-driven—as opposed to rules-driven.

_____ = Total ÷ 5 = _____ = PURPOSE RATING

Chapter 4

Direction

As the director of information systems for a fast-growing insurance company, Eileen uses a facilitative style to manage a team of 10 smart programmers and network experts. She likes her job, but she'd love to love it, and she quickly cites what it would take: a better sense of direction for herself, the team, and everyone else at the company. Right now, it appears that the place is making fast progress to. . . who knows where. "My work unit operates like its own company, and it's important to have that kind of freedom," Eileen says. "But all the work units would be better off if we knew where we were heading as a collective."

Direction seems so basic. You'd never get in your car and start driving around aimlessly; you always start with a destination. Most people even make direction setting the very first thing they do each year. A moment after the clock strikes midnight on December 31, they set a goal or two for themselves in the form of a New Year's resolution. We absolutely fill our lives with dreams and goals: buying that first house, improving our physical fitness, earning a degree, taking a vacation, raising wonderful children, and on and on.

> It appears that the place is making fast progress to . . . who knows where.

Purpose answers the "why" questions: Why am I doing this work? Why are we in business? It defines how we're making a difference today. Direction is all about making *more* of a difference *tomorrow*, and the next day, and the day after that. It answers the "what" questions: What do I want to create? What do we want to create together? What do we need to achieve on our way toward that vision? Think of it as a guidance system. A vision of the future gives you an inspiring, compelling destination. Goals and objectives are the checkpoints and mile markers. And strategies are your agreements on how you'll cover the distance.

Of course, having things like goals and objectives is a lot different from using them. Eileen explained that the CEO and CFO at her company do all the direction setting themselves. They spend a day each year deciding what everyone will pursue as the next 12 months unfold, then package the information into a memo that's sent to all managers. "The top two people decide where we're heading, but we're expected to drive the car," she says. Often she and her colleagues can't even figure out the destination, and when they do, they might not agree with it. It makes for a rough ride. And it points up the fact that whether the direction is meaningful and put to use depends heavily on how it's developed.

> If you don't know where you're going, you'll end up somewhere else.
> —Yogi Berra

Eileen's situation is in sharp contrast to what goes on in a meaningful workplace. There, people share a co-created vision of the future that pulls them together, focuses their efforts, prompts them to take action through commitment rather than compliance, and gets them excited about tomorrow. Goals and objectives serve as a down-to-earth complement to the vision. They bring it closer to people's day-to-day activities, helping them make decisions regarding what to do and how to do it.

Approaches to Direction Setting

Most organizations have something in the way of a vision statement, goals, and objectives, though they might call them by different names. Sometimes these direction-setting elements exist only in the head of the CEO or director. Other times they're spelled out in a crisp document—a strategic plan, perhaps. Still other workplaces commit their direction to wallet-size cards and poster-size wall hangings.

These efforts almost always begin with good intentions, and the people who are involved often feel that their approach is just fine. Even at Eileen's company, it wouldn't be surprising to find the CEO and CFO confident that their annual planning process, in which managers end up with a memo describing 12 months' worth of direction, is accomplishing what they think it needs to accomplish. But is it?

Described next are the most common approaches to direction setting. Read them, study them, and decide which ones sound all too familiar.

Country-Club Approach: A small handful of "senior executives" is involved in developing the vision and creating goals and objectives. The "handful" can even be as small as one or two people. Few others in the workplace are fully aware of the vision, goals, and objectives. (Eileen's company seems to fit this description.)

Problems with this approach: There is no shared vision, no deep commitment to the direction, and in some cases not even an awareness of goals and objectives. People throughout the organization are likely to move in different (and sometimes opposing) directions because they have different ways of seeing the future. The gap between the select few "top" managers and everyone else in the organization is widened.

Event Approach: Efficiency takes center stage as people go about setting direction. A group gets together for one or two concentrated sessions. There's a demanding agenda with clearly established time frames: one hour to develop a vision statement, one hour for the mission statement, two hours for goals, two hours for objectives, and so on. People produce the outputs as they dutifully move through the agenda. When the session ends, so does the conversation on direction.

Problems with this approach: The effort is seen as a task-minded approach to direction setting, in which those who are involved check the steps off their list of things to do. The lack of ongoing dialogue keeps people from getting closer to the vision; there's no opportunity for this to become a shared vision. Goals and objectives become stale and irrelevant.

Bureaucratic Approach: The direction-setting process is an exhaustive series of steps, protocols, forms, spreadsheets, committees, and subcommittees. There's a feeling that this has a lot to do with meetings and paperwork—and very little to do with creating the future. Hands are kept busy, but hearts and minds remain unengaged. Thick planning reports are dutifully generated and consistently ignored.

BELIEVE IT OR NOT

Dial-a-Direction

A facilitator spent two days with a work unit, guiding them as they clarified their mission, vision, and core values. Everything seemed to be going fine.

But when the retreat officially ended, everyone hustled to their cars and zoomed off, leaving behind a solitary soul who rolled up and carried away all the marker-covered flipchart sheets. The facilitator started to wonder whether the ideas had truly resonated with the participants.

He got his answer two months later, in a phone call from the unit manager. "Could you help me out?" she said. "I can't find our mission or vision statements, and I sure can't remember them. Would you happen to have a copy?"

Problems with this approach: Direction setting is done because it's required, and not because it's desired; people approach it through compliance, not commitment. Those thick reports create the illusion that there's a vision for the future and a set of meaningful goals and strategies. People grow cynical toward "vision statements" and goal numbers that were "pulled out of thin air."

Glossy Approach: A small group throws together a vision statement and a set of goals, which are featured in marketing materials and prominently displayed in public areas. Each employee receives a laminated, wallet-size card titled "Our Vision." More often than not, the statement is full of clichés and buzz terms, and the goals sound like something out of a motivational speech.

Problems with this approach: People see this for what it is—an exercise in marketing and public relations and not an effort to set meaningful direction. Cynicism grows. Genuine efforts to create the future get pushed aside because "we've already done that. It's in our company brochure."

Left-Brain-Only Approach: Everyone is rational, logical, and linear as they think through the organization's vision, goals, and objectives. Creative thinking isn't encouraged, and when it emerges on its own, the right-brain thinker is pressured to "be realistic." Anything that strays from established patterns and decision-making models is off the table.

Problems with this approach: Opportunities fail to register on the radar screen, and as a result, the direction ends up being woefully limited. People might agree with the direction, but they don't get excited about it. Achieving goals and objectives becomes a matter of compliance, not commitment. Some of the direction setters get the sick feeling that the future is passing them by.

> Not everything that can be counted counts, and not everything that counts can be counted.
> —Albert Einstein

Negative Approach: The direction-setting process is focused on how to beat the competition, how to knock through barriers, how to deal with problems, and how to avoid unwanted situations. Conversations about the future are grounded entirely in a preoccupation with the past or present. There's plenty of hand-wringing and verbal venting as people focus on how tough things are.

Problems with this approach: Breakthrough opportunities slip by because they're not directly related to the competition, barriers, and problems. Improvement becomes strictly an incremental proposition. The organization risks doing the wrong thing better and better—instead of ditching the wrong thing and doing entirely new things. Fear can paralyze the organization as people worry over what will happen if they "lose" to a competitor or "fail" to deal with a pending problem. Even beating the competition or the problem can wreak havoc because the rallying point suddenly disappears.

In reading about these different approaches, chances are you've found one or two that are fairly descriptive of your workplace situation. Or maybe you realize that absolutely no direction setting—not even bad direction setting—goes on in your workplace. Whatever the case, there are certain principles that should guide everyone, everywhere, when going about this tricky task of creating a picture of the future and developing goals and objectives.

> If we want everyone to be strategically headed in the same direction, doesn't it make sense for everyone to help set that direction?

Making Everyone a Navigator

When you refer to the direction-setting elements in your workplace—the vision, the goals, or whatever terms you use—how do you phrase it? Do you use words like "my" or "our"? Or do you see someone else as the owner?

In my conversation with Eileen, she kept talking about the "CEO and CFO's goals." Not once did her words suggest that she had any sense of ownership. It was a stark reminder that when it comes to setting direction, everyone should be a navigator. From a human standpoint, it's simply the right thing to do. But there's also a logical case to be made: If we want everyone to be strategically headed in the same direction, doesn't it make sense for everyone to help set that direction?

Right now, take stock of your current process for developing and updating goals and objectives. Who's involved, and who's left out? How can more people be included? If you're part of a small group that determines the direction for the workplace, use these questions to frame an honest conversation. When resistance is felt, be ready to propose a small step in the right direction. It's a worn phrase, but Rome really wasn't built in a day. Your meaningful workplace also will take some time.

If you manage an area that has any of its own direction-setting components, become a model for involving employees in the process. In a work unit of, say, 20 people, there's really no reason why everyone shouldn't help set the direction. Even with much larger groups, tools and techniques like the future-search process can be used to get everyone's hands on the clay and still not make a mess. And frankly, even if you make a mess but end up with a vision and set of goals that are deeply owned by everyone in the organization, won't it be worth it?

It's All About Dialogue

When it comes to examples of creating a vision, many books cite President Kennedy's vow to "land a man on the moon and return him safely to Earth." What they fail to mention are the countless conversations among NASA scientists, technicians, engineers, pilots, mechanics, legislators, budget analysts, and many others—conversations in which people developed the vision and made it their own. In fact, many of the conversations occurred *before* the president put the vision to words in 1961.

On an epic scale, it shows that dialogue is at the heart of direction setting. When people have the freedom to come together, and when they have the clarity and courage to share their own personal visions, a group can begin to develop a collective vision. Together, they start to see the future that they all want to create. Excitement builds, and pretty soon people start taking action to create that future.

And if they keep up the dialogue, it gets even better. The vision comes into clearer focus. Businesslike goals turn into commitments and promises. People acknowledge their missteps, enjoy their successes, and learn from it all. They continue to take action, only this time, they're smarter. This doesn't mean that group-think takes over. On the contrary, with wide-open conversation routinely unfolding, people freely share their concerns. The insights that result sometimes add detail to the shared picture of the future.

> Meaningful direction setting defies the tight agenda and the one-day off-site retreat.

There's nothing efficient about all this. Meaningful direction setting defies the tight agenda and the one-day off-site retreat. Sure, people can come together for an hour and discuss something, but honest sharing and listening take so much longer, especially when there's a genuine effort to make this a collective, co-creative undertaking. A one-day gathering can be worthwhile, but only if the dialogue seriously continues long after people drive away from the retreat site.

Bringing It Down to Earth

Of course, you don't have to be launching rockets to have a vision and a meaningful set of goals. And you sure don't need to be the president. Everyone should have a sense of direction, which means that everyone should be involved in setting it. Perhaps you're on a project team that would benefit from a clearer vision. Maybe you're in a work unit whose 15 people have been feeling the need for meaningful goals. Or it could be that you're thinking bigger—say, about the entire organization.

So how do you make it meaningful? For one, as a hedge against any bureaucratic tendencies, keep it simple. Get folks together to talk about direction, not to craft a lyrical and grammatically wondrous paragraph, but to understand people's perspectives on where the organization (team, work unit, division, region, functional area, and so on) is heading and where it should be heading. Here are several general questions to guide the process:

What is your own personal vision for the future? At first, people will provide safe answers that sound more like goals than personal visions: "I'd like to be an expert in e-commerce." "I want to go back to college and get a degree." "Within five years, I want to have hands-on experience in sales and operations."

> Get folks together to talk about direction, not to craft a lyrical and grammatically wondrous paragraph, but to understand people's perspectives.

If given enough time, and with gentle prompting from a facilitative type, the conversation will deepen. People will share personal visions that reach beyond the workplace: "I'd like to be educating kids, maybe as a high-school teacher." "I want to be making a difference in some way in my community." "It would be great to feel as if all my talents and interests were being fully tapped." After people have time to share these thoughts and feelings (imagine how much they'll learn about each other in the process!), the conversation can turn collective.

What kind of future do we want to create for ourselves and our customers? As the dialogue develops, people will naturally springboard from their personal visions. They'll start talking not only about themselves and their workplace, but also about their customers, who are so integral to the meaning keys of purpose and service. Common themes will start to emerge, and as they do, it might be time to start putting things in writing. But again, keep it simple; describe each of the shared themes in several words.

Who else needs to be included in our vision of the future? It might be too limiting to think just about ourselves and our customers. What about our suppliers and other partners? What about the communities in which we live and work? What about society in general? Yes, we're thinking big. But powerful, meaningful visions are about big stuff.

Meanwhile, as more ideas begin to coalesce, add more writing. If at some point all of you decide to call the result a vision statement, so be it. Just remember that we're talking about two different forms of the vision. There's the print version resting in the oak frame, and then there's the shared picture of the future that people hold in their hearts and minds. You can "complete" the vision *statement*, but you and others are always pursuing the vision itself. That's why ongoing dialogue is so important. It keeps the vision exciting, compelling, and relevant. It allows for fine-tune adjustments, and yes, even major changes in the vision when people decide it's necessary. All this leads to positive action in a shared direction on a daily basis, which is what meaningful vision is all about.

What goals and objectives will move us closer to our picture of the future? Start out by reaching agreement on terminology. It doesn't matter how the books define "goal," "objective," "milestone," or whatever other terms are being used nowadays. What *is* essential is that all of you work from the same definitions for the same terms. Also decide on the time frame. Are you talking about goals for a quarter, six months, a year? These might get adjusted as the conversation unfolds, but it's important to start with everyone on the same calendar page.

> In the absence of clearly defined goals, we become strangely loyal to performing daily acts of trivia.

If the vision is clear to everyone, and it's truly a shared vision, direction-setting elements like goals and objectives will emerge with remarkable ease. Again, keep things fairly loose. Watch for themes that start to emerge, then begin to focus these into more specific statements. Whatever you do, don't let the group turn itself into an efficient goal factory. This is routinely done, with three-hour meetings producing five crisp and entirely forgettable goal statements. Direction setting should come from the heart and mind, and that takes time. If time is short, strive to create just one or two meaningful goals—instead of a set of five or six that have been slapped together.

Beating Back Bureaucracy

Some organizations hand off some or all of the direction-setting responsibility to a committee or subcommittee. Both are designed to be representative bodies. Each person is supposed to serve as the voice of a certain constituency. This works fine for certain issues, but when it comes to direction, it's awfully difficult to imagine how someone could represent anyone but themselves.

For one thing, people need to share their personal visions when developing a collective vision, and it's hard to imagine this working in a representative structure. There's no way someone else can climb into your history, values, and aspirations. It's equally impossible for people to feel any deep commitment to a vision or set of goals that have been created *for* them instead of *by* them. You'd get compliance—maybe—and that's about it.

So why do some organizations persist with the committee model? It's familiar, it's a habit, and it rarely makes waves. And you know what? It's not the only thing that has bureaucratized the direction-setting process. Check out these other red-tape warnings:

- Goals and objectives have to go through an exhaustive approval process.
- Vision statements must conform to specific requirements regarding word count, word choice, and formatting.
- There are restrictions on how to use and where to post vision statements, mission statements, goals, and other direction-setting elements.
- Other guidelines "strongly recommend" the types of people (by position) who should be involved in direction setting.
- A written memo instructs managers: "All work units are to submit __ goals (fill in a number) by _____ (fill in a date) to _____ (fill in the name and

address of someone at the corporate office who no one knows). Please indicate the section and subsection of the corporate strategic plan to which each goal relates."

- A detailed "documented procedure" spells out exactly how the "strategic planning process" should unfold.

The Power of One

Many organizations follow the country-club approach to direction setting. That's certainly the case for Eileen, who reported that the CEO and CFO seemed to do it all. In my conversation with her, she struggled to recall the goals that had been handed to her in the latest direction-setting memo. She eventually came up with two out of—well, she wasn't sure of the total number.

It sounded like the worst kind of disempowerment, but the more she talked, the more she began to find some of her own solutions. The CEO and CFO played the goal-development process close to the vest, she said, but for the most part, they kept an open door. It wouldn't be all that difficult to visit with them and get a clearer understanding of their vision and the individual goals. Who knows, she said, they might even get the clue that others wanted to be involved in the process.

> She went through a quick mental checklist and realized that nothing was standing in their way.

Then Eileen started thinking about her own work area. Over the past five months, she and her colleagues in information systems had spent so much time talking about senior management's inept direction setting that they never did any of their own. She went through a quick mental checklist and realized that nothing was standing in their way. Then she started thinking about the possibilities: some research into forecasts about the future of their industry, a series of lunchtime conversations about the future, everyone involved in creating a vision for their business within the business, a small set of significant goals to guide daily activities.

That quickly, Eileen took a step toward making herself a direction-setting partner instead of remaining a frustrated bystander. So can you.

Reality Check: DIRECTION

1 = very strongly disagree   5 = agree
2 = strongly disagree   6 = strongly agree
3 = disagree   7 = very strongly agree
4 = neutral; neither disagree nor agree

_____ A compelling vision of the future draws people in a common direction.

_____ People understand and are invested in goals and objectives that serve as a meaningful, down-to-earth complement to the vision.

_____ Goals, objectives, and other direction-setting elements are routinely used by people to shape what they do and how they do it.

_____ The organization's direction is periodically revisited, reassessed, and refocused.

_____ People at all levels are involved in developing and updating the vision, goals, and objectives.

_____ = Total ÷ 5 = _____ = DIRECTION RATING

Be Sure to Invite the Mail Clerk

"It's not rocket science, but there's a tremendous amount of work involved." And an even bigger return on the investment, if you're willing to make it.

That's the message from Gary Waldorf and Stephanie Giles, California-based consultants who worked with Intuit beginning in the early 1990s. At the time, the company was a one-product wonder producing a personal-finance software package known as Quicken. The consultants helped guide about 100 employees through a year-long process to develop a unifying vision, mission, operating values, and goals.

Their return? People made breakthrough discoveries about themselves, their company, and their direction. And was it a coincidence that Intuit went on to reach the revenue stratosphere in several short years? I don't think so.

The process began with an organizational assessment. Then the group was divided into cross-functional teams of about twenty-five people each. They went off-site, picked team leaders, and spent a concentrated period of time reflecting on what Intuit should be and become in the next 20 years. The groups carefully knitted together their ideas; then the team leaders went to work with the executive team. This was followed by a thoughtful back-and-forth development process over several months, with everyone remaining deeply involved. Eventually, the teams ratified the vision, mission, values, and goals—and capped their work with a well-deserved company celebration.

In keeping with the "it's not rocket science" comment, the lessons learned were remarkably straightforward: Involve the whole organization. Use a direction-setting process that people believe in doing. Exert the necessary creativity. Take the time that's required to do it right.

What's most likely to stir resistance is the notion of widespread involvement in the direction-setting process. Says Gary: "Some companies have a senior manager who says something like: 'I don't want a clerk from the mailroom to be telling me what to do.' Well, it never happens that way. But it just might happen that the person from the mailroom has an idea that will save the company a million dollars."

Chapter 5

Relevance

Allen is a materials engineer for a research lab, but listening to him talk, you might assume that he works for a paper mill. The place requires employees to fill out form after form for just about everything. Even a humble request for low-cost office supplies involves paperwork. Then there are the staff meetings, which are held without fail from 8 to 9:30 A.M. every Monday, and from 4 to 5 P.M. every Thursday—regardless of whether there's anything worthwhile on the agenda. Allen's current project is all about increasing aircraft safety, and when he talks about it, his impassioned tones make clear that he has a deep sense of mission. But he says that with all the paperwork and meetings, it's a daily struggle. He even calculated that about a third of his time is spent on administrative activities that simply add no value. "I'd like to be mission-driven 40 hours a week, but this place simply won't let me."

In the last two chapters, we looked at purpose and direction, which are entirely uplifting. They speak to our deep-down desire to make a difference and our inclinations to create a better future. Now along comes Allen with his story of irrelevant work. It's like a bucket of cold water poured over our heads.

> "I'd like to be mission-driven 40 hours a week, but this place simply won't let me."

It's also reality. In interview after interview, people voiced frustration over rules, requirements, traditions, red tape, and plain old habits (some of them self-inflicted) that pull them away from mission-related activities. "It's a constant struggle," one person said. "I think of it as a daily battle between the important stuff and the unimportant stuff," said another. A third person likened his workplace to a hamster wheel. "We're going around and around. There's lots of motion, but we don't seem to get anywhere."

> Struggles, battles, hamster wheels. Whatever you call it, it's in sharp contrast to what happens in a meaningful workplace.

Struggles, battles, hamster wheels. Whatever you call it, it's in sharp contrast to what happens in a meaningful workplace. There, people spend their time on activities that directly relate to the purpose, vision, and goals. Everything else almost always falls away. When it doesn't, it gets scrutinized. And if it fails to pass the mission test, it gets radically redesigned or dumped.

Does It Meet the Relevance Criteria?

We don't want to be too hard on Allen, but if you really think about his story, it sounds like he's in victim mode. Remember his words? "I'd like to be mission-driven 40 hours a week, but this place simply won't let me."

Surely there are things out of his control, but there's probably a lot he can control, and a lot more ways he can wield some influence. And this doesn't apply just to Allen. Whoever you are or wherever you're at in an organization, there are things you can do right now to make your work more relevant. But first, you need to figure out what's irrelevant.

Back in the chapter on purpose, you were prompted to list all the activities that keep you busy during the typical workweek. If your list is handy, pull it out again—or if you skipped past the exercise, consider making a list right now. Be sure it's sufficiently detailed. Rather than crunching everything into three or four big chunks, try to break your workweek down into at least 15 activities.

Now, take a look at the following five questions. Think of these as "relevance criteria." They're a detector of sorts for uncovering the stuff in your schedule that probably shouldn't be there. Going one by one through each activity on your list, apply each of these questions—and keep a tally on your paper to record how many yes responses each activity generates.

1. Does it help you fulfill your purpose?
2. Does it help you serve your customers better?
3. Does it help your colleagues serve a customer better?
4. Does it bring you closer to the future that you and your colleagues are trying to create?
5. Does it relate directly to one or more of your goals or objectives?

Once you complete this exercise, you'll see from the tally marks how well you're spending your time. And by "well," we're not talking about efficiency. Rather, it's all about determining whether you're doing the *right* things.

It's a likely bet that some of your activities have ended up with no tally marks whatsoever, or maybe you really had to stretch to find any connection to the relevance criteria. But how are you reacting to your discoveries? Most people have one of four reactions whenever their relevance detector goes off. They'll look at an activity that has no tally marks and say:

"This really is unimportant. I'm going to stop doing it now."
or, "Even though it didn't meet one of the criteria, it's still important."
or, "It's unimportant, but I still have to do it. My colleagues expect it of me."
or, "The organization makes me do it."

Let's take a quick look at these responses and what to do about them.

"I'm Going to Stop It Now"

There might be something in your schedule that has a big irrelevance bull's-eye on it, and you're eager to put a halt to it. Let's say you spend a lot of time sorting and resorting files, but you realize it just doesn't contribute to the big three of mission, vision, and customers. Maybe you devote too many hours to making documents look fancy, even though you know that's your own preference and not something that's important to your customers. Or maybe you're always checking and rechecking things once you do them—you're your own worst inspector—and you realize you should just make sure the work is done right in the first place and send it on its way.

> Beware of your habits. The better they are, the more surely they will be your undoing.
>
> —HOLBROOK JACKSON

If you've found anything that sounds even remotely similar to this, great, you have an opportunity. But don't neglect the force of your own habits. They can pull you back to your old ways, even when you know better.

Guard against this right now by writing down exactly what you plan to stop doing. And while you're at it—and this is critically important—write down what you intend to start doing in its place. Perhaps you're going to expand an existing activity that's already related to your vision or mission. Or maybe you'd like to take on something totally new. Whatever it is, make it a formal commitment by jotting it down. Record it in your schedule book, on your computer screen, in your Palm Pilot, on a stickie note affixed to your workstation—wherever. Just be sure to keep it foremost in your mind.

"But It's Still Important"

It can be awfully diffi-
cult to distinguish the
important stuff in our
schedules from activi-
ties that only seem to
be important.

It can be awfully difficult to distinguish the important stuff in our schedules from activities that only seem to be important. This is especially the case when we've done something for a long time and have reached a certain level of proficiency.

Perhaps there's an activity that didn't pass your relevance test, but you feel it's still important. If so, ask several more questions to explore all the angles:

Why is it so important? (Take a second look at those five questions. Are you *sure* that it didn't meet any of the relevance criteria? Perhaps another pass through the relevance detector will find some connection to the mission, vision, or customers.)

What would happen if you stopped this activity entirely?

What would be the impact on your colleagues—would it make their lives more difficult?

Would it hurt product or service quality?

What would your external customers have to say?

If you stopped this particular activity, would you also stop learning and growing?

Would your work be a lot less fulfilling?

Now turn things around a bit. If you did cut this activity out of your schedule, how would you use the freed-up time? How would this new activity help you with your vision and mission?

"My Colleagues Expect It"

Perhaps there's an activity or two that didn't pass the relevance test, but you feel compelled to keep doing it because the people around you have come to expect it. Or maybe they do it with you. That's right, it might be *their* habits that keep you stuck with this irrelevant stuff.

You know that the report you crank out every five days doesn't do a darn bit of good, but if you didn't produce it, there would be howls from all those folks who look for it to arrive on their computer screens week after irrelevant week.

Meetings are another prime example. Remember Andy and his anguish over all those get-togethers? He was frustrated because the meetings seemed to steal time away from the real mission of the organization.

Now put yourself in your colleagues' shoes. They haven't gone through the same analysis, they haven't been reading this book, and frankly, they might have a completely different perspective on things and feel that your "irrelevant" activity is actually quite important. So the worst possible approach is to stop the activity cold—and the best approach is to engage them in dialogue on this whole notion of relevance.

Within that larger conversation, you can then talk about the activity you'd like to stop doing, as well as the way you'd like to redirect the time. Raise these four questions, which are a version of the relevance criteria tailored for groups:

Does it help fulfill our purpose?

Does it help us serve our customers better?

Does it bring us closer to the future that we're trying to create?

Does it relate directly to one or more of our goals or objectives?

As they explore these questions, some interesting things might happen. For one, they might start talking about their deep-down purpose as a work group. They might put on their long-range lenses and starting thinking more seriously about the future. The conversation even could end up focusing on customers and ways to serve them better. All this would bode well for the long-term health of your workplace. And in the process, all of you can decide what to do with the activity that you've called into question.

> **GINNY'S STORY**
>
> When Ginny reflects on her workplace, she sees red tape, irrelevant rules, and cumbersome processes that churn on without end.
>
> Her biggest pet peeve is the meeting that's held for the sake of holding a meeting. "It's a meeting culture," says Ginny, who conducts economic-development workshops. "You have your two-hour session even if there's nothing substantial to discuss."
>
> She likes her job best when she's on the road, far from the bureaucratic hub. "That's when I can focus on what's really important."

Keeping Relevance on the Agenda

So far we've been talking about this as a one-time proposition. But to turn it from an activity into an obsession, which is what it needs to be if you're going to stay mission-driven, you and your colleagues need to make it a regular part of your conversations.

Notice the emphasis on doing this as a collective. Sure, this chapter starts out with you doing an analysis on your own and pinpointing some things you can cut from your own schedule. But so much of what we do involves other people that it's essential to get everyone involved.

Consider making relevance a regular agenda item. Whenever you get together, take stock of what everyone did during the past week, and pose those questions listed earlier. If something fails to register, ask why the activity is so important, and decide what can be done instead that would add more value. Then take a look ahead. What's on tap for the coming week or two? Compare the plan to the criteria, and see what shakes out. Don't be surprised if some of the plans change on the spot because they simply don't match up with the mission.

> Don't be surprised if some of the plans change on the spot because they simply don't match up with the mission.

What's the worst that can happen? Some people might throw up their hands and claim that they can't do this kind of analysis because they don't *have* a clear mission. If that's the case, you'll have the perfect lead-in to another conversation all about purpose and direction—which just might be a good problem to have!

"The Organization Makes Me Do It"

Some of the activities that take up your time might not meet any of the relevance criteria, yet you feel compelled to do them because of reasons seemingly beyond your control. Perhaps there's a policy or rule that leaves you no choice, perhaps it's written into your formal job description, or maybe your traditional-looking performance review builds in the expectation that you *will* do it. All this tends to be magnified in larger organizations or where hierarchy dominates.

Your first challenge is to make sure of your original assessment. Are these activities really required? What will happen if you let them fall by the wayside? Try to distinguish between something you perceive as a "must do" and something you can freely banish from your lineup of activities.

You can also start conversations about these conflicts—and when we're talking about activities that go against the mission and vision, "conflict" is the right term. The preceding section suggests ongoing dialogue with your colleagues. It also might be appropriate to involve people from other work units. If you're getting the feeling that some of your time is being spent on valueless activities, it's likely that others feel the same way. Get folks talking, and you just might start to bring about some positive change.

Want to focus these conversations on three likely irrelevance suspects? Try rules, policies, and paperwork.

Target Worthless Rules

Establish or propose a group to hunt down and kill ridiculous rules. Ideally, the group would get everyone involved in the pursuit, and a serious anti-rule bias would prevail. We want to be mission-driven and not rule-driven, right? Well, what a great way to make the point.

One word of warning: Every rule, no matter how pointless or harmful, has at least one staunch defender. Expert rule-hunters will tell you to build your case before you go in for the kill. Has the sick-leave policy risen to the top of the rule hit list? Gather objective data to show, for instance, how the well-intentioned policy has actually increased sick-leave usage. Want to reform the cumbersome travel-reporting process? Calculate the time it takes for employees to plow through the paperwork, then compare it to the time that's expected with a new and improved process.

Present these cold, hard facts to the powers that be, and prepare yourself for a worst-case wall of skepticism. Be ready to explain how the changes will actually decrease abuses (sick-leave abuse, travel-reporting abuse, and so on) of the system.

Put Policies Through the Mission Filter

Charter or suggest a team to conduct an inside-out review of the policy manual. Encourage them to get widespread input from all areas of the workplace. One question, applied to each and every page of the manual, should drive this process: Does this policy help us or hinder us in carrying out our workplace mission? Anything that hinders should be set aside and scrutinized. If there's no persuasive reason to keep it, chop it.

> Expert rule-hunters will tell you to build your case before you go in for the kill.

Again, a warning: Although individual policies have their defenders, whole policy manuals have platoons of people ready to fire off 10 good reasons why things shouldn't be changed. Do you want to deal with that? Of course not, which is why you need to turn these people into partners. Involve them in the review process. Include on the team at least one staunch defender of the status quo. And always—always!—have your ammo box loaded with facts. Don't push any policy to the scrap heap until you have persuasive data showing how this change will have a positive impact.

TAKE ON THE PAPER

In the story that opened this chapter, it sounds like Allen's workplace was cluttered with forms. If you can relate, look for ways to reduce the paperwork. Instead of taking on the whole paper mill, focus on a single culprit. There are so many possibilities: time sheets, expense reports, requisitions, purchasing orders, maintenance work orders, to name just a few. Most forms call for serious simplification, whereas others can be eliminated altogether. Anything in triplicate should be considered suspect.

> We can overcome gravity, but sometimes the paperwork is overwhelming.
>
> —WERNHER VON BRAUN, PIONEERING ROCKET SCIENTIST

If you have a team looking at the policy manual, they'll probably pinpoint several forms that are crying out for improvement. Or an enterprising (and fed-up) work unit might calculate the hours and hours it takes to fill out that damn (their word) expense report.

Regardless of who spots the need for change, the actual changing should be done by the people who process those forms. For instance, the expense report should be overhauled by people who collect the reports, pull the data, and do the reimbursing. Time sheets should be revised by employees who take that data, enter it into the system, and use it for compensation and other HR functions. Of course, early into these improvement projects, team members need to get input from people who routinely fill out the forms. They are, after all, the customers.

Reality Check: RELEVANCE

1 = very strongly disagree   5 = agree
2 = strongly disagree   6 = strongly agree
3 = disagree   7 = very strongly agree
4 = neutral; neither disagree nor agree

_____ People are able to spend their time on activities that relate directly to the mission.

_____ When people want to get things done, they can move forward without any prerequisite hoop-jumping. The old mantra of "ask for permission" is replaced with "just do it—as long as it fits our mission."

_____ There's a willingness—even an eagerness—to eliminate irrelevant activities. (These can include meetings that plod on without purpose, protocol and traditions that have lost their meaning, and any other activities that keep the organization from pursuing its direction.)

_____ Individuals are sensitive to whether activities or projects best serve the larger mission of the organization.

_____ Rules and red tape are kept to an absolute minimum.

_____ = Total ÷ 5 = _____ = RELEVANCE RATING

A Smart Approach to Stupid Rules

At the Ohio Bureau of Employment Services (OBES), red tape and ridiculous regulations have met their match. That's right, deep in the heart of a public-sector organization, the "Stupid" Rules Committee is leading the charge against workplace bureaucracy. They even have a reviled mascot who represents the red tape—a gremlin. Individuals and work units can get the Gremlin Award when their suggestions lead to the elimination of valueless policies.

The effort has been wildly successful. A special bulletin called the Gremlin Graveyard lists 19 rules and regulations that are now 6-feet under. Interred are all sorts of forms, rework-ridden inspections, and various review processes that were more about control than quality. The changes have saved thousands of dollars, and best of all, employees can now spend their freed-up time on activities that relate directly to the organization's mission.

It's serious business, but it's fun, too. When the Gremlin Award goes out, so does the traveling mascot. OBES Deputy Director Howard Wells makes a tongue-in-cheek presentation there in the work unit, thanking the employees, encouraging them to look for more rules that are ready to RIP, and making them responsible for the care and feeding of the reviled yet cute and fluffy gremlin. They take their charge seriously, even to the point of keeping the gremlin well-dressed. On St. Patrick's Day, you're likely to find it wearing green—appropriate considering all the money that has been saved.

According to Wells, the self-described "Deputy of Subtraction" (as in "subtracting" useless rules from the workplace), any workplace can and should have its own "Stupid" Rules Committee. "What you need is a team of dedicated employees to lead this, a way to get everyone else directly involved, a way to recognize people for making this happen—and a willingness to dump a lot of old forms into the recycle bin."

Chapter 6

Validation

As a packing supervisor for a pharmaceuticals manufacturer, Helen keeps a very busy schedule. She can see product heading to the next stage in the process, and she knows deep down that what they produce does good things for people in need. But even after two decades in the plant, she feels remarkably disconnected from the results of her work. "I've been doing so much at this company for so long," she says. "I just wish I could step back and see the real impact of all my efforts."

Even after all these years at the plant, Helen seems to be estranged from the outputs and outcomes of her work. Perhaps it's *because* of all that time. After investing so much of her life, she wants proof that she really *is* making a difference.

> "I just wish I could step back and see the real impact of all my efforts."

For a lot of people, it's important to have a purpose that's bigger than the work itself, and to have a hand in shaping the future; these are captured in the meaning keys of purpose and direction. People also want to be spending their time on activities that relate to these important pursuits, and not on wasteful work that has more to do with rules, bureaucracy, and stale ways of doing things; this is the essence of the third mission key, relevance.

But there's even more, as Helen shows us. It's embodied in the fourth key of this set. Validation is all about seeing the fruits of our labor. You've heard the phrase "seeing is believing." That pretty much sums it up.

Validation means different things to different people. A person who works in a tannery might get deep fulfillment the moment that saddle is completed—whereas another person in that same tannery needs to see the saddle on a horse with a rider on top. For a nurse, validation might come in the form of a smile from a comforted patient—whereas another nurse eagerly awaits the moment when the patient leaves the hospital because that is how *this* nurse sees her efforts transformed into results.

Getting Out of the Box

Go beyond your corner of the workplace, and discover exactly what you help create and how it's used by customers.

Many organizations insist on using boxes as their main way of organizing. They can be found on those neatly formatted organization charts, but more seriously, people often feel like they're boxed off in one small part of the process—to such a degree that all they can see is their own immediate area. What about you? Use these diagnostic questions to assess your own situation:

Do you sometimes feel cut off from the product or service that your work helps create?

Are you so buried in the beginning or middle of a process that you rarely if ever see the output at the end of the process?

Ever get the feeling that you're the "employee in a bubble," sealed off from whatever it is the organization creates?

If you answered yes to any of these questions, make it your mission to reach out and try to see the output, the results, the product, the service—whatever you want to call it—for yourself. That's right, go beyond your corner of the workplace, and discover exactly what you help create and how it's used by customers.

How this takes shape depends entirely on the business you're in. If you work in the administration office of, say, a canning plant, all it might take is a visit to the production area. There you can engage employees in conversation and get immediate input on how they benefit from your work.

Perhaps your job is to help develop children's activities for a park system, and you realize that for the past three months, you've been holed up in the office. Why not spend half a day visiting with kids and their families to find out how they're enjoying those programs? Or maybe you can become your own customer, participating in one of the programs with one of your own children, or with a nephew or niece or neighbor.

If you install glass in an automobile assembly plant, use some break time to hover around the new cars as they roll off the line, or spin by a showroom and marvel at your work.

Remember, this is all about making visible connections between your work and something that's bigger than your work. There are so many possibilities, whatever your profession. If your colleagues think you're crazy, great, you've caught their interest. Bring them along.

Soaking Up the Moment

Helen talked a lot about the hectic pace of her job. It sounded as if she never took the time to press the pause button. That's the first thing she needs to do to get a sense of validation—and it's something you also might want to consider. Whenever you finish a project, stop to assess and appreciate whatever it is you've created. Step off the treadmill for a few minutes and enjoy a breather. While you're at it, pose a few questions:

Who is better off because of my work?

How are they benefiting?

How will they benefit in the future?

If your ego starts to flush a bit, great. That's exactly what you want to happen.

This might even be a great opportunity to get together with some of your customers—especially worthwhile if you've been cloistered away from them while completing a big chunk of work. Let's say you're a retail analyst who has recently found herself plugged into the Internet most days, disconnected from store personnel. Once that project is completed, try to get away from the terminal and spend some time face to face with the salespeople. Tell them about your recent work, maybe get some input, maybe even get a few high-fives.

> ### CAROL'S STORY
> As a grade-school librarian, Carol has an important and challenging job.
>
> "No two children are alike," she says. "I spend the better part of my time getting to know the kids and trying to find a book that will really get them going."
>
> She has her own built-in tracking system for knowing when it all comes together: "I can see their eyes light up." That's when Carol's eyes light up as well.

"You've Got to See These Results!"

Since validation has so much to do with seeing results, look for opportunities to engage in a bit of workplace show-and-tell. When a major project is completed, pull together everyone who was involved at every stage of the creation process. Let them see the finished product and, whenever possible, literally get their hands on it.

Let's say you've developed a new piece of software. Why not have a "coming out party" where colleagues can drop by and try it out? If the milestone is a new training manual, circulate copies to everyone whose work went into it. Is that new conveyor system finally in place after two months of nonstop work? Before starting it up, put a bow on it (literally) and open it for guided tours conducted by the folks who made it happen. And when we talk about getting together everyone who was involved, make it everyone. Even if someone spent just half a day in the early stages, working on some now-forgotten part of the development process, make sure he or she is a part of the celebration.

> Look for opportunities to engage in a bit of workplace show-and-tell.

As you can see, this is show-and-tell with a very serious purpose. It's the collective version of pressing the pause button. It lets people see for themselves that their hard work has created something significant.

Track Goals and Give Yourself Credit

Goals give tangibility and measurability to our work, so tracking them is one way to experience this notion of validation. Perhaps you have a set of all-important personal goals scribbled on an index card that's safely tucked away in a wallet or purse. Pull it out regularly to check whether you're making progress. And when one of your goals has been reached, pull out a mental party hat and savor the moment.

Many work units and teams have goals. These too should be jotted down somewhere, preferably on something larger than a three-by-five card. The tracking approach may be a bit more elegant—for example, a group might be striving for a first-ring response to all phone calls from customers, or a maintenance team might be aiming to increase the life of Machine X by 25 percent. Goals like these require some kind of process to capture and crunch data, and to translate it into useful information. Whenever major progress toward these goals is made—and definitely when the goals are achieved—it's time to sit back and take in the results.

In my conversation with Helen, she mentioned that her company did have goals. These were tracked on a series of spreadsheets that came out once a month. Each employee received a copy, and more often than not, the sheets were promptly filed in nearby trash cans. The goals had been established by the "higher ups," she said, and besides, "the numbers were so small you'd need a magnifying glass to read them."

Her first point takes us back to Chapter 4 (Direction), which is all about setting direction in a meaningful way. And her second point reminds us that you can't see results unless you can—well, see the results. As long as the goals and objectives are meaningful, turn them into an easy-to-understand score-card of sorts that's routinely updated. Use visuals such as graphs and bar charts to make the results easier to interpret. You can even have a scoreboard that's posted for all to see.

Remember, though, that the idea here is not to compete with other work units. Whatever you do, don't create a scoreboard that compares *your* figures to *their* figures. This will only stoke internal competition, which can wreak havoc with many of the other meaning keys. Simply track progress toward the direction-setting elements that you've created for yourselves.

Hearing from Your Customers

Because customers are at the receiving end of what's produced or delivered, they're uniquely qualified to speak about the impact of your work. Hearing what customers have to say about a product or service is the next best thing to watching them actually use it.

Amazingly, Helen reported that in her 20 years with the company, she rarely interacted with any of her company's distributors or with the medical facilities that received their pharmaceuticals—and never did she hear from the con-sumers themselves who were using the product. The reason: Getting this input is difficult.

> Hearing what customers have to say about a product or service is the next best thing to watching them actually use it.

Actually, it might be easier than you think. Consider organizing a series of liberally defined customer "focus groups." These can be fact-finding conversations in which five or so employees sit down with an equal number of customers. That's right, in this situation, you can dispense with the traditional format of a focus-group moderator and tightly controlled conditions. The idea is to have a loose conversation in which employees can hear how their finished product or service is used—and how it can be better.

You can use the following canned questions to start the dialogue, but the answers will likely prompt some follow-up questions that can't be scripted. Here are a few good openings:

How are you (customer) using our product/service?

How are you benefiting?

What do you love about it or hate about it and why?

As answers emerge, employees will get an earful of honest input. Those who usually feel miles away from the end result of their work will suddenly hear about its impact. That nebulous "thing we sell" will start to take on remarkable tan-gibility. Imagine what this conversation would have done for Helen and her sense of validation.

You might be thinking that an informal customer focus group sounds like a crazy idea, especially if you've never been involved in one. Okay, take a quick count. How many Helens do you know—how many employees in your work area or division or whole organization have never had direct contact with a customer?

Hit the Road and See for Yourself

An informal focus group works great, but let's face it, it's not quite the same as seeing the results firsthand. Perhaps you can arrange an employee outing to witness the company's products or services being used by real customers. It's the ultimate in "seeing is believing," and it's guaranteed to deepen everyone's sense of validation.

This obviously doesn't work for all businesses (life insurance?!), but when it does, it leaves unforgettable impressions. Imagine it: A group from a pub-lishing company—one that specializes in children's books—spends a few hours at a grade-school library. A company that manufactures irrigation equip-ment meets with a group of farmers and sees the product in action. A govern-ment team working on urban renewal leaves its office and spends two days at inner-city service centers; their visit involves plenty of conversations with residents, service providers, and city planners.

This is all the more important when the products are never, ever seen by employees in their finished form because they're assembled at the customer site. A huge industrial press is one such example—the people who make its parts seldom see the whole. Everything is put on a truck, and off it goes. Imagine the deep personal satisfaction of seeing that press in action after you've spent weeks helping to build it.

As you think about the visits to customers' sites, you might be punching your mental calculator and coming up with some fairly prohibitive figures. Yes, this can be costly, but it's an investment. Work to maximize the return by clarifying what you want to accomplish from the outing. Assemble an ambitious itinerary, and team up with your colleagues when it's all over to talk about the lessons learned and to determine the next steps.

Adjusting Schedules and Attitudes

Even when a product or service is created on-site, there are those who may never see it in its finished form. Perhaps it's the data-entry person who never, ever sees the final customer reports. Maybe it's the intake specialist who never sees the healthy patient leave the hospital. Or maybe it's that equipment operator who ensures the right mix of chemicals at the start of the production process.

> Imagine the deep personal satisfaction of seeing that press in action after you've spent weeks helping to build it.

Everyone should have an occasional (at least) opportunity to see the output, wherever he or she works in the system. And that may call for some creativity and flexibility. For example, why not organize a get-together with the data-entry folks and everyone else who's involved in producing those customer reports? You can even invite a few customers, schedule it for lunch, and organize a loose agenda that includes plenty of time for socializing.

For the hospital intake specialist: Reinvent the job so he's also the person who signs out the patients. That way, he can see patients when they come in for treatment and when they leave with (in most cases) a clean bill of health. And how about a day "off" for that chemical-supply specialist so she can spend time at other points in the production process? She'll be engaging in eight hours of dialogue with her internal customers, and they'll get a chance to be with one of their suppliers.

Arrangements like these require a bit of adjustment. Part of this may involve an attitude change ("But we've never done this before!"), and part of it may involve some scheduling gymnastics since people will be temporarily away from their regular jobs. Then again, shouldn't a person's regular job include at least some time to get together with people from other parts of the system and to see the product or service he or she has helped create?

Reality Check: VALIDATION

1 = very strongly disagree   5 = agree
2 = strongly disagree   6 = strongly agree
3 = disagree   7 = very strongly agree
4 = neutral; neither disagree nor agree

_____ People can see the impact of their work.
_____ There are tangible results.
_____ Contact with customers (internal or external) is a routine part of doing business, giving employees a firsthand view of how their products/services are used.
_____ Even when people produce intangibles, they have opportunities to see how their work benefits others.
_____ Following a big project, people are able to pause, get a sense of closure, and savor (however briefly) their accomplishments.

_____ = Total ÷ 5 = _____ = VALIDATION RATING

PART THREE

THE PEOPLE KEYS

We value all who work here.

The People Keys

- Respect
- Equality
- Informality
- Flexibility
- Ownership

Chapter 7

Respect

It's not the dirt or the broken furniture that gets to Larry. It's not even the messy kids or the gum stuck beneath the desks. What really bothers this school custodian is the lack of respect he gets from his colleagues. The teachers and administrators are "adults with Ph.D.s," he says, yet they ignore easy-to-correct problems that crop up throughout the day. And by the time Larry shows up for work at 3 P.M., those little problems can be major disasters. For instance, a sink might get clogged with crumpled paper. Cleaning it would take all of about five seconds, but as Larry puts it, "they figure they'll just leave it for the janitor. Then when I come in at the end of the school day, there's an inch of water covering the restroom floor." When he took his concerns to the school's administrators, no one seemed all that interested. When he asked to have five minutes on an upcoming staff agenda, he was told there simply wasn't enough time. Now he just comes in, does his work, and keeps quiet.

Okay, time for an honesty check. Where do *you* place custodians on the workplace status scale? In the class system that pervades the typical organization, are custodians accorded the same level of respect as the CEOs and presidents and directors and VPs and regional chiefs? Probably not. (I'll bet you've never seen a prized parking space marked "Reserved for Custodian.") How do they fare relative to front-line employees?

> "They figure they'll just leave it for the janitor."

Interestingly, the words *respect* and *regard* (as in "how I regard you") are derived from Latin and French words that capture various nuances of the verb *to look*. How appropriate. When I look at you, or vice-versa, what kind of quick judgments do I make? In what way do "looks"—in this case, physical cues of status—affect how we think about one another?

If Larry, dressed in a worn-out shop outfit, is pushing his custodial cart down the hallway, what goes through the mind of the top manager who walks past in a hand-tailored suit? And what does Larry think? If two other people walk past Larry and the suited manager, what's their mental reaction? Do they hold one of them in higher regard because of the status signal that's sent by the clothing? Do those people passing by offer a cheery hello to one person but not the other?

In a meaningful workplace, everyone holds everyone in high regard, regardless of what they see (tie, big office, fancy car) and what they know (several advanced degrees, big title, close friend of the CEO) about each other. Decisions that affect employees are made with greater care. People's opinions are valued, and so are their judgment and know-how. When there's conflict, it's worked out in a way that keeps everyone's esteem intact. And not insignificantly, the workplace is more pleasant. If I truly respect you and we happen to cross paths, expect a warm greeting—in sharp contrast to the stifling silence that's heard in too many hallways and elevators.

First, Look in the Mirror

Respect works in a reciprocal kind of way. When you give it, it almost always comes back to you. And if you dish out disrespect, guess what? That too will quickly ricochet in your direction. So if you want to boost your organization's collective respect level, your first step is to start with yourself. Be a standout example of respect in action.

> The way you see people is the way you treat them, and the way you treat them is what they become.
>
> —JOHANN VON GOETHE

While it sounds fairly obvious, it's not all that easy to do. You need to pay special attention to how you interact with people, especially with those whose roles in the organization tend to be less valued than your own. You also have to listen to those thoughts and judgments that are ever incubating in your gray matter. All day long, each of us has an ongoing internal conversation. This is where respect rises or falls. If you're sorting people into mental file folders—"important," "not important," "totally worthless," and so forth—you're setting yourself up to be an accessory to disrespect. Ditch the file folders and start thinking and doing things differently.

This internal conversation can be difficult to hear, not because it rarely happens, but because it's always going on. It becomes like background music in a restaurant; you don't really hear it unless you try to hear it. So let's turn up the volume by exploring some pointed questions:

- Every workplace has some people who greet their friends and a few chosen others, and that's about it. What about you? Are you ever selective with your hellos?
- Informal workplace conversations can knit people together, but toss in some disrespect and they can quickly pull us apart. Do you ever engage in water-cooler gossip?
- Most workplace problems are the fault of the system, and *not* the people who are working in that system. Statistical studies prove this. So does the simple reality that very, very few people ever go to work with the intention of screwing up. When something goes wrong in your workplace, how do you react? Do you immediately look for someone to blame, or do you do some deeper thinking to figure out where and why the system is falling short?
- It's easy to make judgments about people based on what they're wearing or how they look. Be honest now: Do you ever do this?
- All too often, change is done *to* people, without anyone involving them in making the decisions or at least getting some of their input. This approach might be efficient in the short term, and it surely fits the old paradigm that effective leadership is all about being swift and decisive. It might even be required in emergencies, when the downside of delay clearly outweighs the benefits of involving others in the decision. Excluding these emergency situations, what's your approach on this? Do you tend to go forward single-handedly and do things *to* people or *for* them?
- Then there's the temper issue. It's perfectly human to lose our cool every now and then, but when it's directed at people, the effects on relationships and

MARTHA'S STORY

Martha spent years complaining about the lack of respect she got as a clerical supervisor at a large marketing firm. Figuring it had to do with the functional area, she went back to school part time and studied computers.

The new skills earned her a job in information systems—where she expected to get some of that long-overdue respect. Instead, what she got was some honest input from a colleague. "He went on and on about how I wasn't showing enough respect for the people around me," Martha says.

She got defensive and stayed that way for several weeks. Then she started to reflect, and it slowly sank in. "I was living with the attitude that if I wasn't getting respect, I sure as heck wouldn't give it," she says. "It had turned into a vicious cycle."

esteem can be devastating. So what about it? Have you ever given one of your colleagues a disrespectful piece of your mind?

The aim of all this is not to make you feel uncomfortable or guilty. It's about self-awareness. Since respect is such a give-and-get proposition, you need to take a hard look at yourself before doing anything else.

"To Me, Respect Is..."

You might be wondering whether Larry and the other people who work at the school ever talk about respect. He said it comes up every now and then in passing, but that's about it. Do they think it's important? I'm not so sure, he responded. Would they be willing to make it the focus for an entire conversation? Again, not so sure. Would such a conversation make a difference? It would definitely be a big move in the right direction.

What about in *your* workplace? Once you have an introspective conversation with yourself, you can take another leap forward by organizing a conversation with colleagues.

What does respect mean to each of you?

How do you know when it's thriving?

What are the warning signs when respect is waning?

Questions like these will prompt vigorous dialogue, and people will start to unload their respect-related stories from past and present work situations. All of this will give life, meaning, and a remarkable degree of tangibility to an otherwise hazy concept.

> If enough time is devoted to this, the group will likely reach a common ground on the look and feel of genuine respect in the workplace.

If enough time is devoted to this, the group will likely reach a common ground on the look and feel of genuine respect in the workplace. This won't happen automatically, of course; you or someone, using a facilitative touch, will have to coax the conversation in that direction. But it's well worth the effort, and from there, participants can develop a list of practical action ideas aimed at boosting the respect level in their work area.

Is Respect a Stated Priority?

You and your colleagues will also want to look for opportunities to address respect in any formal or informal conversations regarding purpose, vision, goals, objectives, values, or working principles. Somewhere in these, respect should be strongly implied—or better yet, explicitly stated and (to the degree possible) defined.

> Your timing and opening have to be just right on this, and if you can tag your comments to some kind of immediate situation, all the better.

If you already have your mission and direction spelled out, and respect is never mentioned, then hoist a red flag at the next major meeting. It's time to pull those wonderful statements out of their oak frames and engage in dialogue to make them more meaningful. This can be done just about anywhere in the organization. If you have a set of working principles for your work unit, for example, do they say something about respect? If not, get talking. If you don't have any working principles, there again, start the conversation. And do it soon—you have lots of work (albeit fulfilling work) ahead of you.

As you read this, you just might be thinking: "If I stop the next meeting to say that we all need to talk about respect, they're gonna send me out to get more donuts—then lock the door." Fair enough. Your timing and opening have to be just right on this, and if you can tag your comments to some kind of immediate situation, all the better.

If the group is anguishing over the steep rise in grievances, for example, you may be looking at the perfect lead-in. "We need to deal with all these grievances," you tell everyone, "but it sure would be nice to begin transforming our relationship with the union so we don't make this our usual way of doing business. The core issue that's involved in all of these is respect—basic respect. I know it's tough to measure, but we have to do something about it." You've set the stage.

A Little Empathy Goes a Long Way

Larry kept saying it throughout our conversation: They just don't understand what it's like. He was talking about his job, bemoaning the fact that the teachers and administrators didn't seem to have a shred of empathy. If only they could do my job for a day, he said.

LORNA'S STORY

"I love where I work," says Lorna, a finisher at a ceramics plant. "There's just a lot of trust here—that's what makes it so great."

Ten years ago, her feelings couldn't have been more different. A rule-obsessive owner kept employees on constant guard. "He treated us like machines," she says.

Then the company was sold, and things changed—dramatically. Lorna: "We knew it would get better when the new owner had the time clock removed. From the very first day, he showed that he trusted us, and he treated us with respect. And we gave him plenty of trust and respect in return."

Maybe they can. And maybe he can experience a bit of *their* jobs. That's right, think about spending a few hours or a whole day walking in someone else's work shoes. Literally try out their job. It's the ultimate exercise in respect building—an opportunity to learn by doing.

Wonder what it's like to work the phones? Want to feel the heat from the blast furnace? Curious about the culture of third shift? It may be a bit tricky to make the arrangements, and you'll surely get some strange looks. But you'll come away with an infinitely deeper understanding of what people do in their jobs. And your respect for them will grow by leaps and bounds.

In many cases, a full day in another job simply isn't feasible. No problem. You can at least open your eyes and ears to what other people do on a daily basis. Visit areas of the workplace where you rarely spend time. Strike up some conversations, and if it's not too much of an interruption, ask for a tour. This might seem a bit out of the ordinary to the people you meet, but it won't take long for them to appreciate your interest. And don't be surprised if they pay you a visit soon after.

Assume the Best

A lot of what has been suggested so far in this chapter is one-time stuff you can do to foster respect in the workplace. There's plenty more you can do that's ongoing. One thing is to be democratic. As one of your general working principles, apply the equivalent of "due process" in the workplace. Whenever negative situations arise and the fingers of blame start pointing, operate under the assumption that people are innocent until proven otherwise.

This is easy to put in print, yet darn difficult to put into practice. But almost always, the situation that seems so cut-and-dried is actually filled with important details—call them mitigating circumstances if you like.

"What's that, Sally is late again?" Sure she is, but it turns out her mother is terribly ill, and Sally is spending nights at the nursing home. "The report is a full day late! Tell Stan that if he can't—" Wait, they had a special request from the CEO to clear the decks and finish the big proposal. Everything else got pushed aside. You get the idea. Steer clear of those knee-jerk assumptions that an employee has done something wrong. When in doubt, give the benefit of the doubt.

Making Decisions *with* People

While we're talking about democracy as it relates to respect, another concept that comes up is involvement. The next time you make a decision, give fuller thought to who might be affected. Then, at a minimum, ask for their input, listen closely to their comments, and make a sincere effort to shape the decision accordingly. Even if your "research" consists of a 15-minute conversation in the break room or several phone calls to folks in the field, you're at least taking a step in the right direction.

Other times, you'll want to be much more thorough in getting input. Why not gather employees for a conversation about the decision at hand? If the workplace is unionized, it might be appropriate to get together with the steward or other union leaders. There may even be an employee advisory group or another team that's ideally suited for chatting about possible decisions and their effects on the organization as a whole—and on individual employees. On still other occasions, you may find that the best decision is not to make the decision—but to hand it off to someone else, preferably a team. Nothing conveys respect more than the vote of confidence that you trust others to make a good (or better) decision.

> Nothing conveys respect more than the vote of confidence that you trust others to make a good (or better) decision.

This doesn't mean that every decision should go through an exhaustive approval process or be passed along to another group. But the purchase of new equipment, for instance, is something that would benefit from wide input. So would a decision on changes to the sick-leave policy. And so would a decision on where to locate the new office. These are things that touch people directly.

Take a Stand

A chapter on respect would be woefully incomplete if it didn't mention courage. The fact is, when it comes to creating a respect-filled workplace, very often what you need are good old-fashioned guts. You obviously have no control over other people's intestinal fortitude, but you're in charge of your own. So here's your

BELIEVE IT OR NOT

Leave the G-String at Home

After an employee came to work wearing what someone considered to be "revealing" clothing, the HR office put together an extensive description of the dress policy. Included was the explicit statement that "appropriate undergarments are to be worn."

At first people laughed. What is "appropriate"? Who enforces the rule? And for goodness' sake, *how* do they enforce it? Then the talk turned serious, and it focused squarely on respect. Everyone had the same reaction: How dare they send a memo like that!

challenge: Whenever you see disrespect rearing its ugly head, take a visible, vocal stand against it.

If you're in a meeting where people are unfairly disparaging the hard work of the clerical staff, speak up in their defense. If another session finds someone strategizing on how to sneak a new policy by the employees, again, speak up in favor of openness and honesty. And when you're in a one-on-one situation where someone's comments or behavior strikes you as disrespectful, again, take a deep breath and give them a diplomatic piece of your mind.

Don't want to be a rabble-rouser? Well, it's all in your approach. Obviously, an in-your-face challenge at the board meeting won't get you anywhere, except maybe on the unemployment rolls. But a subtle, well-placed question just might change the direction of the conversation. Whatever you do, avoid compromising your respect ethic simply to get along.

> **Someone:** Those secretaries are worthless. They had my materials for five days and never finished the project.

> **You:** Did you talk with Chris (who coordinates the clerical group) to find out the reason for the delay?

> **Someone Else:** They always have an excuse.

> **Someone:** I'm gonna talk to them this afternoon.

> **You:** I ran into a delay once, but it was because their system went down for a day. It messed up my schedule, but it wasn't their fault. And really, when you think about it, they do pretty good work. Remember their heroics with the Lambert project?

Becoming Part of the Solution

If Larry happens to read this chapter, it wouldn't be surprising to find him a bit ticked off. For the most part, the ideas and suggestions place the burden on him to help create a workplace that's rich with respect. You can almost hear him protesting: Isn't respect a basic thing that should come automatically? Aren't we all entitled to it? Why should I have to work for it?

Sure, it *should* happen naturally, but so should a lot of other fundamental principles. Respect needs care and feeding, and true to its reciprocal nature, the care and feeding need to start with you. If you lock yourself into an entitlement mindset, holding out for the day when respect finally comes your way, you might be setting yourself up for a long, frustrating wait. Even worse, your feelings might intensify to the point where you start showing disrespect for others. Larry might be headed that way. You'll remember from his story that he now just does his work and keeps quiet.

At the very least, he needs to reknit his connection to his colleagues. He also needs to reflect on his own thoughts to make sure he's not part of the problem. Then he needs to become part of the solution.

Reality Check: RESPECT

1 = very strongly disagree   5 = agree
2 = strongly disagree   6 = strongly agree
3 = disagree   7 = very strongly agree
4 = neutral; neither disagree nor agree

_____ People show respect for one another regardless of rank and title.
_____ When decisions are made, there's a thoughtful assessment of how each option might affect people.
_____ People are treated like adults. There's no patronizing parent–child tone in the relationship among managers and front-line employees.
_____ The golden rule is an implicit working principle throughout the organization.
_____ There's widespread respect for employees' judgment. When challenges arise, people freely decide how to respond—as opposed to always being told what to do.

_____ = Total ÷ 5 = _____ = RESPECT RATING

Chapter 8

Equality

Pull up to the custom-made plastics plant where Susan works, and you'll immediately see inequality. It's in the parking lot, where five spaces have been reserved for the top managers. Walk inside, and you'll find paneled offices for people with big titles and lockers for everyone else. Even the words people use—the frequent references to "upper management," "top executives," and "senior staff"—speak of inequality. So it's hard to see why Susan is feeling optimistic about the state of equality in her workplace, until she tells the story. For years, whenever prospective customers visited the plant, they would have a carefully orchestrated meeting with a small group of upper managers—and only upper managers. Then one fateful day, a would-be client asked to hear from equipment operators and others in production. As management held its breath, the prospect asked question after question, and the employees provided rich answers. Next came a spur-of-the-moment plant tour and more questions and answers. The prospect went on to sign a contract later the same day, and in the process, he opened up plenty of management minds. Three more prospect visits have occurred since then, and each time, folks from the front line have been included in the conversation. "We have a long way to go," Susan says, "but we're starting to feel more like equals."

Susan went on to talk a lot more about equality. She felt that everyone in her company, to a person, would say that equality is a good thing. Yet the way the organization was set up—the top-down structure, its reliance on titles, the look and feel of the meetings, how resources were shared, and so much more—seemed to promote inequality.

> One fateful day, a would-be client asked to hear from equipment operators and others in production.

So did the inertia of tradition. Those manager-only meetings with customers had been going on for years. The top managers were perfectly happy with the arrangement, but everyone else felt cut out of the process. It took an outsider to provide the necessary shock to the system, but even Susan admits that positive change is barely getting under way.

The previous chapter explored respect, which is a very personal proposition—something that often happens one on one. Equality, by comparison, tends to be organizational. In a meaningful workplace, there's no class system driving wedges between people. Everyone is a first-class citizen. In a meaningful workplace, it wouldn't dawn on people to restrict those customer meetings to top management only. Production folks would be a part of the conversation, not to placate the customer, but because it would seem like the natural thing to do.

> In a meaningful workplace, it wouldn't dawn on people to restrict those customer meetings to top management only.

The employees in a meaningful workplace operate with an interesting organization chart. On paper, they might have a supervisor or manager or someone who's in a "box" above them. But operationally speaking, everyone is on the same level. The real org chart is one big flat layer of people. It's not "us" and "them" within the same workplace. It's just "us."

The Danger of "Manageable" Pieces

In a quest for order and control, so many organizations break things into manageable pieces. Look at their organization charts, and you'll see for yourself. There are layers and layers of separate boxes, all put there with good intentions.

Yet this order-by-pieces approach has plenty of unintended effects, most of them bad, including internal competition, confusion over what other work units are doing, a tell-me-what-to-do attitude, fractured communication lines, and an overall lack of holistic thinking. Those manageable pieces suddenly start to turn on themselves, making the sum of those pieces anything but manageable.

And it can get worse. The dependence on hierarchy as the primary approach to organizing often shapes how people relate to one another. A social hierarchy forms—a pecking order of sorts—complete with multiple classes of citizens. Divisions erupt not just between functions and physically separate areas, but between entire employee "classes" within these functions and areas.

The Power of Words

You can often see inequality simply by looking around or by picking up the latest org chart. But to get deeper insights, pay close attention to people's conversations. You just might hear inequality in a few key phrases. Here are some of them:

John and Mary work <u>under</u> Jennifer.
Jennifer is <u>over</u> John and Mary.

"Over" and "under" blatantly reinforce the notion of top-down hierarchy. At their most innocent, words like these can make John *and* Mary feel less important than Jennifer. More seriously, the thinking behind these words can create a one-way relationship in which John and Mary expect Jennifer to tell them what to do. It breeds the opposite of ownership.

I <u>oversee</u> the people in accounting.

We won't dwell on the image of slavery and the historical overtones of "oversee" or its companion word, "overseer." It's bad enough that the word is all about watching and inspecting—basically, about standing by and waiting for people to screw up. It's the opposite of coach, of taking action to help people be successful.

Frank works <u>for me</u>.

If you're Frank's customer, okay, he works for you. But if this is said in the context of a traditional boss relationship, it's all wrong. In fact, the "boss" should be working for Frank, helping him be successful in carrying out the mission. Speaking of which...

I'm his <u>boss</u>.

The word *boss* is used so recklessly. It seems to have become such a part of our workplace vocabulary that we don't give it a second thought. And that's a shame because its meaning is sharply at odds with equality. Listen to Webster: "a person who exercises control or authority; one who directs or supervises workers."

Share this information with your subordinates.

It's becoming less common nowadays, but you still hear the term *subordinate.* Talk about hierarchy. In noun form, it's bad enough, but as an adjective, it's brutal. Back to Webster: "placed in or occupying a lower class, rank, or position; inferior; submissive to or controlled by authority."

Here are some more:
Frank is one of my direct reports.
Make sure this gets to the lower levels.
Tell your people about the upcoming changes.

Using the Right Words

The words we use don't just reflect how we see the world. Used often enough, they also shape the world we see. That's why perking up our ears and hearing this stuff is just a start. As much as possible, we also need to delete these words from the organizational vocabulary—starting with your own everyday conversations.

A mere change of preposition can make a difference: "with me" instead of "for me." So can a simple verb change: "facilitate" or "coach" instead of "oversee." Use this new language in your spoken and written words. The impact won't be immediate, but people *are* listening.

> A mere change of preposition can make a difference: "with me" instead of "for me."

An appropriate next step—a next leap, actually—is to edit the policy manual, employee handbook, orientation guides, and any other printed items. Chances are, you'll find plenty of inequality-inducing words. Get rid of them once and for all.

Of course, a solo attack on the policy manual won't win you any friends, no matter how wonderful your intentions. Make this a group effort, and consider involving people who take the most traditional approach when it comes to hierarchy and workplace language. You'll certainly be opening a can of worms, but you'll be opening some hearts and minds as well.

Rethink Those Job Titles

While you're thinking about language, consider job titles. How are they used in your organization? Are they fairly innocent, or have they become a simmering source of inequality? In worst-case situations, organizations seem more like caste systems, with titles used as labels to tell who fits where in the pecking order. If you see signs of title-flexing, at least be aware of the problem. Turning things around can be a big battle indeed, and not because all those business cards would have to get reprinted. Egos are at stake. ("It took me years to get 'Senior' in front of my VP!")

Your best starting place is with yourself. If the organization imposes a title on you, you can always edit it when introducing yourself to others. "I'm the VP for finance, but I like to think of myself as the Facilitator of Mission-Focused Chaos." "My business card says I'm a quality assurance specialist, but I'm more like the Resident Customer. My job is to be the voice of the customer here every minute of the workday."

Perhaps your informal (real) title can even be printed beneath your formal title. As for your colleagues, your title angst might inspire them to follow suit and come up with something of their own. Issue a challenge and see what happens.

Reinvent Your Get-Togethers

In the story that opened this chapter, Susan talked about the source of her recent optimism: Front-line employees were being included in meetings with prospective customers. It's a reminder that equality (or the lack thereof) often shows up not only in the words people use, but also in the look and feel of employee gatherings.

The old model is still the current model at many organizations: big table, usually square or rectangular, with the "boss" at the "head." (Does that mean everyone else is at the "foot" of the table—and that the head does all the thinking?) The boss sets the agenda and leads the meeting. People are asked for their opinions, and they tactfully give them. Most of the participants are allowed to be there because they have the necessary title or rank. Politeness abounds. Everything seems so tidy. Then the meeting is adjourned on time (efficiency is so important!), marking the start of yet another day filled with passive-aggressive behavior.

WILLIAM'S STORY

When William's company launched a quality-improvement initiative, it was *not* business as usual. "We actually did it the right way!" he laughs. Instead of a management-driven effort, a group was assembled to involve people from all areas and levels of the organization.

The first few gatherings were uncomfortable; never before had employees with such different titles and roles come together in the same place. Yet everyone stuck with it, and within three months the group became widely known as a shining example of partnership. "At our first meeting, we talked about leaving rank at the door," William recalls.

"It takes time as folks rework their relationships. Now that we've been together as a group for a couple years, I can honestly say that we all view each other as equals."

Talk about a paradigm—one that sends an ear-piercing message of inequality. Why not try something different? What about a meeting with no table? What about putting the chairs in a circle? What about having participants take turns facilitating each session? What about not having the boss at the meeting? And what about widening participation so the Susans of the world can add their considerable brainpower to the issues at hand? Any or all of these improvements will help restore a sense of equality, and they'll also make for a more productive, useful get-together.

Unfortunately, old habits die hard, and the old-style meeting is a classic horror-film monster. It just keeps coming baaaaack. So you need to keep coming back as well with meeting techniques that promote equality. If you're the traditional meeting leader, it should be easy enough to dispense with the table. Start out each get-together with a quick check-in from all participants so they have equal voice, at least at the start.

> The old-style meeting is a classic horror-film monster. It just keeps coming baaaaack.

As everyone gets more comfortable, consider bringing in an outside facilitator who can model effective meeting techniques. Remember, though, that any facilitator worth his or her salt will work to get wide input from everyone. If you're used to dominating the discussion, you'll have to wear some mental duct tape across your mouth—and it won't feel pleasant at all.

If other meetings find you in the "attendee" role, your ability to transform things will be tougher to pull off. Take advantage of all opportunities to mention your success with a "slightly different" meeting approach. Offer to help develop the agenda, produce the meeting notes, or even facilitate a segment or two. You might be able to manipulate—er, influence—things for the better by taking on a regular role. If the meeting leader is grousing about a lack of creativity among group members, tell about the effective facilitator who's working miracles with some other group. Enough little nudges in the right direction might be sufficient over time to change the look and feel of these get-togethers.

Haves and Have-Nots

Resources are another battleground where equality often loses. Right now, conduct a quick thumbnail assessment:

Which employees can tap into learning opportunities?

Which have e-mail or Web access?

Who has computers?

Who has old computers and who has the newest, fastest, loaded-to-the-teeth models?

Who gets free uniforms or reserved parking spaces or company cars?

> As long as our civilization is essentially one of property, of fences, of exclusiveness, it will be mocked by delusions.
>
> —RALPH WALDO EMERSON

If you find yourself dividing the workplace as you go through these questions, you're face to face with a major cause of inequality. Unless there's a persuasive reason why only certain people should get certain resources, then everyone should have access. Front-row parking for senior executives because they're senior executives is hardly persuasive. Nor is it justified to restrict e-mail to a certain group because "we're worried that everyone else will use it for personal stuff." (You wouldn't yank out all the phones if someone called home to check up on the kids, would you?)

If your work area is the scene of such inequalities, and you can get rid of them, do it now. In some cases, you'll want to end a "privilege" (special parking)—whereas in other cases, you'll want to open the resource to everyone (e-mail). Even something small, like access to certain data, can be significant in the eyes of someone who has never had the chance to check it out. If you're still stumped as to where to implement changes, get together a diverse group of employees. They'll have plenty of ideas.

Trading in Layers for Projects

One powerful alternative to traditional hierarchy is to adopt a project mindset. Instead of organizing in the traditional layered way, let specific initiatives become the gravity that pulls people together. In the words of one person who has been there: "For six months I might be working on the new prototype. People from all sorts of functional areas are involved, and rather than having a traditional boss, we have a facilitator and project sponsor. Six months later—or sooner, depending on how the project goes—I'm off to another project team."

The beauty of a project-centered approach is that it can start anywhere in the organization. That's right, in fine guerilla-fighting fashion, it can exist even within a traditional layer-upon-layer structure. The approach will attract its critics, to be sure, but there will be plenty of converts and copycats as well. Look around your own corner of the work world for opportunities to organize around a project. If the initiative is such that it requires people from different functions and areas of the organization, perfect.

A lot has been written lately about how to organize around projects. Much of the new thinking and practice has emerged from the surging world of Internet-related companies, where projects have quickly become a proven way to bring out the best in people—and in the process, to create a workplace where equality thrives. For the very freshest insights, check out *Fast Company*. This monthly magazine is a gold mine of ideas and profiles showing how organizations are combining tough-minded performance with a deep respect for human values.

Also grab some of the latest stuff by Tom Peters. He's a project zealot who urges everyone to turn every job into a project. He tells anyone who will listen (and a lot of people who won't): "Projects are the nuggets . . . the atoms . . . the basic particles . . . of the new economy."

A Fair Day's Pay for a Fair Day's Work

The reward systems that most of us live under are a reflection of our enduring class system and our love affair with leadership. The challenge is to create pay practices that support the heart of stewardship, which is accountability and commitment to the well-being of the whole.

—Peter Block,
Stewardship: Choosing Service Over Self-Interest

It's the great untouchable at many organizations, but I'd be derelict not to inquire: What about your compensation system and its impact on equality? If it's strictly a title-driven kind of thing, with pay rates consistently getting higher as you go up in status, well, then it simply reinforces hierarchy. If there's a big compensation divide between a handful of folks at "the top" and everyone else in the organization, again, what you have is a bad case of haves and have nots. And make no mistake, people talk about this stuff. Not because they want a BMW or a vacation home, but because it strikes at the basic principle of fairness.

If you think your organization's compensation system has become a serious unequalizer, and you're in a position to do something about it, you face some tough choices. One option is to do nothing, and you might be fine—though "fine" can be a rather precarious position if your industry is even remotely competitive. This is the high-risk path.

Option two, the path of most resistance, starts with learning. Pull out all the stops to see what other organizations have reinvented their compensation systems. Perhaps you can even visit a few of them to deepen your understanding. Call in a seasoned consulting firm, ideally one that specializes in compensation systems yet respects human values and appreciates the systemic nature of things, and have them examine the situation. Also consider pulling together a cross-section of employees to get them involved as well—though their first, second, and third steps are to learn, learn, and learn about this complex topic.

Get clear on the following: What do you want your compensation system to promote? What should be its underlying values? How does it fit into your overall vision and purpose as an organization? Widely involve people in probing these questions. Once there are answers, the nitty-gritty reinvention can begin in earnest.

Reality Check: EQUALITY

1 = very strongly disagree   5 = agree
2 = strongly disagree   6 = strongly agree
3 = disagree   7 = very strongly agree
4 = neutral; neither disagree nor agree

_____ People throughout the organization genuinely feel that they're on the same level, regardless of how things look on the organization chart.

_____ All individuals are considered to be equally important . . .

_____ . . . and actions at all levels reflect this core value.

_____ At meetings and other gatherings, titles tend to fall away, opening the way to free-flowing dialogue.

_____ There are no physical cues of inequality, such as special parking spaces for high-ranking employees, dramatically different work areas and working conditions, and recognition reserved for certain groups.

_____ = Total ÷ 5 = _____ = EQUALITY RATING

Equality Starts in the Parking Lot

When Jim Bushman drove into the parking lot on his first day of work, he could have taken one of the spaces reserved for senior executives. As one of two partners who had just bought Cast-Fab Technologies, a producer of industrial castings and fabrications, he had the credentials. Instead, Bushman put his car in another space and immediately put an end to reserved parking.

Soon after that, he had all the time clocks removed. He says simply, "They seemed to be a downer for everybody."

That was in 1988, and ever since, Cast-Fab has been transforming itself into a model of workplace respect and equality. The changes reflect Bushman's core philosophy, which he boils down to one sentence: "People come in and do things right on purpose."

It's a radical philosophy when you consider that not too long ago, engineers made nearly all the decisions on how work would get done. They'd design the process, decide what tools would be used, and tell production workers how to do it. It reflected a fractured system, with different functions remaining in their own silos. And it made some people rightfully feel like second-class citizens.

This approach followed the time clock onto the scrap heap. With Bushman's encouragement, Cast-Fab literally brought all the different functions together by creating work teams. Each team includes people from engineering, production, scheduling, and purchasing, and they all work in the same location. Hourly employees are among the team leaders. Before, people from different functions would rarely talk. Now it happens all the time. Stop by Cast-Fab any morning, and you're likely to see a welder having coffee with an engineer.

One production employee had been with the company 20 years when he finally became a member of one of these work teams. It marked the first time, he said, that anyone had ever asked for his opinion on how the work should get done.

As respect and equality continue to grow, there has been a profound change in people's relationships. Ten years ago, it was taboo to talk to your boss's boss. Now it's commonplace. Before, coming in late meant another note in the discipline file. Now, people go to their supervisor and talk about it so the reasons are fully understood.

Bushman's nutshell advice? Bring people together. It makes a difference on a personal level, and it's good for business.

Informality

At the company where she used to work, Shelly was affectionately known as the social director. It started when she organized a lunchtime birthday party for a colleague. It ended up being so much fun that Shelly became the go-to person for workplace social gatherings. That was five years ago, and she has since moved on, working as an engineer at an assembly plant. Her job isn't much different, but the workplace sure is. There's a strict dress code, all sorts of protocol, and an overall feeling of stuffiness. When she began her job as a billing supervisor, her colleagues kept greeting her in formal fashion by using her last name. "I must have said it a hundred times, 'Please call me Shelly.' But the formality runs so deep over here that they had trouble getting used to it."

Shelly's story has very little to do with party hats and birthday cakes. It's more about the personality of the organization. As she put it: "I'd like a workplace that isn't so stifling."

In so many interviews, people explained how their workplaces seemed burdened down by excessive formality. The word *stifling* came up again. So did *oppressive* and *stuffy*. The way they described things, it seemed like formality had taken precedence over people.

> In a meaningful workplace . . . no one deifies a set of heavily starched traditions.

What happens in a meaningful workplace is entirely different. No one obsessively follows rigid or politicized ways of doing things. No one deifies a set of heavily starched traditions. And though people take the work seriously, they don't take themselves too seriously.

Informality is evident in the way people personalize their work areas. You'll see family photos, drawings from the kids, knick-knacks that have special meaning to someone. People can wear formal business clothes if they want to, but there's no unbending requirement—only the expectation that everyone will use his or her best judgment. (If I have a meeting with Mr. or Ms. Formal, I'll adjust and wear a suit.) You can even hear the informality. It's in the hum of casual conversation and the laughs that lift above all the seriousness.

Why Is This Important?

You might be wondering what all the fuss is about. Who cares whether an organization is full of formality? If it's okay with the people who work there, why worry about it?

First, you're *assuming* that all that formality is fully acceptable to everyone in the workplace. Unless you've asked folks directly, who can tell for sure? It's a likely bet that at least one Shelly is in your midst.

> Rather than deal with forms, massive rules and regulations, we just slap some dough down, put some sauce on top of it and try to keep the customer happy.
>
> —LOUIS PIANCONE,
> PIZZA ENTREPRENEUR

But more important, even if people seem to accept the formal way of doing things, that might not be what's best for the workplace. At first glance, formality seems like a hazy and fairly innocent concept. Yet it can shape the way things are done on a daily basis and end up making life more difficult for employees and customers.

For instance, formality gets into our work processes. It can string them out with time-consuming approvals and check-offs, all because protocol dictates that certain people get to review the work as it moves along. Innocent stuff? Not when it's viewed by front-line employees as a lack of trust in them, or when it leads to longer process times that keep customers waiting.

Then there's dialogue. In an excessively formal workplace, there are often unwritten rules on who can talk to whom. Certain topics are off the table. Even when conversation gets under way, it often ends up being more of a one-way flow, with tradition and protocol deciding who gets all the airtime. The result? Many problems are left to simmer beneath the surface, either because people feel they can't bring them up or because they're not thoroughly addressed once they're uncovered. Also missed are opportunities to build relationships, seize opportunities, show appreciation, develop a shared vision, and much, much more.

Where formality reigns, you also often find excessive hierarchy. Communication is a top-down proposition. People have to go through "channels" to get things done. They feel the need to play "politics." All this can have a serious effect on respect and equality, two of the other people keys.

Don't Take My Word for It

The preceding section is *my* answer to why informality is so important. But you need to formulate your own answer that's tailored to your own situation. If you can involve your colleagues in this process, all the better.

On a whiteboard or piece of paper, create a four-column grid, as shown here. Start out by focusing on the first column, brainstorming all the signs of formality in your workplace. List them separately going down the column. If you think something might be a symptom of formality but you're not sure, include it anyway.

Now focus on the second and third columns. For each sign of formality, decide whether it helps or hurts employees or customers. You'll be thinking about your underlying purpose as an organization, your vision of the future that you and others are striving to create, the down-to-earth goals and objectives you might have—all of which are embodied in the mission keys. You also should be thinking about respect, equality, and other meaning keys. If you decide that something does help or hurt, define how, then capture your analysis by writing it down on the grid.

IRENE'S STORY

"Walking into our office is like walking into a mausoleum, people are that stiff," says Irene, a secretary for an engineering firm.

On her first day she was taken aside and "encouraged" to wear more formal attire. A year after being there, she worked up the courage to suggest a holiday party— something informal at a local restaurant. It turned out that a party *was* being planned—a formal wine and cheese mixer at a local art museum.

"Every time I leave the office at the end of the day," she says, "I feel like I need emergency oxygen."

Signs of formality	How formality helps employees and/or customers	How formality hurts employees and/or customers	How can we improve the situation?

The last column is all about action. Focus on those signs of formality that seem to be causing harm, and analyze *why* they exist in the workplace. Only after digging deep to uncover root causes should you move into developing some potential action ideas.

This exercise leaves formality with nowhere to hide. It prompts people to take a fresh look at their situation and honestly determine the impact on employees and customers. Now you can see why it's so important to turn this into a group activity. Even an hour or so of conversation at an upcoming meeting will make a difference because it will put the issue of formality on everyone's mind.

The Small Stuff Can Be Big Stuff

This analysis—even if you give it just a passing thought—makes clear that formality tends to be deeply rooted in an organization's culture. You'll recall how frustrated Shelly became when trying to get her colleagues to dispense with the formal greetings; she simply wanted to be called by her first name. It's a powerful reminder that when it comes to bringing informality to the workplace, you might want to set your expectations low. Start small, and begin with the one person you can always count on: yourself.

One quick, visible tactic is to add a few informal touches to your workspace. A friend of mine started his solo effort with a color shirt. That's right, *a color shirt*. The workplace had an unwritten rule that all men should wear white shirts, and one day he looked in his closet, took a deep breath, and put

> Smile. It makes people wonder what you're thinking.
>
> —Anonymous

on (god forbid!) a nonwhite shirt. "It seems so foolish to anguish over such a thing," he says today, "but you have to appreciate the work atmosphere." And yes, he made progress. "No one said a single word about our white-shirt obsession or about my civil disobedience, but you know what? Within several months, at least half of the guys were wearing color or striped shirts." His next challenge? "No tie."

At another organization, this one a rather stuffy financial-services firm, a budget analyst covered his filing cabinet with tiny magnetic words. Even the most reserved visitors couldn't resist the urge to compose their own silly sentences and poems, and within a few weeks, everyone was stopping by to check out the latest literary works. (A nice counterbalance to their focus on numbers, don't you think?)

While we're speaking of words, and thinking again of Shelly, you also might want to watch your language. Is there an excess of "Mr." and "Ms." references when people talk with each other? Someone has to start using those first names, org-chart rank be damned. Maybe it should be you. And what about meeting protocol? Does everyone wait in polite silence until Mr. or Ms. Bigtitle talks first? Does this person sit at the head of the table while everyone else dutifully sits at the sides?

If you yourself happen to be Mr. or Ms. Bigtitle (you know who you are!), think about making some changes. A round table, or a circle of chairs without a table, sends a physical message that we're all in this together. And a round-robin check-in, with each person giving a three-minute update, is a good way to get folks talking. So is sugar—really. Bring a big bag of candy to the next meeting. Simple? It sure is, so why don't you try it?

A Change of Scenery

If you can't bring some informality to the workplace, try bringing the workplace to the informality. Perhaps you can organize a picnic, for example, and encourage people to bring their families. Without many of the formal cues, like wood paneling and wingtips, people just might start relaxing and mingling. Some of this informality will find its way back to the workplace.

If you want to keep it for employees only, schedule the picnic during regular work hours. That's right, shut the place down and head someplace where people can get away from their work and focus on each other. If a picnic seems too big of a leap for your hyper-formal organization, try holding a meeting off-site. That quarterly session always held in that austere conference room can seem oh so different in a lodge setting with an all-glass wall overlooking a scenic ravine.

CHRIS'S STORY

When Chris talks about the ingredients of a meaningful workplace, he always comes back to one thing: sugar.

His office has an annual tradition called the Festival of Treats, in which employees come to work loaded down with cakes, cookies, and candy. The event is held in September— a typically slow month for the office.

The sugarfest gets people eating, to be sure—but also talking. In some cases, people who've kept their conversations to an occasional hallway hello finally get the chance to chat. "It always succeeds in loosening us up," says Chris.

To Whom It May Concern: Please Lighten Up

Is an obsession with formality slowing down the internal communication process or leading to miscommunications? Some memo-writers are afflicted with a condition known as "excessive verbiage syndrome." They insist on utilizing prodigious terminology and phrasing, and they also show an inclination to repeat themselves and make the same point twice, as opposed to utilizing an approach to communication that is absent of confusing sentences like this one. (Crystal clear, ain't it?) Other memos, especially ones that relate to policies, often sound like they're written by an attorney—probably because in most cases, they are.

You'll score a minor victory for informality if you edit your own internal writing. Write like you talk. Be crisp, clear, and conversational. If writing isn't your thing, hand the job to someone else. And if it's already someone's job, encourage him or her to ease up on the formality. It may even be worthwhile to have memos and letters "test read" by someone who's known for directness. If that person has trouble figuring out what the note says, it's time to start rewriting.

There also may be too much formality in how the information is presented. Are memos printed on official company letterhead, complete with the full name and title of the sender—even when it's just another memo *du jour* from someone everyone knows? If so, lighten up. Save the letterhead for contacts with external customers. In fact, if employees have e-mail, skip the hard copy entirely and reach them electronically. (This will even give them the chance to respond. You *do* want a response, don't you?)

> If you have the chance to skip written communications entirely and meet with people face to face, do it.

Last but not least, if you have the chance to skip written communications entirely and meet with people face to face, do it. You may still want to have a handout, but there's no substitute for the personal touch when you're conveying an important message.

Is Your Policy Manual Full of Formal Decrees?

In some cases, formality is written right into the policies of the organization. Flip through your organization's employee handbook and see for yourself.

Start with the dress code. Is it more formal than it needs to be? If so, why? And what would happen if the whole code were tossed out the window? If a wholesale dumping isn't possible, how can the rules be significantly relaxed?

Next, look for guidelines on how to format memos or other written documents. Find anything? If so, your formality alarm should be ringing wildly. Unless there's a persuasive reason why written stuff should follow a common format—such as a requirement by an industry auditing group whose standards you *must* obey—why bog down the communication process with worthless formality?

And what about protocol? Are there any policies or other written statements that provide guidelines—a more accurate word would be "decrees"—on how to follow the chain of command? You know what we're talking about: "If you have a suggestion, first consult with your immediate supervisor. The supervisor will then . . . ." Anything that reinforces a rigid top-down mentality should be exorcised like the demon that it is.

Okay, easier said than done. It's especially tough when the policies are tightly held by a small group of senior managers, which is usually the case in formality-infested organizations. If you're one of those "seniors," what's stopping you? Pinpoint the one policy that seems to be the best candidate for white-out. Bring it up at the next meeting, and make your best case. In the process, you'll draw attention to the issue of formality in general and the policies in particular. You just might end up with some allies (even one would be nice) who'll also make a mission of attacking excessive formality.

> ## JIM'S STORY
>
> "It sometimes seems like I work at a social club, and yet we get tons of work done!"
>
> At the engineering firm where he's a computer specialist, Jim and his colleagues spend a lot of time at what appears to be socializing. A *lot* of time! The workplace is designed with open areas to bring people together.
>
> "When we need to discuss something, it's no big deal," Jim says. "You'd probably hear a lot more laughing than you do at most companies, but that's just the way we operate."

If you're not one of the chosen few, you need a different strategy—and a lot more patience. Diplomatically point out how a certain written policy is not only making the place too formal, but also having a negative impact on productivity and customer service. If you can make a link to the bottom line, you'll have a case. Anything else will sound like garden-variety griping.

Reality Check: INFORMALITY

1 = very strongly disagree

2 = strongly disagree

3 = disagree

4 = neutral; neither disagree nor agree

5 = agree

6 = strongly agree

7 = very strongly agree

_____ An open-door policy is practiced by everyone, not because business books encourage it, but because it feels like the natural thing to do.

_____ When it comes to workplace attire, people exercise their good judgment, wearing whatever is appropriate for the situation.

_____ People are comfortable decorating their workspaces with photos, plants, cartoons, posters, and more.

_____ It's not unusual for a major project to turn into a major pizza party—with the work still getting done.

_____ There's a widespread feeling that work and fun can go hand in hand.

_____ = Total ÷ 5 = _____ = INFORMALITY RATING

The Serious Side of Fun

At RewardsPlus, "tee time" has special meaning. During late December, employees celebrate the holidays by creating their own miniature golf course, with 18 improvised holes spread throughout all the departments. Forget beepers and cell phones—what you need at this company is a putter.

Then there's the boat. Every other week when weather permits, a different group of employees gets together for a cruise around Baltimore's inner harbor. Oh, and did we mention the baseball games?

RewardsPlus might be one of the funnest businesses around. It's also one of the fastest growing, and make no mistake, they take their work very seriously. Launched in the mid-1990s, the company is a business-to-business e-commerce provider of employee benefits. From 1996 to 1999, employee ranks grew from six to 100, and projections show more of the same as the years unfold.

All this growth, interestingly, has a lot to do with all that fun. An informal atmosphere gets people talking. The more they talk, the more they learn and the closer they become. It translates into better products and services. It's not just a boat ride. It's a chance to get to know one another and share ideas away from the ringing phones and whirring disk drives.

Of course, informality hasn't been the only key to the company's success. Ownership and direction also come into play. All employees receive stock options, and there are meaningful goals and objectives for the organization, the departments, and individuals.

The results show up in ways both big and small. In 1996, when the company had just six employees, one of the newcomers came up with the crazy idea that the Internet would redefine the marketplace. Empowered to develop his vision, he ended up single-handedly changing the focus of the business plan.

Other examples come to life every day. When the main phone lines get heavy incoming traffic, people from other work areas happily pitch in. It doesn't matter that answering the phones isn't their regular job. It's *their* company that's getting the call.

Flexibility

It's spelled out in the consulting firm's employee handbook: Work hours are from 8 A.M. to 5 P.M. Monday through Friday. So Carl, a senior consultant, knew the cards were stacked against him when he approached his rule-driven supervisor one Friday afternoon. Carl had worked 60 billable hours that week, and he wanted to come in at 10 A.M. on Monday—just two hours past the usual starting time. He explained his request and waited while a long pause filled the room. The supervisor knew all about Carl's intense workweek, yet he responded by quoting chapter and verse from the employee handbook. "If we bend the rule for one person," the supervisor said, "we'll have to bend it for everyone."

In my interview with him, Carl spent a good 15 minutes talking about other ironclad policies. Then he started a new rant about the extensive written procedures that dictated exactly how he and his colleagues were supposed to go about their work.

> The supervisor responded by quoting chapter and verse from the employee handbook.

It's easy to roll our eyes and label him just another employee who can't play by the rules. But when you think about the real theme of his story, some interesting questions begin to surface.

Do all these rules help employees? Do they help customers?

If not, why do we keep them?

For that matter, why do we want to populate the workplace with people who "play by the rules"? Our goal is to be mission-focused, right? Shouldn't we expect people to "play by the *mission*"?

Wouldn't it even make sense for employees to break a rule or even abolish a rule every now and then if it freed up their potential and meant better service to the customer?

In a meaningful workplace, mission and people come first, and the rules are there only to the degree that they help. They're few in number, and they bend easily. This has nothing to do with having a "loose" environment where people eagerly abuse the "lack" of rules. It has everything to do with creating a workplace built on trust, support, and freedom.

What do *you* think? Is it better to spend precious energy to stop people from doing the wrong thing, or to give people the flexibility they often need to do the right thing?

Rules Will Fill the Mission Void

Carl's situation is not unique. In fact, you probably have a story or two of your own about inflexible rules. Why is it that so many workplaces are so rule-infested?

> If we succeed in maintaining focus, rather than hands-on control, we also create the flexibility and responsiveness that every organization craves. What leaders are called upon to do in a chaotic world is to shape their organizations through concepts, not through elaborate rules or structures.
>
> —MARGARET WHEATLEY

A big reason has to do with mission. When it's unclear, or when it's shared by only a handful of people, there's nothing to hold people together. They have no unifying purpose, no shared vision, no common set of down-to-earth goals. Mission provides gravity; it pulls people together. Without it, people can't help moving apart, going in different directions. And when that happens, the powers that be invariably pull out the rules. It's all they have to rein people in, to restore a form of order. Rules are even convenient—look, they're right here, neatly packaged in a handy binder.

In Carl's situation, he had worked a 60-hour week and wanted to come in on Monday two hours after the regular workplace starting time. The "no" from his supervisor sounded like a classic case of "reining in," but perhaps there was more to the story. Had there been any conversation about Carl's schedule for Monday morning? If they were a mission-focused organization and the time away wouldn't interfere with any client engagements (Carl works as a consultant), what was the big deal?

The organization as a whole didn't give much time or attention to customers, Carl said. Sure, they spent many hours working with clients, often at client locations. But in terms of a deep sense of purpose and direction, with customers being a big factor—well, they talked a good game, but their behind-the-scenes actions said something else. The rules, no matter how arbitrary, always came first.

The moral to this story? Don't neglect those mission keys: purpose, direction, relevance, and validation. A strong and widely shared mission may very well be your best way to put rules in the background—and to keep new rules from surfacing.

The Twin Traps of Efficiency and Consistency

The lack of a shared mission explains much of it, but not all of it. Another culprit is our preoccupation with efficiency and consistency.

It's so tempting to reach for the rules and apply them as almost a knee-jerk reaction. It's quick and easy—sort of a fast-food approach to dealing with people, with the same unhealthy results. Whenever there's a "situation"—someone spends a couple of hours playing online blackjack, say, or coffee gets spilled on a keyboard—out comes another decree. The rules proliferate, and before long, the rules rule.

> Consistency is the last resort of the unimaginative.
> —OSCAR WILDE

The alternative to all this requires dialogue, something that was markedly missing from the conversation between Carl and his supervisor. It requires a willingness to see shades of gray, to acknowledge that all situations are different. It even calls for an admission that rules should exist to serve people, and not the other way around.

As for consistency, well, you've probably heard it yourself: "If we let you do it, we'll have to let everyone do it." This phrase is used so often that its advocates fail to see the obvious. Maybe we *should* let everyone do it. Will it be good for people? Will it be good for the mission? If so, why *not* let everyone do it? Even if it benefits just one person and doesn't affect other people or the mission, why not?

Make Flexibility Everyone's Business

Your first challenge in addressing all this is to make flexibility not just your concern, but everybody's business. The best way to do that is by getting folks to talk about it—and not in a gripe session around the coffeemaker. Arrange a widely inclusive employee conversation that digs deep into this issue of rules, mission, and how the two might be at odds.

Here are some prompts guaranteed to stir constructive dialogue:

"Flexible workplace" can be open to wide interpretation. What exactly does it mean to you?

When have rules or policies hampered people's ability to carry out their mission, or pursue their vision, or achieve their goals? What changes would be needed to clear the way?

If these mission elements don't exist, simplify the question: When have rules or policies interfered with things that are important to customers? Again, what does this suggest in the way of needed changes?

What about procedures? Do these suffer from inflexibility? If so, what should we do about it?

> To err is human, to forgive is against company policy.
> —Anonymous

On this latter question, try to get specific examples. "Well," says Bob, "the shipping procedure leaves a lot to be desired. We could be doing so much on the Internet, but instead, our approach is entirely manual." Claire chimes in: "That's right. We're following our procedures to the letter, and we got high marks for it from the auditor who came through last week. But our customers don't care about that. They want the fastest, surest delivery at the best cost—period. And we'd improve all those measures if we could just throw away the old approach and do something that takes advantage of the latest technology."

You'll notice in the preceding questions that there's a bias toward action. People are urged not only to talk about the current situation, but also to propose improvements. This is a critically important part of the conversation. Without it, expect to engage in a major gripefest, with people leaving more distressed than when they came in.

But be careful. You need to balance this action orientation with sufficient analysis. If the dialogue uncovers a rule or procedure that seems especially harmful, take the time to explore *why* it was created in the first place, and why it still exists. The resulting insights will steer you to the right actions.

Making the Most of "Test Cases"

There's a lot that can be done on an ongoing basis as well. For starters, remain alert to situations in which organizational rules, policies, and procedures are put to the test. These are opportunities to conduct on-the-spot flexibility tests—and to set the stage for change in the right direction. Does it seem as if the rules have become more important than people? If so, promptly address the situation, and always take the people's side.

Case in point: Martha, who works in operations, arrives from lunch 35 minutes late. The rule on this is ironclad: Lunch is from 11:30 A.M. to 12:30 P.M. Delays and tardiness are unacceptable. But it turns out that Martha was breaking bread with an important client—the very first time an operations employee met for any length of time with a customer. It's a new practice the company is testing after a survey showed that customers wanted more contact with folks from operations.

So what's the right response? Give Martha a verbal smack for breaking an established rule? After all, she *was* late; everyone saw a big "out" next to her name on the traffic board. Or does it make more sense to re-examine the old rule and either ditch it or add considerable flex?

Just Say No to New Rules

The same diligence should be applied to keep new rules from surfacing. Perhaps you've heard of the "rule creation reflex." It's a serious condition that can afflict well-intentioned managers who face difficult situations, and it triggers a response in which they rush to a notepad or computer or dictation device to create a new written policy.

Example: An employee is spending work time and work equipment to browse Web sites like www.adult.com. Unfortunate Response #1: Browsers are removed from the computers of virtually all employees. Unfortunate Response #2: Employees who are allowed to keep their browsers are

---

SARAH'S STORY

Sarah sells advertising for cable TV, and she loves her work. It offers constant challenges and the chance to meet regularly with external customers. So why is she angry?

"I'm going through hell trying to figure out how they'll pay me on maternity leave. (When she shared her story, Sarah's first child was due in two months.) My income is mostly commission, so when I'm off, I'll really be struggling. My immediate bosses are very flexible, but corporate is another thing. They're totally fixated with rules and tell me my income structure can't be changed."

Sarah doesn't think she should get special treatment. Rather, she thinks the rule book should get special attention—and revision—so it allows greater flexibility.

BELIEVE IT OR NOT

The Open-Toe Ruling

Several VPs got together to discuss their company's staggering turnover rate. They figured it had a lot to do with the strict dress code—the owner was such a stickler for formality that the rules on workplace attire were like something out of a Marine Corps handbook.

The VPs quickly decided that each Friday would be "casual day." They got the owner's grudging go-ahead, and a new rule on casual days made its way to the already hefty policy manual.

Then the personnel manager met with each work unit to explain how things would work. That's when the question came up: "Can we wear sandals?"

Yes, the personnel manager responded.

"Open-toe sandals?"

continued on page 101

issued a list of permissible Web sites, along with the requirement that Internet research should be kept to a maximum of 30 minutes per day. Result #1: The company seals off a massive pipeline of useful information. Result #2: Employees complain about "corporate" and begin finding ways to sneak their Web searches.

So what's a better approach? One way is to deal with these isolated situations on a case-by-case basis. Sounds pretty inefficient, doesn't it? It'll probably happen with some other person, and you'll have to address the situation all over again. Well, maybe you will and maybe you won't. The point is, in a quest for efficiency, do you want to send the message that you don't trust anyone when you really have issues with only one person? Of course not. Efficiency is overrated anyway. Have a private conversation with the source of your concerns, and involve them in shaping the solution.

Get Creative with Schedules and Technology

Many workplaces are pursuing a slightly different kind of flexibility through flextime and telecommuting. The pros almost always outweigh the cons, and with telecommuting, advances in Internet technology are making it more and more attractive.

One approach—and it's truly radical at some organizations—is for a wide cross-section of people to come together and figure it out for themselves. That's right, there would be no prescribed 8-to-5 or 9-to-6 or some other artificial chunking of time. People would create a timetable that works best for their workplace and customers in general, for their work lives in particular, *and* for their lives beyond work. Doing this right takes time, of course. People first need to revisit (if necessary) and refine (very possible) their mission. Then they should obsess over the needs, wants, and hopes of their customers— and use the insights to deepen their understanding of their mission. Then they should get crystal clear on their specific goals. Only after all this will people have the necessary grounding to develop their own work schedules.

This has its limitations, of course. If you work as a mail carrier, to cite one of many examples, customers have clear expectations of when they want you showing up, and you sure can't provide your service by phone. Yet many organizations *can* exert an extreme amount of flexibility—and everyone benefits when they do.

> The personnel manager paused, looked down at the freshly written policy, then made her declaration: "You're permitted to wear open-toe sandals, but only if the toenails are covered with nail polish."

Procedures As Fossils

When procedures are committed to paper as "our way of doing things," they have a way of getting fossilized. Three years later, that original approach remains the same in documented form, and people either ignore what's in print or mindlessly follow it because it *is* in print.

If people are doing the latter and there's a better way—and three years later, there definitely should be!—it's time for change. Pull together a team of employees to look at the documented methods and the approach that's *really* being used in the organization. (From what I've seen, the written procedure and the real procedure often bear no resemblance!) Set some priorities, focusing on the significant few procedures that have the biggest impact on customers. Ideally, get together with customers to find out exactly what certain processes need to deliver—not to "meet expectations" or "conform to requirements" but to make customers positively tingle with hypersatisfaction.

As processes get overhauled, tweaked, or tossed out entirely, the big book of procedures will get updated. Just remember: The moment a procedure gets tucked away in a neat binder or database, it starts getting old. Within a year, it might be downright ancient.

Making Flexibility a Priority

As this chapter winds down, you might be wondering about Carl's own degree of flexibility. Was he open to different ways of doing things? When situations arose with his colleagues that called for a change of plans, was he supportive? Or did he find himself exerting the same kind of inflexibility embodied in the larger system?

He told a revealing story. A colleague had proposed delaying a client report because they still needed some data. The client wasn't expecting the report just yet; it was Carl and other team members who had set their own deadline. Carl had pulled out their project plan and waved it like a rule book, urging everyone to stick to the timetable. Someone then asked Carl what was more important, sticking to an old schedule or ensuring a high-quality report? He opened his ears and his mind, quickly realizing that he had his priorities mixed up. He quietly put the plan back in its folder, and the team went to work figuring out how to get the remaining data.

Reality Check: FLEXIBILITY

1 = very strongly disagree

2 = strongly disagree

3 = disagree

4 = neutral; neither disagree nor agree

5 = agree

6 = strongly agree

7 = very strongly agree

_____ Good judgment is the guiding principle when applying rules and policies. People accept the subjectivity that goes with this.

_____ If a rule, policy, or procedure stands in the way of awesome service to a customer, people do what's best for the customer.

_____ Issues and problems involving one or two people are addressed on a case-by-case basis—and rarely result in the creation of new workplace rules.

_____ When it comes to applying rules and policies, common sense is valued more than consistency.

_____ Policies and procedures are in place, yet people fully understand that specific circumstances may require different approaches.

_____ = Total ÷ 5 = _____ = FLEXIBILITY RATING

Ownership

When Barry got a job as a scheduler at a distribution center, he brought along a simple philosophy: To get ahead at work, you have to get along with your supervisor. And to get along, you have to go along. So he routinely looked to his boss for direction, and when situations called for Barry's judgment, he went straight to the supervisor and let him decide. But now things are changing. Thanks to his 18 months of front-line experience, Barry knows the scheduling process inside out— and he has ideas in mind for making it better. That's the good news. The bad news is that his supervisor has shown very little interest and seems to want Barry to keep doing things the way they've always been done. "I have absolutely no control over what I do," Barry says, admitting that his "go along to get along" philosophy has turned on him. "Now that I'm trying to use my brain, the supervisor and I have become adversaries."

Few concepts have drawn more attention, generated more books, and sparked more workshops than empowerment. And nothing else—not even teams, which may be the only concept that has stirred more dialogue and motion—has been tougher to put into practice.

Part of the reason is that the meaning of empowerment has been distorted. A lot of the guidance—those books, workshops, magazine articles, and so on—has been dumbed down into "five steps" or a single "proven formula." These simplistic approaches are easy to package and market. But they ignore the depth and complexity of change that needs to occur for empowerment to become not just a new set of skills, but an organizational way of thinking and being.

> "Now that I'm trying to use my brain, the supervisor and I have become adversaries."

Some managers have added their own distortions, happily defining the concept in ways that fit their comfortable paradigm of "us" and "them." You'll hear talk of empowerment being "tailored to fit" an organization, but too often, this is code for saying that the people who do the work will simply get a few more privileges. Perhaps they'll receive more frequent updates of decisions, policies, and events that affect the organization. Maybe they'll have more opportunities to be involved in process-improvement teams. Or they might be allowed to participate on a steering committee of some sort, or to stuff their ideas into a suggestion box, or to attend a big banquet that honors employees for all of their hard work during the past year.

The biggest reason empowerment is so difficult to achieve might have to do with the concept itself. As it is commonly practiced, and as Webster's interpretation suggests, empowerment is inherently paternalistic. It's about people who are relatively high up in the organization selectively *giving* things to other people—information, resources, decision-making authority, control, and so forth. It boils down to a bestowing of power, something that not only fits the old us-and-them model, but also perpetuates it.

> You'll hear talk of empowerment being "tailored to fit" an organization, but too often, this is code for saying that the people who do the work will simply get a few more privileges.

This explains why people in "empowered" workplaces can still feel like second-class citizens. They know what's happening. They can see through "empowerment" that is really a controlled, orderly doling out of resources that may or may not have any real value.

For all these reasons, this fifth people key is called ownership rather than empowerment. It embodies the vision of a wide-open information network that reaches everyone, substantial authority and responsibility for all, and an environment where people can make their own decisions on what to do and how to do it. It also has a lot to do with equality. When people are thinking and acting like owners, it's not a matter of waiting until a higher-up gives them something or allows them to do something. People can just take it or do it.

Keep the Other Keys in Mind

This vision of ownership extends far beyond the safe brand of empowerment that many companies pursue. So you might be wondering: Wouldn't it lead to utter chaos?

Yes it would, and it usually does—not because people don't try hard enough or lack sincerity, but because their thinking is too restricted.

The worst thing you can do is to focus exclusively on ownership, to view it in isolation from the other meaning keys. If it's simply dropped into a rule-driven, permission-seeking workplace, chaos *will* ensue. And people will grow more cynical toward change in general and "empowerment" in particular.

Perhaps more than any other key, ownership needs to be pursued hand in hand with other meaning keys. Consider the following:

- When people share a clear understanding of their purpose, a compelling vision of the future they want to create, and a small set of meaningful goals, all of their efforts become sharply focused. This is the kind of environment where ownership thrives. The last thing you want is to slow people down by having them jump through rule hoops, wait for permission, and scrape for resources.
- Respect also comes into play. It's a big hedge against individuals going off in different directions because they're more likely to make decisions *with* people and to weigh the full impact before taking action.
- Ownership calls for ongoing support—not the paternalistic form of boss giving the employees what they need once a request is made, but daily, informal collaboration among people in all areas and positions of the organization.
- Then there are the community keys. All of them contribute to ownership, but dialogue, service, and oneness are especially important. These keys ensure that people work together as they pursue their mission.

As you can see, there's a lot more to ownership than just ownership. But don't let that scare you away from it. There are specific, practical things you

KEITH'S STORY

What do farming and teaching have in common? More than you might think, says Keith.

Growing up on a family farm, he had a long list of daily chores. But he also had wide independence, and he loved it. "I knew what had to be done, but *how* I went about my work was largely up to me," he recalls.

Today, as a tenth-grade English teacher, he thrives on that same kind of ownership. The school system sets clear expectations and goals, to be sure, but the teachers are able to develop their own teaching plans. "What I want to shape is how my classes unfold, and that's exactly what I can do."

can do to make ownership an integral part of your work life and workplace. They're the focus of the rest of this chapter.

Asking Versus Taking

A lot of the current literature makes it sound like a workplace is either empowered or unempowered, with no in between, no gray area. People tend to label themselves accordingly, and when they decide that they're unempowered, they adopt a sort of victim mentality. This seems to be happening in the opening story with Barry, who is rightfully tired of checking his brain at the door. Remember his words? "I have absolutely no control over what I do."

A comment like this suggests that Barry is becoming an unwitting accessory to paternalism. He is essentially affirming that his boss has all the power, and if he sticks with this belief, nothing will change.

> Do you seem to be endlessly waiting for a boss or someone else in management to come to their senses and "empower you" once and for all?

What about you? Do you ever complain about the lack of ownership in your workplace? Do you sometimes feel like a victim because so much of the communication comes in the form of directives from on high? Have you ever thought about how wonderful it would be to change certain things about the way you do your work, *if only* you had the authority? Perhaps you've had these feelings for years. If so, has anything changed? Or do you seem to be endlessly waiting for a boss or someone else in management to come to their senses and "empower you" once and for all?

To break free of this paradigm, Barry has to change his own thinking, and then his actions—as difficult as that might be. He needs to step away from the model of asking permission and *take* some ownership for himself. This is not an endorsement of a workplace coup that'll have him reworking his resume later that same day. Rather, he needs to think fresh about the situation, analyze what's happening (especially in the context of that old boss–employee model), and uncover areas of his work where he can begin to exert his brainpower.

Once again, apply this to your own situation. Perhaps you're constantly asking permission, seeking direction, or waiting for someone else to take the lead. If so, why? Could it be that a lot of this, or at least some of it, is self-imposed? Reflect on what you do and how you do it. Then pinpoint one thing you can do differently right now that will make full use of your own judgment and decision making. Make it happen, then repeat the process again and again.

That's right, instead of focusing on what you cannot do and blaming it on the uncaring supervisor, determine what you *can* do and *possibly* can do, and work from there. Your confidence will build as you achieve small successes, and your colleagues (including your "boss") will not only start appreciating your brainpower, but also may come to expect you to make decisions and take action on your own. As all this happens, you'll be better able to see the faults that are inherent in the old boss–employee model. And your example might help others see as well.

Helping Others Achieve Ownership

If you listen to those passing workplace conversations, you'll hear plenty of talk about empowerment. It sometimes seems like a form of workplace therapy as people share their latest sagas of control-minded supervisors and rigid ways of doing things.

This venting can provide some very temporary relief of pent-up frustrations, but when it's only venting, it can make matters worse. It can turn the victim mentality from an individual feeling into a collective belief. So instead of just Barry checking his brain at the door when he comes to work, everyone does.

On the surface, everything may appear to be just fine. But the deep-down impact can be devastating. An unspoken arrangement is at work in which people do as they're told in exchange for having management take care of them. The gap between thinkers and doers becomes a chasm. The potential for creative synergy goes unrealized. And when quitting time rolls around, people rush to the exits, eager to reclaim their brains so they can become whole again.

> An unspoken arrangement is at work in which people do as they're told in exchange for having management take care of them.

It sounds so grave that it's hard to realize how one person can change this dynamic. But it can be done. In fact, one person with a different perspective is exactly what's needed to jolt the collective perspective.

Perhaps you're that person. While listening to those informal conversations, pay close attention to your own thoughts and words. Use this deeper awareness to keep yourself from feeling and acting like a victim, and whenever you can, try to refocus the dialogue on possibilities. Help people use their brainpower then and there to figure out what they *can* do to achieve a sliver of ownership in their part of the workplace.

Get More Hands on the Clay

You may have noticed that a certain word keeps coming up in this chapter: brainpower. For ownership to thrive, there has to be an appreciation for the substantial experience, creativity, and IQ that everyone brings to the workplace. That's right, everyone—not just those with diplomas on the wall or letters after a name.

The best way to put this into practice is by involving people—in developing plans, goals, initiatives, improvements, breakthrough ideas, new systems, whatever. Every day brings new opportunities.

Perhaps you're anguishing over some customer complaint information, and you'd like to analyze what's happening and figure out how things can be done better. Rather than jump to conclusions on your own, openly share the information, then assemble a group and work to improve the situation together. Maybe you want to change the layout of the workplace, and you're in a position to file the request and make it happen. Resist the urge to do it alone, and get your colleagues together so all of you can determine what kind of workplace design will work best for everyone.

This has nothing to do with the kind of token or symbolic involvement that happens all too often. You know the kind: Front-line employees are brought together so management can tell them what has been decided, or there's an opportunity for employees to share their opinions in a one-time session. The kind of involvement that fosters ownership is of the co-creative variety. It takes everyone's brainpower seriously and makes the most of it straight through to the finished product.

Your organization or work unit might have periodic "all-hands" meetings. With everyone together, it's a great opportunity to nurture genuine ownership. Instead of having everyone sit around while one or two people (usually the manager or someone from human resources) drone on with informational updates, create an *all-brains* session. Put the updates in a handout, and use the time together for roundtable dialogues where people, regardless of position and title, can exert their creativity to come up with new ideas.

By the way, all this applies equally to managers *and* to the Barrys of the world. Even though Barry's front-line position might make it impossible for him to organize something like an all-employee gathering, he can still make it his business to solve problems and develop improvements in a truly collaborative way.

The Challenge for Managers

Of course, whether we like it or not, there are certain things that only managers can do to nurture genuine ownership. This is especially the case in organizations that are heavily layered or divided by functions, and wherever there's simmering internal competition. Here are some of the issues—and practical ideas for addressing them in order to increase ownership.

> When you make the finding yourself—even if you're the last person on Earth to see the light—you'll never forget it."
>
> —CARL SAGAN

WHAT DO YOU HAVE TO HIDE?

In many workplaces, information is not accessible unless and until a higher-up gives permission. Flip this around entirely: Make everything accessible unless there's a persuasive reason to do otherwise. (Obviously, personnel files should remain restricted.)

An open approach fosters inclusion. If I'm seeing the monthly sales figures or last week's defect rates or the results of that recent customer focus group, I feel like a part of the enterprise. There's no "us" (the second-class citizens) and "them" (those people who get all the information). It also makes for better decisions, and it can spark constructive dialogue among employees as they share information and talk it over.

Financial information is often the last to get out from under lock and key, yet when it does, employees show a remarkable ability to integrate the numbers into their daily decision making. Sure, open-book management requires training, you *do* need to figure out how to keep the info away from arch competitors, and years may pass before people become fully at ease with financial concepts. But a change is felt the moment the books open up.

CUSTOMER INFO: A MEANINGFUL PLACE TO START

If the notion of an open-everything atmosphere gets palms sweaty, a good place to start is by sharing any and all information that relates to customers. You probably have letters from customers. Post them to the intranet, send them out by e-mail, or paper the walls with them. The same can be done with customer e-mails, transcripts of focus groups, survey results, and so on.

If the organization uses some kind of customer satisfaction index, turn it into a key organizational indicator and get everyone watching. If a few work areas use the information to seed an improvement conversation, and they go on to implement a few action ideas (no matter how seemingly small), have them write a one-pager describing their approach. Then include this with the next batch of customer info.

Do Away with All Those Sign-Offs

Conduct a thorough "approval audit." Put your processes under a harsh spotlight to find out how much organizational energy is expended "approving," "giving clearance," and "signing off." All these process speed bumps are more than just speed bumps. They send a signal that people can't be trusted, that they have to be watched.

Does this sound familiar? "The work order has to go to the supervisor, then to the maintenance chief, then to the facilities manager. It takes an average of 36 hours to move up the chain of command, and if the machine is down, our order backlog starts to climb. Why don't they just trust the operators and front-line maintenance folks?" The delay is bad; the message on trust is much worse.

The approval audit can be gradual, going from one process to the next to uncover sign-offs that do more harm than good. Flowcharting or something less formal is all you need, though you'll probably have to do some detective work to figure out why certain approvals are there in the first place. (Sometimes they're imposed by other organizations—like an OSHA regulation that requires specific signatures.) Make this an inclusive process, and wherever you can, put the approval power in the hands of the folks who are closest to the work. Workflow will quicken, but the gain in empowerment will be even greater.

Reality Check: OWNERSHIP

1 = very strongly disagree   5 = agree
2 = strongly disagree   6 = strongly agree
3 = disagree   7 = very strongly agree
4 = neutral; neither disagree nor agree

_____ People view themselves as owners of their work and act accordingly.

_____ The people who do the work shape how that work is done.

_____ Everyone is kept in the information loop. Nearly all information (except for select items like personnel records) is widely available.

_____ Change is done *by* people instead of *to* people. Co-creation is the method of choice for setting direction, developing ideas, and seizing opportunities.

_____ Front-line employees routinely make their own decisions and judgment calls—instead of going to their supervisors for permission or step-by-step instructions.

_____ = Total ÷ 5 = _____ = OWNERSHIP RATING

This Company *Does* Know Jack

Most companies have a meeting room or a conference room. Jellyvision has "couch world."

That's what they call it. When the company's 61 employees get together every other week, they gather in a space that looks like the sofa section of a furniture store. As for a dress code, well, let's just say you'd find plenty of sandals, baseball caps, and T-shirts.

Jellyvision makes what they call "interactive experiences," like the computer game *You Don't Know Jack*. Creative talent abounds at the company. There are writers, editors, audio technicians, graphic artists, and musicians. When Kate Powers joined Jellyvision as a writer in 1997, she thought she had gone to workplace heaven. "I was astonished by the extent to which people are kept in the loop, how people are so respectful and friendly and informal. I honestly couldn't believe this company was for real."

Of course, it takes hard work to build this heaven, and much of it goes against traditional workplace practice. For starters, Jellyvision has an open-book policy with employees on just about everything, including financials. "We share the good, the bad, what's happening," says Vaiva Vaisnys, director of human resources. "If it's a roller-coaster ride, we're on the coaster together."

And then there's dialogue. At Jellyvision, people routinely come together to talk about issues, problems, and opportunities. For instance, instead of slapping together a sexual-harassment policy on her own and packaging it in a forgettable memo, Vaisnys assembled a diverse group to talk about it and develop something meaningful. They took four months, but the dialogue raised awareness and gave everyone a sense of ownership over the issue.

There's a group searching for new digs for the growing company. Another is developing training for the various disciplines. Another is taking a hard look at the review system. It's all about dialogue.

There are even whiteboards in the restrooms. A new question is written down each week, and answers appear as the days go by. No, this isn't communication in the traditional sense. But that's the whole point.

PART FOUR

THE DEVELOPMENT KEYS

We value growth.

The Development Keys

- Challenge
- Invention
- Support
- Personal Development

Chapter 12

Challenge

When Steve was hired by a small consulting firm, he brought along a newly minted college degree, an eagerness to please, and a deep desire to stretch his skills. There had been vague promises that he would be sent to a client site for a three-month consulting assignment, but word soon got around that he had strong writing skills, and the senior consultants liked the reports and letters he put together. Before he knew it, Steve was "exiled" to a cubicle, as he puts it, where he spent eight straight weeks rewriting one of the firm's training courses. It's not that writing was a chore for him. In fact, he could do it easily—so easily that he started getting bored. He held out hope that more interesting work would soon come his way, but it never did. Instead, he got another writing assignment . . . and another . . . and another . . . .

It happened ten years ago, and today, Steve looks back on the story with a grim sense of humor. He can imagine what he must have looked like during those cubicle days—hunched over, a blank look on his face, blazing away at the keyboard to crank out yet another revised training book.

The good news is that Steve's fortunes soon changed. The bad news is that many other people remain in exile doing the familiar or easy thing over and over. It makes for easy workdays, but it rarely makes for meaningful days. People want to be challenged.

This isn't strictly a personal proposition, either. Sure, it affects individual people like Steve, but hardly ever does just one person feel the impact. The lack of challenge tends to be a widespread problem—a reflection of how a workplace does business. It usually results from our tendencies to fit people

> He held out hope that more interesting work would soon come his way, but it never did.

into narrow, neatly defined roles, and to keep them in those roles because they can do their work so well.

Perhaps you've seen a workplace where challenge is sorely lacking. People complete their tasks—and yes, "tasks" is the right term—in an almost robotic manner. It's as if they're on autopilot, going through the motions with neither their hearts nor minds engaged. As the months fly by, days become a dull routine, and the Steves of the world slowly but surely atrophy. Then there's the price that's paid by the organization. A chronic lack of challenge leads to a collective dumbing down. The immediate work suffers, and serious innovation always seems out of reach.

> Conquering any difficulty always gives one a secret joy, for it means pushing back a boundary-line and adding to one's liberty.
>
> —Henri Frédéric Amiel

It's completely different in a meaningful workplace, where people have all sorts of opportunities to hone their many skills, use their know-how, and tap into their deep interests.

The challenges can come from the inside ("How can we eliminate downtime on our packing line?"), the outside ("What can we do to tap into that new market?"), or a combination of the two ("How can we speed up the time it takes to answer call-in inquiries from customers?"). Challenges can focus on roles ("Would you be willing to facilitate this meeting?"), functions ("Want to learn the new design software?"), or something else ("What's your read on this customer data?"). They can be big ("We have to cut waste by 80 percent or we'll keep losing money."), small ("Will you be a part of the project team?"), or in between ("Are you willing to form a project team?").

What About You?

The fact that challenge comes in all sorts of shapes and sizes raises an important question: What challenges you? That's what the list on page 117 is all about.

Scan it, and note the three or four actions or conditions that are your biggest sources of positive challenge. You can record your top choices by placing a checkmark in the "Important Source" column. If there's something else that puts the wind in your sails—something beyond the list—don't hesitate to add it.

	A Very Important Source of Positive Challenge for Me	Currently Available to Me, Currently Exists
Getting involved in new projects		
Working with a new group of people		
Developing entirely new ways of doing things		
Taking old processes and reinventing them		
Using new equipment		
Developing new equipment		
Leading a project		
Organizing a project		
Learning something entirely new		
Applying what I've learned (this includes using newly learned skills)		
Exploring the leading-edge developments of other organizations		
Improving upon and implementing some of those developments		
Trying to solve a workplace problem		
Having a compelling vision		
Having a set of down-to-earth goals		
Keeping an eye on a set of scorecard-type measures		

Next, take an honest look at the current situation by posing a second question: Are you really being challenged? We're not talking about the workaholic's kind of challenge, where you're swamped with too much work and too little time to do it. The focus here is on an entirely different kind of "demanding." Does your brain get a daily workout? Are your talents and skills routinely tapped and stretched? Do you sometimes find yourself in that *dis*comfort zone where you're doing things that seem new, even foreign, and you have to learn on the fly?

Go back through the list, and flag the things you're able to do at least once in a while, or that seem to exist in your workplace. You can use the right-hand column to make a checkmark record of your observations.

KWESI'S STORY

Kwesi's most meaningful work experience also happened to be his most exhausting.

He served as assistant manager of a city-wide campaign to pass a school levy, and it took every ounce of energy he could muster. The situation called for long days (and long nights) as campaign workers stuffed envelopes, made calls, paid door-to-door visits, and strategized.

"By the time it was over, everyone was ready to drop, and yet it felt great," Kwesi says. "We had truly taken on the challenge."

Taking Charge of Your Own Situation

It's so tempting to sit back and wait for challenge to come your way. Steve admitted doing as much. But he also said that things started to change for the better only when *he* took action.

Fed up with yet another writing assignment, he approached the senior consultants with a detailed plan for putting together a team to research new database technology, developing a new consulting service based on this, then piloting it with a couple of new clients who were waiting in the wings. At first, the proposal stunned the other consultants. Who was this newcomer to be suggesting such grand plans? Steve made a strong and well-researched case, however—so good that even the skeptics saw it as a wise course of action. And that's how Steve broke free of his long service as the resident writer.

Perhaps you've discovered from your analysis that some of your most important sources of challenge really do exist in the workplace and are available to you. If that's the case, your challenge (there's that word again!) is to make the most of them. For instance, maybe your mind truly gets engaged when you're organizing a project—and you realize that there are workplace opportunities to do just that. Then get going. You'll be doing what you can, right now, to strengthen your sense of challenge.

Do it even if you have to start with a small, short-term project in your immediate work area. In fact, something small might be perfect, allowing for a quick success (relatively speaking) that you can then leverage to bigger things. And do it even if you first have to convince other people that it's the right thing to do. Sure, you can view this as a silly game of jumping through hoops. In some cases, it will be. Steve saw it as building a case to show how the organization would benefit more by having him involved in other activities. It worked for him, and it can work for you, too.

Analyze First, *Then* Take Action

Let's say you went through the list and found something alarming: None of your top four or so sources of challenge are available to you in the workplace. If so, you might be tempted to wring your hands and conclude that nothing can be done—or to do just the opposite and jump headfirst into some kind of action that may or may not make a positive difference.

Instead, take some time right now to analyze. Ask yourself *why* this is the case. For instance, let's say some of your most fulfilling challenges at previous workplaces have come when you've been able to lead or organize projects—but where you're at now, these kinds of opportunities don't seem to be available. Well, why not? Keep peeling back the layers, asking why as many times as possible, until you come to a root cause. Then figure out how you can deal with that root cause.

> The greatest enemy of your creative powers is smug complacency— being satisfied with less than what you are capable of doing.
>
> —NIDO QUBEIN

I'd like to get involved in new projects. This would really provide a fulfilling sense of challenge for me, but there don't seem to be any opportunities.

Why's that?

Because the same people are always selected, and unfortunately, I'm usually not one of them.

Why not?

Maybe it's because I'm not very well-known around the workplace. Everyone in my immediate work area knows me, of course, but most of the really exciting projects are cross-divisional. And I'm just not a "big name" in other areas.

Why aren't you?

Well, I've done a lot of good work and have good skills. I guess I haven't done a very good job of getting beyond my own work area and building a network of folks from elsewhere in the company.

You can see where this is going. By doing some diagnostics on the situation, you can understand the deeper issues that are at work. Out of this, you'll get a clearer sense of what you can do to improve things. Follow this process for all of your most important sources of challenge.

Steve talked about doing this. He figured he had to come up with something, or he'd remain the resident writer indefinitely. He kept asking "why" to better understand his situation, and he came to realize that people in his workplace were given new opportunities only when they built a water-tight case showing how the business would benefit. So he went about the time-consuming work (during free minutes stolen from his writing projects and some extra hours in the evening) to do just that.

AMY'S STORY

"There will never be a dull moment."

With those words, Amy's editor welcomed her to her first day as a daily-newspaper reporter. By the end of the week, she was covering big stories in city politics and community affairs.

But that was three years ago, and now, Amy recalls her editor's never-a-dull-moment comment to explain why the job seems empty. "I never thought I'd say this, but I can do the job *too* well," she says. "Sometimes I just seem to be on auto-pilot as I interview someone or write a story. I'm waiting for the *real big* story to come around—something that really tests my skills."

I Think I Can, I Think I Can

Once you've analyzed your situation and decided on a course of action, it helps to solidify your intrinsic resolve by creating some personal goals. Even a single goal in the right direction can make a big difference. It's your commitment to overcome the boredom and desperation that can result from doing the same thing over and over.

So what'll it be? What do you want to accomplish in the next four workweeks? That's long enough to accomplish something significant, yet short enough to keep your feet to the fire. Pull out a piece of paper, and make a promise to yourself.

In terms of phrasing, be specific and set deadlines so you'll know beyond a shadow of a doubt when you've turned the goal into reality. And keep your goals up to date, adding new ones as you chalk up the achievements. It sounds like a lot of work because it is—but you'll get a new spring in your step each time you remember that these are entirely *your* goals.

What Can *We* Do About It?

So far in this chapter, we've been focusing entirely on the individual. This makes sense when you consider that challenge is such a personal proposition; what gets *you* engaged and excited might be very different from what gets someone else fired up. But it's not enough. What's needed in the long term is a *challenge culture*—a workplace that understands why challenge is important, that appreciates the fact that different people are positively challenged in different ways, and that makes a conscious effort to make challenge an everyday reality.

If you're in a position to do so, it might be tempting to start tossing out challenges. But a far better approach is to do what you can to create an environment where people freely figure out what kinds of challenges are right for them—in other words, to make this everyone's responsibility. A conversation with colleagues is the best place to start. These simple questions will open things up:

How do people want to be challenged? In other words, what are their most important sources of positive challenge? The list on page 117 can be used to jog the thought process. It's important that people fully explain what is important to them. Press for specifics to understand exactly what they're talking about.

Are they finding and taking advantage of these challenges in the workplace? If not, why not? This is a vital part of the conversation. Take the time to dig into the situation and uncover those root causes. Only by doing so can you and your colleagues hope to answer the next question.

What can we do to improve the situation? Some of the solutions might be very individualized—it might come to light, for example, that Mary should be on the new project team, or that the John is the right person to attend the upcoming three-day workshop. Other action ideas will have a more collective feel, requiring everyone's involvement and benefiting the whole group. These can even be turned into co-created goals.

> Contrary to what we usually believe, the best moments in our lives are not the passive, receptive, relaxing times—although such experiences can also be enjoyable, if we have worked hard to attain them. The best moments usually occur when a person's body or mind is stretched to its limits in a voluntary effort to accomplish something difficult and worthwhile.
>
> —MIHALY CSIKZENTMIHALYI, *FLOW: THE PSYCHOLOGY OF OPTIMAL EXPERIENCE*

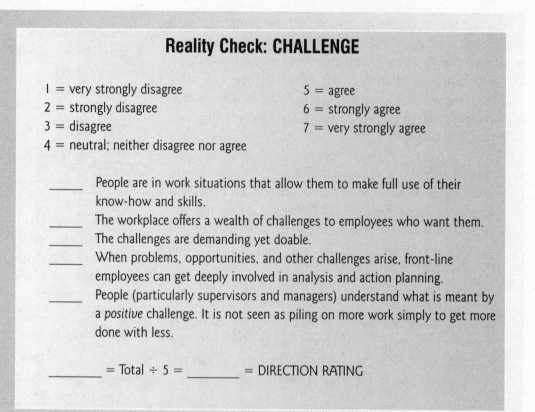

Reality Check: CHALLENGE

1 = very strongly disagree	5 = agree
2 = strongly disagree	6 = strongly agree
3 = disagree	7 = very strongly agree
4 = neutral; neither disagree nor agree	

_____ People are in work situations that allow them to make full use of their know-how and skills.

_____ The workplace offers a wealth of challenges to employees who want them.

_____ The challenges are demanding yet doable.

_____ When problems, opportunities, and other challenges arise, front-line employees can get deeply involved in analysis and action planning.

_____ People (particularly supervisors and managers) understand what is meant by a *positive* challenge. It is not seen as piling on more work simply to get more done with less.

_____ = Total ÷ 5 = _____ = DIRECTION RATING

The Challenge of Choices

Imagine a company where new employees spend four days delving into their organization's history, getting into the details of their mission, envisioning the keys to service excellence, and engaging in rich dialogue on their role and how it fits within the larger organizational picture. And no, that's not a typo—four days really *are* devoted to this. It happens at Albany Ladder Company (a division of National Equipment Services), which supplies and distributes ladders, lifts, scaffolding, and light construction equipment.

Company president Tony Groat teams up with other senior managers to facilitate these four-day gatherings. When talking with Tony, you hear a lot about efforts to make the workplace meaningful. He believes that the most vibrant organizations are those that challenge people and give them the freedom to make a positive difference.

Albany Ladder doesn't just walk the talk when it comes to this stuff—they run it. The four-day program, called Choices, involves about twenty people at a time. They come from all over the company to engage in conversations, activities, and a variety of surprise events. Past sessions have included a whitewater-rafting trip that taught unforgettable team-up-or-else lessons. At another session, program veterans transformed a company store into a five-star restaurant, serving dinner to Choices participants as a way of showing how people with a vision and follow-through can turn the ordinary into the extraordinary.

Some companies would balk at the cost and logistical challenge of having people away from their regular jobs for four days. For Albany Ladder, it's a small investment in the most important part of their business: people. "People start feeling like owners," Groat says. "They realize that what happens is a product of the choices they make."

Chapter 13

Invention

As an inspector for a municipal regulatory agency, Beth takes her work seriously. So seriously that she developed a reputation for her by-the-book, take-no-prisoners inspections. Then one day something clicked. A business owner sat down with her and unloaded all of his frustrations about the inspection process. She nodded in a false show of empathy and tried to wrap up the conversation, but he kept talking—and she started to listen. For the first time, she began to see the inspections from a completely different angle. That's when she realized there were all sorts of opportunities for making life easier, for both the inspectors and the people whose sites were being inspected, without sacrificing high standards. When she got back to the office, she gathered her colleagues for a conversation about one part of the process: forms. There were tons of them, all of which took precious time and caused frequent errors and rework. It seemed to Beth and several others in the group that four of the forms could be consolidated into a single one-pager. Beth's supervisor seemed skeptical of the change, and the supervisor's manager was flatly opposed. The inspectors soon received a formal memo instructing them to get back to their "real work" of doing inspections.

> Beth's supervisor seemed skeptical of the change, and the supervisor's manager was flatly opposed.

Because Beth works for a public-sector organization, it's easy to blame her situation on bureaucracy. But the underlying message is hardly unique to government workplaces. So many organizations, including plenty in the private sector, seem to be held in a death grip by the status quo. They do the same thing over and over, often justifying it (as in Beth's case) as the real work.

Some people are so busy doing their immediate work that they don't have time for anything else. Forget whether what they're doing is the right thing or whether they're doing it in the best way possible. The hamster wheel is going around too fast. No one seems willing or able to climb off and rethink what they do and how they do it.

In other cases, the workplace culture prizes sameness and conformity. This is what kept IBM in white shirts for so many years, until their success formula suddenly turned on them. They hurled themselves into change as a matter of survival.

Even places that claim to be improvement-minded often have little to show for it. A big reason is the low-hanging fruit phenomenon, in which improvement initiatives focus on small processes that don't make much of a difference in the big scheme of things. This is fine as a starting place, to get people using new improvement skills and know-how. But a "think small" approach can become a status quo of its own, leading the workplace into an endless loop of marginal improvements. Worse, it can keep people busy doing the wrong things better and better—when they should really be junking useless processes and creating entirely new ones that add value.

> A "think small" approach can become a status quo of its own, leading the workplace into an endless loop of marginal improvements.

A meaningful workplace takes advantage of the low-hanging fruit, to be sure, but it's not afraid to reach for the high stuff. In other words, there are continuous improvements of the daily, incremental variety as well as breakthrough innovations. The search is always on for newer, better, faster, smarter. As for risk and failure, they're regarded not as *possible* consequences of invention, but as an *expected* and *acceptable* price to pay.

A Passion for Possibilities

So where can a workplace find the considerable fuel it needs to power up all this invention? The answer, quite simply, is you. Your own gray matter can run creative rings around the world's most powerful computers, but only if you let it. And that's where attitude comes into play.

Thomas Edison, the Wright Brothers, and countless others who left their marks on the world never asked for permission to be creative. They went out and did it, whether working in a drafty room or on an even draftier beach. Okay, so maybe you're not out to create the next light bulb or airplane. But you can follow their lead and exert your inventive spirit and skills wherever you are.

Operate every day with an inventor's passion for possibilities. Keep your eyes wide open to problems that are crying out for creative solutions. And when you see an opportunity, seize it—or even better, assemble a team and go after it together.

Is that indexing mechanism showing unusual signs of wear and tear?

Does the phone system seem to strain whenever there's a surge in call activity?

Has a new technology opened the way to some break-through innovation that could put your organization light years ahead of the competition?

> The free, exploring mind of the individual human is the most valuable thing in the world.
>
> —JOHN STEINBECK

Or, in Beth's case, is there a way to cut down on the paperwork in order to make life easier for everyone involved?

There are so many possibilities—everything from incremental improvements to entire process overhauls to wild discoveries that rewrite the future. Look around, pick an opportunity, and start inventing now.

Making Time for Invention

All this talk of possibilities might sound exciting, but if you're like most people, you probably have a schedule that's jammed with your "real work." How can you possibly find time for improvement and innovation? Well, if you can spare just a few minutes right now for a quick analysis of your schedule, you might come up with an answer. That's what the chart on page 129 is all about.

You might already have a jump on this. Chapter 5 suggested that you list your typical weekly work activities, then put them through the ringer of five important relevance questions:

Does it help you fulfill your purpose?

Does it help you serve your customers better?

Does it help your colleagues serve a customer better?

Does it bring you closer to the future that you and your colleagues are trying to create?

Does it relate directly to one or more of your goals or objectives?

If you compiled an activity list, dig it out. If not, write the activities in the left-hand column of the chart. Then take each activity one at a time, and place checkmarks in any of the other columns to indicate how it adds value. Is it essential to your immediate work? Does it allow you to serve your external customers better, now or in the future? Everything is spelled out on the chart; simply work from left to right as you evaluate the worth of each activity.

You might find that a single activity applies to more than one column, so you'll have multiple checkmarks in a single row. It also might happen that an activity doesn't seem to add any value. Don't try to push it and place a checkmark where one doesn't belong.

Once you've completed the chart, look for any activities that don't have any corresponding checkmarks. Are there persuasive reasons why these activities should remain a part of your schedule? Does this "regular work" add any value, or is it just motion? If you're bluntly honest with yourself, you have a golden opportunity. Stop the meaningless motion, and turn the time over to invention.

Does this "regular work" add any value, or is it just motion?

Now take a close look at columns 2–5. These are all about making things better and creating the future, which is at the heart of invention. If you don't have any checkmarks in these columns, or if you have just a few, be on the alert. You might be leading a work life that's dangerously free of invention.

Lastly, look at column 1, where you've put checkmarks to note the day-to-day work that helps you achieve your underlying purpose. This is important stuff, so it can be uncomfortable calling any of it into question. But a schedule that's dominated by these kinds of activities can put you at risk of having a chronically short-term vision. All the focus is on doing the work of today, at the expense of creating tomorrow, the next month, the next year, the next decade, and so on.

All this might point you to some difficult choices. You surely don't want to neglect essential activities, but you *do* want to achieve a balance between the short and long term—between doing the work, figuring out ways to do the work better, and deciding whether you should be doing certain work in the first place. So what about it? Are there certain important day-to-day activities that you can trim down so you can sneak some time away for invention?

1. Essential to my immediate work; allows me to achieve my underlying purpose 2. Allows me to serve my external customers better—or it might in the future 3. Allows me to serve my internal customers (colleagues) better—or it might in the future 4. Relates to the vision; moves us closer to the future we want to create 5. Helps us achieve a meaningful goal or objective					
Typical Weekly Activities (List each activity on a separate line)	1	2	3	4	5

Is There Room to Create?

In addition to finding the time, you also might want to set aside some space just for improvement and innovation. This not only has practical value, but also sends a message throughout the organization that invention is important.

It can take shape in many different ways. If there's an unused conference room somewhere, consider making it the default place to go for anyone who wants to let their creativity breathe free. Equip it with flipcharts, markers, a whiteboard, magazines, an Internet-connected terminal, perhaps even a "creativity tools" guidebook. The room can even have a unique look and feel. Make it a different color, toss in some comfortable chairs, and decorate accordingly. Perhaps the first blast of invention should be for folks to come together and decide what this space should look like.

Then open the doors and—wait. Even if people want to get creative, they may be too busy doing their "regular work." Then a team will show up . . . then a pair of people . . . then another team . . . then an individual who wants to get away from her work area to think about an opportunity . . . then she'll return a day later with two colleagues. Before long, the place will be humming.

If it isn't within your power to set aside an entire room at your workplace, you can still have your own personal space. Get creative with this. Your "space" could even be a simple binder where you jot down your wild ideas and inspirations.

Get More Brains Around the Table

In the story that opened this chapter, Beth had something of an epiphany. She realized that her city regulatory agency could maintain high inspection standards without inflicting so much paperwork on the inspected organizations. She even involved some of her colleagues, and together they got inventive and developed a way to consolidate four separate forms into a single page. Then her supervisor questioned the wisdom of such a change, and the supervisor's supervisor put a stop to the whole notion. It was back to business as usual.

In telling the rest of her story, Beth had a few ideas on why this happened—and what she could have done differently. It turns out that those colleagues she pulled together were her several close workplace friends. They didn't represent a good cross-section of the inspectors who used the forms, and when everyone else found out about the "secret" improvement conversations, they got angry. Who was Beth to run off and change *their* forms?

As for the supervisor, the first time he heard about the improvement idea was when Beth handed him a draft of the brand-new one-pager. Ideally, she shouldn't have to seek permission to invent, and we can make a case that her supervisor should support her regardless of how he feels, as long as the change benefits customers. We can even quarrel with the term *supervisor*, which calls forth the image of someone who spends most of the time telling people what to do and catching people when they do something else. But it still would have made sense for Beth to at least keep her supervisor in the information loop. After all, he too is a colleague.

Beth had the right idea in conferring with at least a few other people, but she could have gone a lot further—by setting up a team, perhaps, or by giving more of her colleagues an opportunity to be a part of this dialogue. The challenge is to make change a process that's done *with* people or *by* people

The Neutral Facilitator

The next time you're in a group that's struggling with a titanic problem, or looking longingly at a distant opportunity, consider bringing in a neutral facilitator. Outside facilitators come with extensive group-process know-how, and their bag of tricks includes tools and techniques for sparking wild creativity. Good facilitation has an almost magical way of making the most of people's gray matter.

instead of *to* them. Yes, this takes more time in the short run. But the greater brainpower leads to better ideas, and support for the change will steadily grow as the improvement or innovation takes shape.

Making Invention Your Real Work

Perhaps you can relate to Beth's situation. Or maybe you can empathize with the supervisor or someone else in her organization. Whatever role you're currently in, there are many more actions you and others can take to make invention more prominent in your workplace.

REACH OUT AND TALK WITH SOMEONE

Maintain an ongoing dialogue with other work units, offices, divisions, functional areas, or wherever else there are people whose paths you rarely cross. While you're at it, why not get together with people from other organizations? It's so easy to do at chamber of commerce gatherings, conferences, outside workshops, and elsewhere.

A random conversation at that conference mixer might tip you off to new technology in your industry. A scheduled one-hour huddle with several colleagues from another part of the plant might trigger the breakthrough revelation that will solve a long-time problem. Even e-mail "conversations," though a poor substitute for face-to-face dialogue, can be used to bounce around ideas.

> **Book Tip**
>
> Tom Peters' *The Circle of Innovation* is a combination workshop and wake-up call. Filled with big ideas and countless examples, it's a must-read for people who need to take innovation seriously—and that's all of us.

LEARN FROM THE INNOVATION ZEALOTS

Keep an eye out for organizations that truly live up to the billing of "hypercreative." Their stories are often told on the pages of *Fast Company, Fortune, Business Week, Harvard Business Review,* and many other publications, so you won't have to look far. If several catch your eye, get on the Web and do more research. Call for their annual reports and anything else they're willing to share.

Did an article extensively quote the operations manager or HR director or someone else? Send him or her a note expressing your interest, then follow up with a call. The ensuing conversations will give you a chance to go well beyond the article, and the insights could prove illuminating. You may even want to arrange a visit. Obviously, a competitor won't fling open their doors to you, but others may be flattered by your interest and eager to show off. Some companies have regular tours, so all you'll need to do is show up at the appointed time.

Whenever possible, make these visits with at least one of your colleagues, so you can exchange ideas with someone who understands where you're coming from. And when you return to home base, synthesize your observations, share them with others, and start incorporating any of the stand-out things you saw into your own way of doing business.

Promote It

Put invention in the spotlight whenever you can. Communicate a crystal-clear message that creativity is not just permitted . . . not just required . . . but absolutely vital to the health of the organization.

In newsletters and on intranets, include a section that profiles new developments, whether they're minor tweaks or total overhauls of processes, procedures, equipment, whatever. If you have periodic get-togethers with colleagues to review your progress and look ahead, *voilà*—you have another chance to send the innovation message. Make it a regular agenda item. Share information on recent instances when people stretched their creativity and the status quo to come up with something new.

> Progress always involves risk; you can't steal second base and keep your foot on first.
> —Frederick Wilcox

This might even be the time and place for a team presentation or a conversation about a team charter that's being developed. Or maybe there's a consensus that the workplace is filled with obstacles to invention. Use some of the meeting time to engage people in honest dialogue to pinpoint these barriers, analyze why they're occurring, and develop specific action steps to eliminate them once and for all.

Set a Course for Creativity

To brighten the spotlight on invention, write it into at least one goal—whether that goal is for a work unit, location, region, or the whole organization. This may be the first time that improvement and innovation are put on the same priority level with revenue generation, market share, customer return rates, and other traditional goal categories—so this promises to be an eye- and mind-opening conversation.

Expect a contingent of skeptics to ask or at least think: How can everyone get their real work done if they're so busy making things better? Answer: Making things better *is* the real work. Others will struggle with this goal-setting conversation because, let's face it, innovation can be tough to measure. It just doesn't have that bean-counting tangibility.

If any of this surfaces during goal-setting conversations, you're in luck. It's the perfect lead-in to a conversation on this topic, and if everyone is open and honest, you'll see the mental light bulbs going on one after the other. Folks will realize that process measures *are* possible.

For example, you could cite the number of newly chartered improvement teams, the number of employees serving on these teams, or the number of teams implementing their improvements. As for outcomes, a simple system can be put in place to track how innovation has contributed to traditional targets like reductions in costs, or gains in market share, or increases in customer loyalty.

Redefine "Failure"

As you and others pursue improvement and innovation, expect failure. And when it comes, don't punish it—encourage more innovation. The stock market offers the perfect metaphor. There are daily ups and downs, but over time, it pays off big. What you need are patience, a long-term perspective, and an occasional bottle of Maalox. Every single stock takes an occasional plunge, and so will your organization's investment in invention. The question is, are you going to sell immediately, or will you hang in and reap the long-term benefits?

Prediction: If you're a manager, people will be watching to see how you respond to those creative "losses." Prediction: If you can stomach your way through ten "bad" investments in innovation, the eleventh one will be a smashing success. A thought: That breakthrough on try 11 might be traced to all the learning from tries 1–10.

JIM'S STORY

It happened a decade ago, but Jim can still feel the excitement.

He and more than a thousand others had come together for an introductory presentation by the new agency director. "He emphasized one point over and over: 'You have permission to make mistakes.' Talk about proposing a different culture! Before then, it was well-understood that you covered your backside, and that meant trying absolutely nothing new."

The director's comments marked the start of a slow but sure change process. "For the first time in a long time, people started to experiment in the name of better service to their customers."

Reality Check: INVENTION

1 = very strongly disagree	5 = agree
2 = strongly disagree	6 = strongly agree
3 = disagree	7 = very strongly agree
4 = neutral; neither disagree nor agree	

_____ Risk-taking in the name of improvement and innovation is strongly encouraged. Mistakes are seen as a fair price to pay for personal and organizational development.

_____ The organization truly values right-brain thinking.

_____ The workplace abounds with opportunities to be creative.

_____ People are open to new ideas, trends, and approaches. The "way of doing things" is always evolving, and sometimes it's done away with entirely.

_____ Improvement and innovation are seen as everyone's business—and not the restricted domain of people with certain credentials or titles.

_____ = Total ÷ 5 = _____ = DIRECTION RATING

Support

Jerry is tired of waiting. Nearly three months ago, he asked his supervisor for help in getting certain data needed by his process-improvement team. The supervisor promised to have it within 24 hours. Then the day turned into a week . . . then a month . . . and another month. In his role as team leader, Jerry went back to her a few times. At first, she blamed the delay on her workload. Then there were other reasons: she couldn't find the data, it was too old to be useful, and so on. The excuses kept coming, then the supervisor started asking questions about the team and its direction. She had chartered the team herself, but now it appeared she was doing her best to make it go away. Jerry and his teammates went elsewhere to get the data and were only partially successful. They ended up using what they could find and making assumptions about the rest.

As Jerry told the story, he seemed downright bitter. He couldn't understand why the supervisor would be so unsupportive, and he vowed that the next time, he'd go around her to get whatever was needed—assuming he'd be willing to take on another team assignment. Talk about a sad ending to a promising story. Surely his improvement team began with a spirit of challenge and invention. It took just one stonewalling supervisor and three short months for Jerry to join the legion of workplace cynics.

> The supervisor had chartered the team herself, but now it appeared she was doing her best to make it go away.

People need all kinds of support as the workday unfolds—practical, down-to-earth stuff like data, information, time, money, space, tools, and technology. Yet all too often, what they get are questions, delays, and excuses. In worst-case situations, support can even become an arena for political game-playing, internal competition, and plain old manipulation.

In a meaningful workplace, there's a near obsession with getting people what they need to be successful. Whether we're talking about routine work or something on par with the Manhattan Project, employees go about their business fully aware that no one's going to be penny-pinched to exhaustion, or put in an endless holding pattern while their request sits in someone's "in" box, or left to flounder by an inattentive project sponsor.

When Support Is Lacking

Before going any further, let's explore the big mystery that's embodied in Jerry's story. Why did the supervisor put up such resistance?

Being a newly minted cynic, Jerry assumed the worst. The team had worked entirely on its own until the data search became an issue, making enough progress that people in other work areas were starting to take notice. They were doing such a good job, he theorized, that the supervisor felt threatened. By dragging her feet at a key point in the improvement process, she kept the team from becoming a success story—something that would have brought attention to the team members and put some of them in competition with the supervisor for promotional opportunities.

> Everyone needs help from everyone.
> —Bertolt Brecht

Who knows whether there's any truth to this conspiracy theory? It wouldn't be the first time that someone put his or her own aspirations ahead of everything else. But there are many more possible reasons to explain a lack of support. These might be cropping up in Jerry's situation and in your own workplace.

People are too busy.

There's nothing conspiratorial about this. Sometimes people are simply too occupied with their everyday work to provide support, especially if the request is fairly complex. The challenge for the person seeking support is to allow enough lead time, to anticipate questions and have ready answers, and to provide key information in a concise format.

They don't understand why it's needed.

Jerry admitted that he never made a clear case for why the team needed that data. In fact, he initially asked for the supervisor's help in a two-sentence e-mail. This might work fine for some people, but others will want more background before they're willing to help out.

The workplace has a play-it-safe culture.

The status quo can get jostled when people provide support. In Jerry's situation, the data they needed had been tightly held by the accounting office for years—and seven of the nine team members worked elsewhere. Perhaps the supervisor simply didn't want to make waves.

> We've all seen workplaces where divisions, units, and individuals go head to head for scarce resources and rewards. In these environments, providing support amounts to selling out.

The workplace is seriously fragmented.

The "manageable pieces" approach to management has turned so many organizations into jumbled collections of divisions, units, offices, and cubicles. This can make support a complex proposition, not only because it can be unclear where to go for what's needed, but also because a request from some *other* work area might be seen an unimportant.

There's a strong strain of internal competition.

Fragmentation is bad enough, but it gets markedly worse when combined with internal competition. We've all seen workplaces where divisions, units, and individuals go head to head for scarce resources and rewards. In these environments, providing support amounts to selling out.

People rarely engage in dialogue.

Now for the real mystery of Jerry's story: Did he ever sit down with his supervisor to have a bluntly honest conversation about the much-needed data? No. He blamed it on a workplace culture that practiced one-way, do-as-your-told communication. Openly talking about it never seemed to be an option, he said.

Building Your Case

It's a fair bet that right now, there's something you need in the way of support. Maybe it's simple: a new type of wrench, or an updated version of a software package, or a new uniform. Or perhaps you need access to a restricted database, funds for a week-long workshop, or money to bring in an outside facilitator who can help resuscitate a flat-lining project.

Regardless of how big the request is, be ready to explain why it's needed and how it will benefit you and the organization. If that wrench would halve the time it takes for some laborious step in the process, have your proof close at hand. If that outside facilitator has worked miracles on similar projects, document the stories in a crisp summary and have it readily available. Without getting too squirrelly with the numbers, try to show how the investment will be good for the bottom line. This applies not only to individuals, but also to teams, as Jerry will be happy to tell you.

You may have made requests before, only to see them get stonewalled or turned down. If so, you might be experiencing the same kind of bitterness that Jerry did. Don't let your feelings lock you into inaction. Analyze what happened, then use your insights to change your approach and, possibly, *who* you approach the next time around.

The Risk of Asking for Permission

Now that we've talked about building a case to get support, it's time for a huge caveat: Don't let your pursuit of support become an exercise in always asking for permission.

> The people who work beside you, and the many others in different divisions and units, just might have what you need.

This can happen easily, especially in organizations that have a well-defined chain of command. The front-line employees who need something go to their supervisors, the supervisors go to their managers, and so on up the hierarchy. By mindlessly submitting to the top-down structure, people end up strengthening it. Support becomes ever more elusive as the bureaucracy grows.

That's what happened to Jerry. He seemed to get caught up in the protocol and hierarchy, dutifully asking his supervisor for help in getting the data. Perhaps he could have gone straight to the accounting unit, which housed the data in the first place. There were two people on the team from accounting; maybe they could have made the request. He learned his lesson, though. Remember his vow to bypass the supervisor the next time he needed data or something similar?

No one's urging Jerry (or you) to snub the hierarchy to the point of getting fired. But there's something to be said for looking beyond your "immediate supervisor" for support. The people who work beside you, and the many others in different divisions and units, just might have what you need. And by going to them directly, you'll be doing your part to strengthen other meaning keys, including equality and oneness.

To Give Support, First Open Your Mind

So far in this chapter, we've focused on *getting* support, but that's only half of what it takes to strengthen this key in the workplace. You also need to *give* it whenever and wherever you can.

In doing so, it's important to be aware of the organizational structure and how it shapes your thinking on this. If you're a manager in a workplace that still operates in top-down mode, you might be inclined to focus all of your attention on supporting the people "below" you. These are your colleagues, so definitely go ahead and support them. But don't forget that there are many other folks in the organization who might need some help from you, if not now, then certainly in the future. Your challenge is to operate with a constant appreciation for the interconnected, systemic nature of the workplace—and not to let hierarchy distort what you do and for whom.

> We cannot live only for ourselves. A thousand fibers connect us with our fellow man.
> —HERMAN MELVILLE

Hierarchy poses a similar risk for people who are not managers. They can easily conclude that because no one is "below" them, they're in no position to provide support. The result? People end up missing easy opportunities to help one another, not because they're uncaring, but because the top-down mindset blinds them to the possibilities. Over time, this can even create a front-line culture in which individuals focus exclusively on their own needs, which is the exact opposite of the unity of purpose that's so essential to a meaningful workplace.

Making Support Routine

Spend some time thinking about your own history of providing support to your colleagues. How has the workplace structure and culture affected your actions? With this awareness, what can you do differently to provide more support to more people in your workplace system? How can you get started on this right now?

If you need some ideas, read on.

The Vital Role of Team Sponsor

You might recall from Jerry's saga that the stonewalling supervisor was also the sponsor of the improvement team. When it comes to support in team environments, sponsors fill an important role—often a make-or-break role, as the story illustrates.

Effective team sponsors don't have much of a hands-on role, but the few things they do can make a big difference. If you're one of them, take your role seriously. And if you're on a team that has gone adrift, open a dialogue with the sponsor immediately—or if you don't have a sponsor, get one.

> Effective team sponsors don't have much of a hands-on role, but the few things they do can make a big difference.

The sponsor creates the team charter and then stands out of the way while the team goes about its work. Where it gets tricky is knowing when to get involved. The wisest sponsors take their cues from the team, staying out of team meetings but providing help when it's requested—to address barriers, needs, or opportunities. And if the team doesn't proactively keep the sponsor up to date, it's up to the sponsor to keep the communication lines open and active.

As the team's work moves forward, sponsors can serve as the link to other work areas and teams. But most important, they serve as the team's primary connection and spokesperson with key leaders in the organization. In some cases, support will require a nod from the powers that be. A good sponsor who's equipped with a solid case for *why* the support (information, time, funding, expertise, tools, whatever) is needed can get the job done.

Team Check-Up

Speaking of teams and support, now might be a good time to assess the current status of all projects. Are any of them crying out for help?

If you're a sponsor in the formal sense, get up-to-date information and provide what's needed—or at least do whatever is in your power to move teams closer to getting the needed support. If you're not the sponsor but can still help out, go for it. If it's unclear what the team needs, or if there are problems getting it, get together and talk about it. Open dialogue can work wonders.

If you glance around and it appears that all projects are cruising along at warp speed, don't assume the best. You might be in a workplace where people are uncomfortable or fearful asking for support. Periodically talk with team sponsors and team members, and put the support issue squarely at the center of the table. Make it easy for them to explain what they need and why. Several simple questions can get things rolling: What kinds of barriers are you running into? What would help you and others make even more progress with this project? How can I help you be successful on this?

As the responses unfold, listen carefully. Some people might hesitate to flat-out report, for example, that someone somewhere is hoarding data and keeping it from the project team. Apply an attentive ear and some well-crafted follow-up questions to uncover the real situation.

PUTTING RESOURCES WITHIN REACH

Take stock of what's being hoarded, hidden, and otherwise kept from employees. Is it an industry newsletter that's under lock and key for crazy reasons? ("They'll only use it to find their next employer.") Is it a database or a computer? ("We can't trust people with such sensitive information.") Is it certain equipment? ("Only trained operators can touch that stuff.") Is it Internet access or e-mail capabilities? ("They'll use it for personal business, and it'll distract them from their regular duties.") Is it access to various parts of the office or plant? ("We can't have people wandering all over.")

There are so many possibilities—and so many excuses. But how many of these restrictions are truly justified, and how many are merely an exercise in control? Sure, it's fair to say that only trained operators can touch certain equipment. But if the case can be made that wider access would be good for everyone, why not make training available to those who want to learn? At best, limits constrain people's movement and thinking. At their worst, they send the message that people are not to be trusted.

Start somewhere, *anywhere*. Take a look around, be honest with yourself, pick out a situation where you can widen availability to needed resources, then make it happen.

SANDY'S STORY

Sandy worked as a computer specialist at a company that produced slick business presentations. She did her best to keep pace with a rapidly changing industry, but her boss stood in the way.

She explains: "The company belonged to an industry association, and the group's newsletters were about the latest tools and techniques in our field. But my boss kept everything under lock and key. He didn't want to distribute it because it had help-wanted ads, and he was afraid we'd leave the company. So we missed out on all the valuable information in the newsletter."

When Sandy moved on, she found that her new employer subscribed to the same newsletter and encouraged employees to read it. "They have enough faith in their work environment that they don't have to worry about me rushing off."

Get Obsessed with Technology

The nontechnical folks just might bring the freshest, wildest ideas for applying new technology.

Set up an ongoing dialogue group—a think-tank of sorts—to focus entirely on technology. Put particular emphasis on information systems and anything even remotely related to the Internet. This group would have a threefold mission: to stay up to date on the latest advances, to pinpoint opportunities for applying those advances in the workplace, and to excite others about the possibilities.

Members can come from a single work unit or from a wider range of functions and work areas—as long as they bring a rich mix of perspectives. Technical acumen should not be a requirement. In fact, the nontechnical folks just might bring the freshest, wildest ideas for applying new technology. Still, the group should include at least several people who spend most of their days and nights using and learning and obsessing over the latest technology. These folks will play a key role when it comes to bringing the latest and greatest developments to the workplace.

Giving and Getting Enough Prep Time

As new assignments and projects get under way, avoid throwing people into situations without adequate time to prepare. Start off with a conversation to find out how they'd like to get ready. If they're totally happy starting out cold, and the situation can allow it, no problem. But if other things are needed on the front end—training, shadowing, coaching, whatever else—invest the time and money.

Perhaps you're the one taking on the new assignment. If so, you might have to start the conversation. If the work unit has a tradition of tossing folks into new jobs, and you just know that *everyone* would be better off if you could spend two days shadowing the person who has filled that role for years, step forward and say so. The same is true even if you're not taking on any new assignments but feel you could do your current job better with more training. Build your case, then take the initiative and ask.

INVEST IN PEOPLE

Some organizations nickel and dime invention to death, whereas others do just the opposite and toss cash in all directions. Why not strike a middle ground? Have a clear, collective direction that everyone understands, coupled with a bias toward investment.

Ideally, spending authority should be widely shared. Here's a policy that briskly walks the talk: "Each employee has the authority to spend up to $_,___ each year for a workshop, a new piece of equipment, new software, a learning-filled visit to another organization, or whatever else *they* decide they need to do their job better."

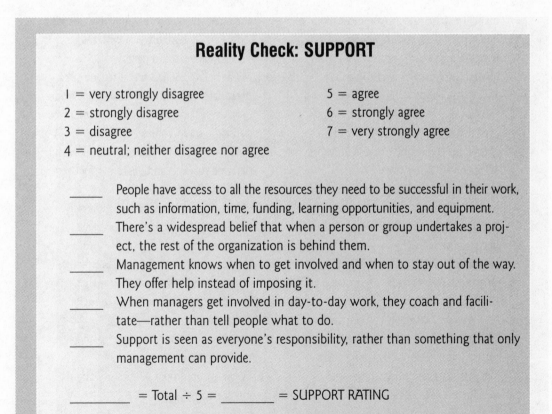

Reality Check: SUPPORT

I = very strongly disagree

2 = strongly disagree

3 = disagree

4 = neutral; neither disagree nor agree

5 = agree

6 = strongly agree

7 = very strongly agree

_____ People have access to all the resources they need to be successful in their work, such as information, time, funding, learning opportunities, and equipment.

_____ There's a widespread belief that when a person or group undertakes a project, the rest of the organization is behind them.

_____ Management knows when to get involved and when to stay out of the way. They offer help instead of imposing it.

_____ When managers get involved in day-to-day work, they coach and facilitate—rather than tell people what to do.

_____ Support is seen as everyone's responsibility, rather than something that only management can provide.

_____ = Total ÷ 5 = _____ = SUPPORT RATING

Conversation Instead of Evaluation

In Multnomah County, Oregon, the publicly elected county CEO and her staff have led an effort to enrich the workplace for all 4,900 county employees. Part of this has involved a complete overhaul of performance reviews for the county's department directors and the people who work in the CEO's office.

In fact, the term *performance reviews* hardly even applies anymore. They're more like ongoing, two-way performance *conversations*, facilitated by Bill Farver, the CEO's chief of staff. He draws from the following questions to seed the dialogue—and to discover what he and others can do to help their colleagues be more successful.

1. Who are your primary customers? How do you get feedback from them?
2. What professional work accomplishments during the past year are you most proud of?
3. What have been your major learnings over the past year?
4. In what professional areas or skills would you like to improve?
5. How would you like to see your job evolve in the coming year? Are you getting an opportunity to use your best efforts and skills at work?
6. How would you assess your overall leadership skills?
7. What assistance do you need from Beverly and Bill? (Beverly Stein is the publicly elected CEO of Multnomah County.)
8. What issues would you like to raise with Beverly and Bill?
9. How can we make better, more personal contact with staff in departments around projects and issues of concern to them?
10. What basic assumptions have you questioned in the past year?
11. What was the most difficult issue you dealt with this past year?
12. How's your sense of humor? How's your balance of work with the rest of your life?
13. What can Beverly and Bill do to reduce the stress on you and your department? How can we support you better with your employees and peers?
14. What does RESULTS mean to you on a personal level? (RESULTS is a countywide initiative calling for widespread employee participation in addressing service improvement, data-based evaluation and decision making, and customer-focused performance measures.)
15. How has your thinking about diversity and its value to the county evolved over the past year?
16. What personal insight have you had about yourself in the past year that has changed the way you think about or do "your job"?
17. How do you most enjoy giving and receiving recognition?
18. What are you most passionate about in your work?

(For more information about workplace renewal in Multnomah County, turn to pages 176-177)

Chapter 15

Personal Development

After six years as a buyer for a chain of clothing stores, Sandy knows her job inside-out. In fact, she can practically do it with her eyes closed—which is exactly why work has become so meaningless for her. "My brain is turning into mush," she says. Determined to improve the situation, she attended a three-day seminar on retail marketing. More recently, she has been trying to take on some additional duties as a way of learning more about the business. Sandy knows that some of her colleagues at the company also feel stuck in a personal-development rut, but there's enough to like about the workplace that for her, it would be hard to leave.

The development keys include challenge, invention, support—and personal development. They're all about the ongoing development of the organization's products and services, the methods for creating these things, and the people who do the creating.

> "My brain is turning into mush."

It makes perfect sense, but in too many workplaces, nearly all the development effort focuses on only two of the three: the products and services, and the methods for producing them. In worst-case situations, "development" is nothing more than a quest for efficiency. Even well-intentioned efforts aimed at innovation, reengineering, and process improvement often end up dealing exclusively with the inanimate aspects of the workplace—hardware, software, processes, tools, specifications, data, and so on.

The message this sends is that all these "assets" are more important than people. And over time, people like Sandy—who are the real brains of the organization—start to atrophy. They also start to polish up their resumes.

A meaningful workplace develops equally in all three areas: *what* is produced, *how* it's produced, and *who* produces it. Training is seen as an investment, not as an expense. Learning opportunities are everywhere. Anyone who wants to can become a learner. People are encouraged to try out new skills and tools and roles, even if there's a temporary price to be paid in terms of efficiency.

As for what people can learn and how they can grow, this is partly determined by the mission of the organization. But within that, employees are well-empowered to set their own development directions. Deep inside, they feel that they're not simply existing in the workplace—they're flourishing.

Yes, It's *Personal* Development

The choice of words for this meaning key may have caught your attention. Most people talk about professional development. Why call it *personal* development?

One reason is the simple fact that "professional" is a loaded term. Too many workplaces distinguish between their "professional employees" and everyone else, and they end up creating a class system that reinforces division. The term *professional development* might be interpreted as something reserved for people with special credentials or certain titles, but that's *not* what is meant here. Everyone should have opportunities to develop.

A second reason for the choice of words is to convey that this is indeed a *personal* proposition. We're talking about *your* development. *You* need to take responsibility for it. Sure, your colleagues should be a part of the process, and the organization should invest in your development and support you. But the last thing you want to do is sit back and expect your boss, or the human-resources office, or a training unit, or anyone else to take care of you.

> We're talking about *your* development. *You* need to take responsibility for it.

I'm not saying they don't have your best interests in mind. Perhaps they do. But by counting on them to manage your development process, you're buying into the notion that an organization should look after its employees. This caretaker model—which some have even likened to a parent–child model—leads to a workplace made up of a handful of thinkers and many doers. Over time, it can even create an entitlement culture in which people dutifully do as they're told in exchange for being taken care of. This is a workplace where people truly check their hearts and minds at the door.

Have You Been Learning?

The story that opened this chapter is full of insights into personal development. For one—and this is a big positive—Sandy seems well aware of what's happening in her work life, and she's eager to take charge and do something about it.

What about you? Have you stopped to analyze what's going on in your own work life? There's no need to spend hours with a career counselor, or complete one of the many commercial inventories and assessments that promise to remake your career. Rather, take stock of your personal development here and now.

Start by creating a timeline that extends from your very first workplace experience to the present day. Draw a horizontal line across the middle of a flipchart sheet or an 11-by-17-inch piece of paper. The far-right point is today, the far left is that first job. Now divide it into time intervals—draw marks on the timeline to show each year, or five years, or decade.

> Recognizing what we have done in the past is a recognition of ourselves. By conducting a dialogue with our past, we are searching how to go forward.
>
> —KIYOKO TAKEDA

Above the line, write down all the jobs you've ever held, from that first paper route or babysitting job to the position you hold today. Now think of any major events that occurred on your workplace journey, and jot down these as well. Perhaps you went back to school for an advanced degree, maybe your long-time employer went belly up, or it could be that you had an awakening at some point and hurriedly quit a dead-end job.

After you've recorded all these milestones, focus your attention on the space below the line. Here, write your "learning achievements." In other words, what did you learn from each of these milestones? Include specific skills ("learned the ins and outs of control charts"), new ways of thinking ("Stan showed me by example how to empower others to make decisions"), and general life lessons ("finally figured out how to exert my own independence and creativity in the workplace"). And if you're having trouble figuring out what you learned along the way, well, that might be a lesson in itself. But chances are you've learned plenty. Take the time you need to rewind your memory and replay some of what went on during those past years.

Once the bottom half is completed, synthesize the information and try to draw some conclusions.

What themes emerge?

Were there years when your learning opportunities seemed few and far between? If so, what caused this?

As time went on, have you picked up the pace of your personal development, or just the opposite—and why?

Which workplace situations offered the greatest chance for development?

What did *you* do along the way to promote your own personal development?

What are the implications for your *future* personal development?

> One of the reasons mature people stop learning is that they become less and less willing to risk failure.
> —John W. Gardner

How Will You Keep Learning?

Our personal development is often steered by our careers, our workplaces, and our jobs. It can sometimes feel as if our work is pulling us along, forcing us to learn things and develop skills in areas that simply don't fit our deep interests. Let's take a few minutes to flip things around and let your development vision lead the way. Create a new timeline, this one extending three or so years into the future.

Start with the bottom half first. What personal-development milestones would you like to achieve as the months and years unfold? This is a private opportunity to be entirely honest with yourself, so don't hold back. Write down specific skills, general know-how, specialized expertise, sweeping life lessons—whatever you consider to be an important part of your own development. And when you're done, take a wide-angle look. What major themes or patterns seem to emerge? Take time to do this thoroughly, crystallizing your ideas into a clear vision of your immediate personal-development future.

Now go to the top half of your future timeline. Your challenge at this point is to think *how*. How will you make this vision your reality? Write down vocations, professions, workplaces, jobs, projects, activities, pursuits, and whatever else you think would make possible your ideal personal development. There's no need to devote a lot of ink to this; a handful of carefully developed ideas should be enough. But you *do* need to keep your mind wide open to possibilities.

If you're completely honest with yourself and true to your vision, expect some surprises. That impending project that once seemed so distasteful might offer rich learning opportunities that perfectly fit your vision. Or maybe there's a new position opening up somewhere in the organization, and wouldn't you know, it offers most of the personal-development opportunities you wrote down. It could even be that your snap analysis points you to a completely different calling. Are you ready to act on your discoveries?

Be Wary of the Learning Paradigms

When it comes to learning, society seems locked into some self-defeating paradigms. One is that we learn until the age of 18 or, if we go to college, a few years later. Then a new phase of our lives begins, and if we're fortunate, we get to use what we learned. It's as if the first two decades of our lives are all about development, after which learning becomes almost incidental, something we do in passing.

With technology changing so rapidly, people have been forced to sharpen their technical skills. That's a small part of development, but it's better than nothing. And there's more talk about the need for lifelong learning. But there's still a dominant mindset that education is something we do early in life.

The other paradigm relates to *how* we learn. In too many cases, education is designed around the view that people are empty vessels who need to be filled with information. This was the method of choice in the days of the one-room schoolhouse, with its three R's, its primers, and its learning by rote. And it still dominates. Just peek into any classroom nowadays, and in most, you'll see rows of desks facing the front. Order and control are still the top priority in many schools—more so than a desire to instill passionate curiosity and a love of learning in the people schools should serve.

This empty-vessel model is still so dominant that it's no surprise to find it shaping how we learn in the workplace. All too often, development is still called "training." It usually involves a group of 20 or so people who spend one or two days glued to their chairs, facing the front, while a so-called expert tells them everything they need to know. Then they return to their jobs, with all those old pressures and problems, and it's back to business as usual.

EILEEN'S STORY

As purchasing manager for a glass distributor, Eileen worked hard to turn the unit into a self-directed work team. "Every day was something new," she recalls. "We had good days and bad days, but all of them were learning days."

After a while, though, the learning started to slow as the team truly became self-directed. Eileen switched to a classic coach's role, but she felt that her own development pace had slowed to a crawl. "I looked for other opportunities in the company, but they simply weren't there."

Determined to keep learning, Eileen updated her resume and soon moved on.

Learning Is a Means to an End

You'll recall from Sandy's story that she attended a three-day workshop on retail marketing. It provided useful information, she said. But did she actually use any of it? Well, when she got back to the office, there was a backlog of e-mails to answer . . . a report due in a couple of days . . . and a presentation two weeks later. The workshop binder ended up on the shelf, and so did all those new ideas.

It's tempting to say that Sandy didn't try hard enough to use some of what she had learned, but it's worth noting how the training unfolded. According to Sandy, all three days had the look and feel of an old-style information dump. Sure, it was valuable information, but it seemed like the instructors simply wanted to get through every page of the participant notebook—without any real concern over whether people were really learning, let alone whether they would use the information once they returned to their workplaces.

> I hear and I forget. I see and I remember. I do and I understand.
> —Confucius

There's a lesson in here for workshop organizers, instructors, facilitators, and everyone else who's involved in education. Ideally, learning sessions should be designed around *using* the information.

- Instead of trying to fill people's brains with as much information as possible, turn the presentation into a conversation. Allow people to explore with each other, in pairs and small groups, how they can use their new ideas and insights in their workplaces.
- Instead of having a one- or two-day session, break it into six or eight mini-sessions over two months, with people deciding at each exactly how they plan to use their new knowledge—then reporting how things went. This turns the learning process into a series of progressive experiments, and it turns learners into teachers.
- Instead of having people come together for the session, only to return to their own corners of the work world when the session ends, try to organize people into small networks so they can stay in touch and keep learning together as the months and years unfold. If it's an outside workshop and everyone works in other organizations, they can use e-mail or phone calls to stay connected.

So What Can You Do?

Taking charge of your development is your first challenge. Recognizing the dangers of those education paradigms is your second challenge. The third challenge—and this has to be a lifelong proposition—is to do something about it. Here are some practical ideas.

USE IT ASAP

Whenever you attend a workshop or something similar, identify two or three significant ideas, insights, or skills you learned and apply them as soon as you return to the workplace. If writing down your plans makes it more likely you'll carry them out, do it.

Perhaps you can even huddle with your colleagues, share the information, and get them involved in the learning and using process. Even before the workshop ends, you can start on this by getting a partner or building a small network. Tell each other how you plan to use your new information, then stay in touch to keep yourselves honest—and to keep the learning process rolling.

FIND THE TEACHER BESIDE YOU

Workshops are a traditional approach to learning, and done right, they're a good approach. But each and every workday can be its own mini-workshop, if you let it. Who knows, the colleague who's working next to you might have something to teach you—an idea, a skill, a software package, whatever. If you want to learn something from that person, step forward and ask. Chances are, he or she will be honored by your request, and your personal-development process will be richer for it.

To make the most of this, an organization can even form its own internal "faculty" of resident experts. A directory listing people's special skills and expertise might be all that's needed to form a connection between someone who wants to learn and someone who's ready to coach. A list can be handed out periodically with a newsletter or as a stand-alone, or it can be routinely updated on an intranet.

> To teach is to learn twice.
> —JOSEPH JOUBERT

This same faculty can be used for organized workshops or informal dialogue sessions. This will require more preparation, especially since the instructors and coaches may not have any formal training experience. An experienced workshop facilitator can work with them ahead of time to ensure the session runs smoothly.

Learn by Doing

In addition to learning from what people know, look for ways to learn from what they do. You might recall that Sandy took on additional duties to deepen her understanding of the business. Are there similar opportunities in your workplace? What about spending an afternoon using a different piece of equipment, or helping someone with a database, or sitting in for the first time on a brainstorming session with a client? Figure out what fits your learning wish list, then make the arrangements.

> Seek out people who can offer rich insights into the challenges or opportunities you're currently facing.

Reach Beyond the Organization

If you can't achieve all of your personal-development goals within the workplace, hit the road just as Sandy did. Seek out people who can offer rich insights into the challenges or opportunities you're currently facing.

If the latest conversations have been about a sense of purpose (or the lack thereof) in the workplace, spend a few hours at a place where mission is everything. What about a local nonprofit social-service organization? These are the folks who know mission. Looking to strengthen the sense of workplace unity? Arrange a get-together with the coach and several players of a local championship sports team. What they do may be worlds apart from your business, but they'll have rich lessons in *how* to do it.

Also take advantage of the various conferences and workshops offered by countless organizations, universities, trade schools, and chambers of commerce. You're guaranteed to find a learning opportunity on just about anything. A Web search will turn up all sorts of possibilities. Start by visiting the sites of several associations for your industry, and check out the cross-industry groups like the American Society for Quality, the Association for Quality and Participation, the Society for Human Resources Management, and the American Society for Training & Development.

BRING IN NEW KNOW-HOW

Organize a series of learning opportunities for all employees. Bring in outside speakers who are experts in their areas, either for monthly "learning lunches" or slightly longer learning forums, and build in time for dialogue among small groups of five or so people. The presentations can even be videotaped, so folks who can't attend can still get the information.

> Bring in outside speakers who are experts in their areas, and build in time for dialogue among small groups of five or so people.

Topics can be based on the personal-development goals people have shared with each other—and on issues that are weighing heavily on your industry and organization. If you're in the steel business, for instance, and new trade policies have just been negotiated between the United States and Japan, people might be eager to get the inside scoop from an import–export expert. If there's a feeling that meetings are lasting too long and producing too few results, perhaps it's time for a session with a guru on meeting effectiveness. The small-group dialogue at the end will give people the opportunity to figure out how they can act on the information when they get back to their work areas.

TURN TECHNOLOGY INTO A LEARNING TOOL

Make maximum use of computer technology and the Internet to foster learning. The Web offers a vast wealth of information, and anyone who knows even the rudiments of effective searching can learn in minutes what just a few years ago required hours and hours in a library.

Online mail lists (also known as listservs) can put you in touch with thousands of others with a single e-mail, and online bulletin boards let you pose questions to the world. Not bad for what amounts to a very minimal investment. If your company is in the knowledge business at all—and what company isn't?—everyone should have computer and Internet access.

If the present looks bright, the future is positively blinding. Distance learning is quickly coming of age as programmers develop new ways to make sessions more interactive. We're *not* talking about Web-based training that's little more than a series of sequential overhead slides. We're talking about two-way audiovisual capabilities in real time, so even if the instructor is in Australia and you're in Topeka, you can still attend, interact, and benefit.

ZANNA'S STORY

Involved in public
relations for a national
health agency, Zanna
rarely sits still.

One day she's
overseeing special-event
fundraising, the next
day she's meeting with
a would-be donor, the
next she's developing
a media plan. Many
days find her doing a
mix of all these things
and more.

"It's nonstop
variety and nonstop
learning," Zanna says.
"I wouldn't want it any
other way."

Making Development a Group Endeavor

In talking about her workplace, Sandy mentioned that some of her colleagues also felt like their brains were turning into mush. They said as much when they heard that she was attending the three-day seminar. And the issue still comes up every now and then, usually in a frustration-filled conversation at lunch.

Many organizations make personal development a very private effort involving just the employee and the boss. It's often tangled up with a person's semi-annual or annual performance evaluation—an age-old process, by the way, that tends to feel like a flawed apology for not maintaining constructive dialogue during the past six or twelve months.

Why not make personal development a collective process? Instead of those behind-closed-doors conversations with just two people, or those lunchtime gripe sessions, make it a topic for a constructive group conversation involving all employees from the work unit, team, or office.

Get together and create a simple flipchart sheet with three columns titled "How we want to grow," "What we can share with each other," and "Where we can go for everything else." Use the first column to record people's personal-development goals for, say, the next 12 months. This is much like a needs assessment, though it goes far beyond the narrow definition of "needs." The conversation shifts gears with column two, as people put their heads together to determine how they can help each other. ("You want to learn the new packaging process? I'll be more than happy to show you!") This is the time to uncover all those hidden gold mines of knowledge and skills.

In all likelihood, not all the personal-development goals (column 1) will find a match with internal expertise (column 2). So column 3 will prompt the group to figure out what can be done. Perhaps someone knows of an upcoming workshop or a worthwhile book. Someone might even chime in that her best friend's cousin, who's an expert in such-and-such, will be in town a month from now; perhaps he can come over for a brown-bag learning session. As personal development becomes a group initiative, the possibilities truly begin to multiply.

"Here Are *Our* Learning Needs"

Some organizations conduct learning-needs assessments, which raises an important point while we're on this topic of getting more people involved in setting the direction for personal development. Try to avoid the old approach of having a consultant conduct one-on-one interviews with a random sampling of employees. People are adept at telling consultants what they think are the right answers, and consultants can be only too happy to oblige so they can get on with their next interview.

Why not open the assessment process to dialogue? Bring people together and have a conversation to uncover exactly what they need and want to learn. Make the organization's overall vision and mission—along with specific work-unit goals—a prominent part of the conversation. Also talk about people's deep interests. All this should come together to shape the learning plan.

There are some hazards here. One is the risk of creating a learning wish list that extends for pages and pages and pages. The conversation should include time at the end to establish a doable list of top priorities. Also be watchful for the boss-dominated conversation, in which people censor themselves because of who's in the room. If the company wants to hire a consultant for the needs assessment, encourage the use of an outsider who can facilitate these conversations without the "boss" on hand.

Reality Check: PERSONAL DEVELOPMENT

1 = very strongly disagree
2 = strongly disagree
3 = disagree
4 = neutral; neither disagree nor agree

5 = agree
6 = strongly agree
7 = very strongly agree

_____ The workplace provides people with all sorts of opportunities to learn and grow.

_____ People take responsibility for their own personal development.

_____ Variety (trying new equipment, building new relationships, varying your work, and so on) is encouraged because it fosters learning and development.

_____ Internal job-changing is valued as a way for people to develop their skills and experience.

_____ Training is seen as an investment—and not as an expense.

_____ = Total ÷ 5 = _____ = PERSONAL DEVELOPMENT RATING

PART FIVE

THE COMMUNITY KEYS

We value togetherness.

The Community Keys

- Dialogue
- Relationship Building
- Service
- Acknowledgment
- Oneness

Dialogue

Heather couldn't figure it out. It was her first day of work at a financial-services company, and aside from a few quick greetings from people she met on a 10-minute office tour, everyone seemed so reserved. It happened the next day, and the next, and the next. Heather soon learned that it had nothing to do with her—and everything to do with the culture of the organization. "I call this place a talk-free zone," she says. "We have your garden-variety conversations about everyday things, but we don't really talk about things that matter to our work and our workplace." A year into her job, Heather tried to gather a small group to talk about a flawed billing process. She thought an informal conversation would lead to at least some improvement and perhaps set the stage for a formal process-improvement team. It never happened. "Everyone I approached said the same thing: If we talk about this, they'll think we're trying to rock the boat."

It's sad to say, but Heather has lots of company. The talk-free zone extends to all sorts of organizations, regardless of size, location, or mission. Even at places where conversation is fairly common, it can be anything but dialogue. Idle chit-chat is not dialogue. Traditional debate is not dialogue. One-way flows of information are not dialogue. Ping-pong discussions are not dialogue. Perhaps you've seen verbal ping-pong players in your workplace—or maybe you're one yourself. A person pontificates for a minute or so, shuts up to allow the other person to talk, uses this time to plan what to say next, then inhales deeply and starts talking all over again.

> "I call this place a talk-free zone. We don't really talk about things that matter to our work and our workplace."

Dialogue goes so much deeper. In fact, it's less of an activity and more of a philosophy. In a meaningful workplace, when employees need to work through a problem or issue or opportunity, they have freedom and opportunities to engage in open conversation. A big title is not required for "admission" to a conversation. Nor are there any artificial litmus tests on intelligence ("They just won't know where we're coming from."), experience ("They haven't been around long enough."), or affiliation ("They're not in our work unit, so why should we invite them?").

Instead, there's a recognition that most problems and issues and opportunities involve many people and can benefit from many perspectives. Let's get together and talk about it—all of us. As for the character of these conversations, honesty and respect are core principles. People get a chance to share their opinions and ideas and whatever else is on their minds, and there's a willingness—ideally, an eagerness—to hear what everyone else has to say.

Now Hear This: Start Listening

Dialogue has more to do with open ears than with open mouths, so to begin strengthening it in your workplace, sharpen your listening skills. Listen so that you truly hear and understand what people are saying—and pay close enough attention so you can figure out what they're meaning to say even if they're beating around the verbal bush. You should be working so hard at it that beads of sweat practically pop out of your forehead.

> Most conversations are just alternating monologues. The question is, is there any real listening going on?
> —LEO BUSCAGLIA

Listen to those comments about the product or service. Listen to that gripe about the new recognition process and the resulting internal competition. Listen to that suggestion for improving the process. Listen to that complaint, even if—especially if!—you've heard it over and over again. What is *really* being said?

It's not easy being a great listener, which is why these tips are so important:

- When someone is talking to you, let him or her entirely finish the comment. If the person pauses and seems to have more to say, don't rush to fill the silence. Let the person collect his or her thoughts and continue.
- Make a point of asking questions. You'll deepen your understanding and help to move the conversation forward.

- As the dialogue unfolds, listen to the internal conversation you're having with yourself. Be alert to the judgments you're making about the person's personality or delivery. Focus all of your attention on the content of the message.
- Reserve judgment on the content until you've heard the full story.
- Do your best to see things from the speaker's perspective. Besides learning *what* the person is saying, also try to figure out *why*. Try this simple question: "Why do you feel that way?"
- Practice. Like any other skill, listening needs to be developed over time. But it's well worth the effort when you consider that effective listening can help you in just about every area of your life.

> **Word Check**
>
> The word *dialogue* brings together the Greek terms *dia* (through) and *logos* (word, thought). Dialogue is all about achieving a deeper level of understanding through a process of collective sharing and reflection. Much more common in the workplace are "discussions" in which people eagerly share their ideas but keep their ears and minds closed.

Finding a High-Interest Topic

You'll recall Heather, whose story opened this chapter. She tried to assemble her colleagues for an informal conversation about a failing process, but no one seemed willing. You have to wonder, were they unwilling to engage in any kind of dialogue, or was it the topic that made them so reluctant? The immediate challenge for Heather—and for you—is to pinpoint an issue that's likely to draw people into conversation. Use it to get the talking and listening under way. Start with the one topic that seems to be the most manageable, then construct a dialogue that widely involves employees.

Let's say there have been sporadic debates regarding software. Some want to upgrade, others want to buy new products, still others are satisfied with the status quo—but everyone seems to have an opinion. By default, the status-quo people have been "winning" because no action is being taken either way. It sounds like a problem, but it's actually a great chance to set a precedent for healthy dialogue *and* to resolve the software issue.

Think about the current situation in your workplace. What topics are getting heavy airtime around the proverbial water cooler? Jot down the possibilities, then look at the list and find one "lukewarm" topic—something that's warm enough to generate wide interest, yet not so hot that it will scare people away.

Most people would call Roberta a health-care quality consultant, but she's really a "connector." Much of her work involves bringing people together so they can better serve each other and their customers.

One assignment took her to a nursing home where there seemed to be sharp differences in care levels between first and second shifts. During the first shift, 30 long-term-care residents wore adult diapers—while the number nearly quadrupled during second shift.

"I brought together staff from both shifts and gently guided the conversation," Roberta says. It marked the first time in a long time that the two shifts sat down to talk and learn from each other. As the second shift adopted some

continued on page 163

Installing an "Opportunity Radar"

Let's assume you pinpoint that lukewarm topic, get folks together, engage in great conversation, and end up reaching a wonderful outcome. Everyone is satisfied. It all sounds good, and it is, but don't be fooled into thinking that dialogue has sprung to life in your workplace. It's a long-term undertaking. You and others must stay on constant alert for situations that are calling out for conversation. And when they show up on your radar screen, you need to jump into action.

Have folks been voicing random concerns about a newly released product from an arch competitor? Get together, talk about it, and decide what to do. Is a first-of-a-kind situation pointing up some problems with the sick-leave policy? Well, team up and work things out. Is John running around the office telling everyone who'll listen about a brand-new software package that knocked his socks off at a recent industry conference? Sounds like we should devote some time to this as a group. Who knows, that software might revolutionize certain aspects of how we do our work.

Whatever you do when situations arise, avoid the inclination to work things out immediately with little or no involvement from others. Make a habit of pulling people together, talking about it, and opting for a group decision.

By the way, if meaningful conversation is a rarity in your organization, pursue it with slow and gentle steps. Keep in mind that it marks a radically different approach for many people. Most of us are comfortable with fairly vacuous discussions—not because we like them but because they're familiar. Anything more will feel like a sudden jerk out of the collective comfort zone. Think of initial conversations as subtle icebreakers rather than epic exchanges. Simply getting together may be more important than getting into deep conversation.

Don't Leave Anything to Chance

Even lukewarm topics can heat up very quickly, pitting people against each other, uncovering concerns that had long been dormant, and stirring up new issues. And oddly enough, that might be an extremely healthy development. Do you want folks to stay stuck in their passive-aggressive postures? ("Gee, Mary, sorry I didn't get you that report on time." "Gosh, Chris, I just don't know where that spreadsheet is." "I'd love to help, Bob, but my schedule is jammed that day.") Or would you prefer to get the angst out in the open where it can be worked through constructively?

If you think an upcoming group conversation might get unwieldy, establish a specific and doable goal for the get-together, and communicate it to everyone not only several days before the session, but also as soon as the session begins. ("Let's decide whether to continue using the Pro Design software in its current version . . . or upgrade . . . or buy entirely new software.") This will help frame the conversation, but don't be surprised if the "frame" gets adjusted once folks get together. Different people just might have different perspectives on what the session should accomplish.

When the conversation gets rolling, consider having a neutral facilitator on hand to guide things along. If people go off on tangents, record the topics on a flipchart "parking lot" for near-future dialogue—very near future, perhaps even during this same meeting. If Mary and Chris harden their positions and start sniping, let them. Good dialogue taps deeply into emotions, and emotions aren't tidy. A skilled facilitator will give everyone time to share his or her ideas in full, then move the entire group back to its focused goal.

Keep It Going

It's easy to think of dialogue as an event, but it needs to become an ongoing process. Try to make rich conversation as routine as possible. If you have regular staff meetings that are afflicted with one-way flows of information, carve out a portion of the agenda for free-flowing conversation. A new topic can be addressed each time, with participants setting the agenda.

of the first shift's practices, there was a sharp decrease in the number of residents wearing diapers—and a steep climb in their self-esteem.

Roberta had once again succeeded in her "connector" role. "That's what feeds my soul and spirit," she says.

HAL'S STORY

After 20 years with his current employer, Hal is a self-described "raging cynic." He tells of a workplace where closed-door conversations are not just the norm—"they're the rule. If doors didn't exist, our company wouldn't exist either."

There's also a list of taboo topics. "You never talk about executive perks," he says. "And you never question the rules or policies."

If the budget will allow it, what about buying lunch each month for the work unit and using the time together to engage in conversation? It's probably not the best time to deal with deeply contentious issues—who wants indigestion?—but an informal atmosphere will automatically lower those communication barriers. Maybe there's a certain time each week when folks, for whatever reason, have some collective free time. See it as an opportunity to get everyone together for conversation.

> There are no "five easy steps" to constructive dialogue. But there are some easy-to-use tools that can enrich workplace conversations.

Equip Yourself for Conversation

You can tell by now that there are no "five easy steps" to constructive dialogue. But there are some easy-to-use tools that can enrich workplace conversations.

Want to unload a wealth of wild ideas? Try classic brainstorming. Need to get ideas from people who may want to remain anonymous? Bring several stacks of stickie notes to the meeting to combine brainstorming with confidential writing; then have participants post and sort the ideas into common categories, creating what's called an affinity diagram. Want to identify all the action steps required for a given implementation? Start out by developing a tree diagram, then use the info to develop a Gantt chart. The latter will spell out who does what and when.

Now for a note of caution: These tools, simple though they may be, are easy to misuse. Brainstorming is fairly common, yet it's one of the most abused techniques in the meeting toolkit. With classic brainstorming, participants are supposed to fire out their ideas in bullet-point fashion, with no comment or criticism from others. Yet so many brainstorming sessions get bogged down as someone hears an idea and wants to pontificate on why it will or won't work. In the end, the brainstorming process gets undermined, and those mind-stretching ideas that would have transformed everything remain under wraps. The tip here—and this applies to all the tools—is to learn how they work and then stick to the guidelines as the session unfolds. An Internet search or a trip to the library will turn up all sorts of resources that explain these tools in detail.

Another warning: Tools are a good way to harness the energy that comes from strong ideas, opinions, and raw emotions. But don't expect them to turn a passionate person into a pushover, and even more important, don't even try to turn down the volume on people's passions. If anything, you want folks to get more enthusiastic and more excited and more committed to their ideas.

The Open Space Method

In addition to the tools, there are more extensive group processes (sometimes called technologies) that can foster constructive dialogue. One of the most powerful is the "open space conference," and at the very least, you should learn more about it. When it comes to fostering ownership, creativity, and unity among diverse people, the open space approach is stunningly simple and effective. Quite literally, it gives participants the ability to shape the conference to their own needs.

How does it work? First, the organizers develop a compelling theme for the conference. Participants then come together, starting in a big room that's filled with one wide circle of chairs. Plastered to the wall is an oversize conference schedule—but it's blank. Available meeting rooms are listed in the columns, and time slots are noted horizontally. Participants are prompted to work with the theme and identify topics for discussion that they'd like to lead as the day unfolds. Each of these volunteer "conveners," as they're called, then writes a session title and name on a flipchart sheet, reserves a space and time on the meeting schedule, posts the title sheet so others can sign up, and comes to the center of the circle to explain the topic to everyone else.

It doesn't take long for the schedule to fill up with topics, each with its own convener from the group. Then people mill about in what has the look and feel of an open marketplace. They can freely decide which sessions they want to attend, putting their names on the appropriate sign-up sheets. After each session, the convener compiles succinct notes that report highlights and all agreed-upon actions. These are usually compiled at the event on one of the nearby laptop computers, so all participants can leave with a still-warm photocopy of the conference proceedings.

Are there any rules that govern these sessions? Sort of. They're expressed in four refreshing principles and one law:

1. Whoever comes are the right people.
2. Whatever happens is the only thing that could.
3. Whenever it starts is the right time.
4. Whenever it's over, it's over.

> ## An Essential Key
> Dialogue has special importance in efforts to create a meaningful workplace. That's because it has a big influence on so many other meaning keys. Think about it: Healthy dialogue can lead to support, service, relationship-building, direction, challenge, invention, and more.

The Law of Two Feet: Every person can move to another place. If you're in a place where you cannot contribute, go to where you can.

Setting Yourself up for Conversation

Speaking of open space, how is your workplace designed—and what impact is that having on dialogue? Is the work area conducive to conversation, or does it cut people off from each other? I'm not saying you should toss out the furniture and turn the work area into an airplane hangar, but if the space is nothing more than a labyrinth of cubes or a block of offices, you've got problems.

One solution is to create a space where people can go for conversation. If you want to call it a lounge, fine, but its purpose goes beyond lounging. Stock it with several flipcharts, markers, tape, and stickie notes. As for furniture, equip the room with chairs, but keep tables to a minimum. (They'll be just another barrier.) Perhaps seed some conversation by headlining a flipchart sheet with a provocative question: "What kind of technology will our work unit be using in 25 years? Write your ideas here . . . ."

A space like this is great for unplanned chats. In fact, spur-of-the-moment exchanges can be among the most fruitful. Yet the space is also ideal for planned sessions. In fact, by having some serious conversations in the new space early on, people will forever think of it as the dialogue room.

Party Your Way to Dialogue

If Heather's "talk-free zone" sounds all too familiar, you might see attempts to start good dialogue as something akin to oral surgery without anesthetic. So turn the pain into a party. That's right, pull folks together for some kind of social gathering. Perhaps there's a birthday coming up—a good excuse to buy a cake and lure everyone into a common space. Maybe next month marks the first full year with that prized account—sounds like a fine reason to have a party.

Look for *something* that calls for celebration, but make sure the festivities are held at work during regular work hours (lunchtime is perfect). This ensures that even Joe, who would never in a million years go to the local restaurant for a gathering with his work-mates, will see what's going on and be just a few footsteps away. Also remember to keep things simple and, well, restrained. Joe may not be the kind of guy who'll eagerly don a cardboard party hat while hanging out with colleagues. In fact, the very sight of party hats might prompt him to walk the other way. Remember that your mission here is to get folks talking. Design the gathering accordingly.

As soon as the festivities wind down, take advantage of the thaw to get folks together and talking once again—but for something a bit more serious. If your opportunity radar has been operating, you'll know the perfect topic for drawing folks together.

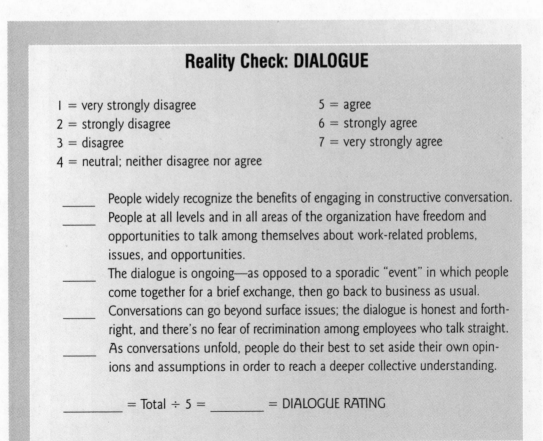

Reality Check: DIALOGUE

1 = very strongly disagree	5 = agree
2 = strongly disagree	6 = strongly agree
3 = disagree	7 = very strongly agree
4 = neutral; neither disagree nor agree	

_____ People widely recognize the benefits of engaging in constructive conversation.

_____ People at all levels and in all areas of the organization have freedom and opportunities to talk among themselves about work-related problems, issues, and opportunities.

_____ The dialogue is ongoing—as opposed to a sporadic "event" in which people come together for a brief exchange, then go back to business as usual.

_____ Conversations can go beyond surface issues; the dialogue is honest and forthright, and there's no fear of recrimination among employees who talk straight.

_____ As conversations unfold, people do their best to set aside their own opinions and assumptions in order to reach a deeper collective understanding.

_____ = Total ÷ 5 = _____ = DIALOGUE RATING

CHAPTER 17

Relationship Building

You can tell right away that Jim values relationships. Reflecting on some of his past workplaces, he always comes back to the people he met and the things they accomplished together. He's still in touch with some of his colleagues going back 15 years. Then he starts talking about his current workplace, and the tone changes. "This is a place that values efficiency above all else," Jim says. "It certainly sees no value in people building relationships with each other." Departments—he calls them silos—get together only when the most pressing matters require them to do so. They efficiently transact their business, then go back to their separate areas. It's the same with individuals, Jim says. People seem interested in getting together only when the work at hand makes it absolutely necessary. "I don't go to work to find a best friend," he says. "I just think it would be more fulfilling, and more beneficial from a business standpoint, if we actively worked to foster relationships."

We've learned a lot since the days of scientific management, when workplace improvement had more to do with developing the most efficient way for a worker to shovel coal—and a lot less to do with people, community, and relationships. But you know what? There's still a strong strain of depersonalization in the workplace. We're no longer obsessing over time-and-motion studies, thank goodness, but

> They efficiently transact their business, then go back to their separate areas.

some people still view workplace relationship building as an inefficient distraction from the real work.

Then there's Jim. For him and countless other people, the social aspects of the workplace are so important. And as he said, this isn't about going to work to

> You think *effectiveness* with *people* and *efficiency* with *things*. I've tried to be "efficient" with a disagreeing or disagreeable person and it simply doesn't work. I've tried to give 10 minutes of "quality time" to a child or an employee to solve a problem, only to discover such "efficiency" creates new problems and seldom resolves the deepest concern.
>
> —Stephen Covey, *The Seven Habits of Highly Effective People*

find bowling buddies or best friends. It's about working in an environment that allows people to get together, to learn from each other, to help each other, to grow together. Let's face it, people (including the coal shoveler) are social beings. A workplace that denies this might be efficient, but it surely won't be effective in the long run—or meaningful to those who work there.

A meaningful workplace abounds with opportunities to build relationships. Perhaps it's projects that bring people together. Maybe there's a common area where paths can cross. Or maybe the work is such that you can't help but be with people as the day unfolds. Ideally, relationship building flourishes not only inside the organization, but also beyond—to include suppliers, customers, the community, and various other stakeholders. The bottom line is, employees get the chance to mix with a variety of people, regardless of how it happens.

Renew Those Long-Lost Contacts

Asked what simple steps he had taken on his own to foster relationship building in his corner of the workplace, Jim hemmed and hawed. He cited his busy schedule and the fact that his work kept him in a fairly secluded part of the building. But after a while, he admitted what these were: excuses.

When it comes to relationship building, there's no substitute for action, and it has to start with you. Right now, get a pen and jot down the names of three workplace people you've lost touch with during the past few months or years. These can be colleagues, customers, suppliers, community members, trade-group friends, whoever.

Pick up the phone and call them as soon as possible—preferably now, unless it's the middle of the night, in which case you've just added to your to-do list for tomorrow. If they're close by, perhaps you can skip the phone and stroll over for a visit. If they're in a foreign country and a long-distance call is out of the question, you might have to resort to e-mail. However you do it, reach out and get back in touch with some of these long-lost contacts.

"Want to Team up on This?"

Challenging work situations are a golden opportunity to start building relationships—and to get other folks doing the same. The next time you start some daunting task, reject the urge to deal with it all by yourself. Our lone-ranger culture prizes solo heroics, yet the best results tend to involve two or more people. And besides, things are so complex these days that just about any issue is too big for just one brain.

Have any big projects on the near horizon? If so, who can help? It's never too early to start building your project network. Get in touch with those people now. Putting off a decision about new equipment? Consult with others, and you'll get the input you need to make a truly informed choice. You might even want to have *them* make the decision. Forget the go-it-alone mentality. It stunts relationship building in the workplace, and besides, it's bad for business. Pull out that pen again and list the names of some prospective partners.

Remember, They're *Meet*ings

Judging from what they're called, meetings should be the ultimate opportunity to build relationships. Talk about ideal conditions: They're one of those rare times when folks are together *and* away from their phones, computers, and routine work. Of course, we both know that this opportunity is hardly ever leveraged. Jim described the meetings at his company as dull affairs in which people discreetly watch the clock while waiting their turn to talk—the same description that so many people give.

Your challenge is to transform those routine meetings into relationship factories. For starters, think about the agenda. Work some time in for a break—perhaps an extended break with snacks—so people have time to mingle. What about the room layout? Will there be a 10-ton conference table separating everyone? ("Please pass the binoculars so I can make eye contact.") Opt for a circle of chairs with no table. And if meeting attendees will be headed to different locations following the session,

PAT'S STORY

For years, Pat had dreamed of owning her own business. When she got tired of dreaming, she took action and made it happen, opening a storefront cafe.

It proved to be everything she ever wanted in a job—except for one thing. She found herself making decision after decision all by herself.

At first she enjoyed the autonomy, but the good feelings gave way to another dream: "I wanted community." Pat spent more and more idle time looking out the front window—her metaphor for wanting to reconnect with the outside. She eventually sold the cafe and took a job with an employee union.

circulate names, phone numbers, and e-mail addresses to everyone. Perhaps you'll foster some contacts, which can lead to relationships.

Of course, there's even more you can do to make the most of meetings. If the organization has just reached a milestone of some sort—or if there's a personal milestone, like a birthday—take some time to celebrate. Yes, have a cake, candles, and—well, a piñata would probably be taking things a bit too far. If folks are fairly new to each other, make sure there are introductions, and prompt them to share more than just the standard "who I am" and "where I work." It's amazing how seemingly minor connections ("You mean you ride a Harley too?!") can be the starting point for a relationship.

Finally, give careful thought to the meeting process, and design it to bring people together. If the whole thing is a one-way flow of information, with one person at the head of the table doing all the talking, kiss any relationship building goodbye. If people are engaging in dialogue, all the better. If they have a chance to divide into smaller workgroups for closer conversation, better still. Throttle up your creativity to maximize the number of person-to-person contacts that unfold during the session.

When No Involvement Is the Best Involvement

Now that you have some ideas on what to do, here's something *not* to do. If you're a manager or supervisor and there's a dispute among employees, avoid rushing in like an overly attentive parent to help work things out.

For one thing, a quick-to-the-rescue response implies that people are unable to solve their own problems—that they are, in effect, children who need a wiser person's guidance. And worse, it sends a message that people are not empowered to resolve their own relationship challenges in the workplace. They just might conclude that they have a similar lack of authority in other areas—say, in making day-to-day decisions about their work or reshaping their work processes to make them more effective and efficient.

If someone who's involved in a situation approaches you for help, avoid taking sides. Listen to his or her concerns, and

BELIEVE IT OR NOT

Gym Class All Over Again

When the manager of a 30-person division went on a health kick, he decided to take "his people" along. He began a lunchtime regimen of outdoor walks and encouraged the division employees to join him. Participation was "voluntary"— much like participation in fundraising efforts and attendance at the annual office party. Before long he had 30 "volunteers," many of whom muttered boss-related comments while they walked.

ask several well-placed questions to open their hearts and minds to new ways of looking at things. If the dispute seems to be getting out of hand, it may be time for an outside facilitator or someone else who's well-versed in dispute resolution. Keep in mind that even the worst person-to-person problems have the potential to strengthen relationships. We've all heard stories about two people who were the worst of enemies, went through some kind of transforming event, and are now the best of friends. It's all in how you deal with—or let others deal with—the situation.

Turning a Supplier into a Partner

So far we've been talking about relationships in terms of what happens inside the organization. But if you're going to be serious about this relationship-building stuff, you have to look to the outside—and that means tightening your connections to suppliers.

> If you're going to be serious about this relationship-building stuff, you have to look to the outside.

If you count on anyone on the outside to provide you with products or services or both, there's no time like the present to get started. Don't just pick up the phone, call your contact at Ideal Supply Company for five minutes of idle chit-chat, then get back to business as usual. Rather, work to build deep, strong relationships. Sure, it can—and probably will—start out with a phone call. Then it can move on to visits involving several people from "our organization" and some from "their organization."

Early on, there will be some fairly predictable getting-to-know-you conversations. ("Oh, so *you're* the one who's always on the other end of the line. It's great to match a face with the voice.") But pretty soon, and with little effort by anyone, the dialogue will turn to mutual goals. ("If the packaging were narrower, it would be easier to ship." "Funny you should mention that. We were just talking about that earlier today. Tell us more about what you have in mind.") If the get-togethers and other contacts are frequent enough, the supplier will become more of a partner, and both of you will enjoy big win-win benefits. You may even get help in areas that you didn't expect. ("We'd be more than happy to share our new team-launch workshop materials with you.")

Closing the Door to Strengthen Our Bonds

All the preceding action ideas are steps in the right direction. Perhaps you want to take a leap. If so, shut the organization down for one day, and spend the time getting to know one another. That's right: Close the place and spend an entire day building relationships. If you work in an air-traffic control center or a neonatal intensive care unit,

> Just when you think that a person is just a backdrop for the rest of the universe, watch them and see that they laugh, they cry, they tell jokes . . . they're just friends waiting to be made.
>
> —Jeffery Borenstein

this isn't feasible. But the vast majority of places *can* stop operations for 24 hours. And those that can't can get creative to figure out how to get away for at least a few hours, even if the gathering doesn't involve everyone at the same time.

There are all sorts of ways to use that shut-down time to open the way to relationship building. How about an open-space conference? Or try an all-day fair where work units and functional areas set up booths to tell the rest of the organization what they do. Or hold a learning day that allows for peer workshops and several sessions with outside experts. If you really want to broaden things out, invite suppliers and customers.

Obviously, whenever you shut the doors, the bottom line takes a hit. And it's darn difficult to calculate the net return on a day of—well, let's call it what the critics will call it—nonwork. But it's an interesting thing to contemplate. How much is it worth to have operations and marketing *finally* talking with each other? What's the value of the breakthrough idea that emerged from a spur-of-the-moment conversation between the engineers and machine operators? And won't life be nicer—a lot nicer!—now that everyone has had a chance to see that the folks from legal are really and truly approachable.

The Computer as Connection Builder

In his interview, Jim mentioned that his workplace values efficiency above all else. You can almost hear the chorus: "We don't have time to build relationships! We're too busy doing the work." Well, it is possible to be efficient in building relationships. This is rarely the best way, but it's doable. And as you may have guessed, it involves computers, networks, and the Internet. There are so many communication tools out there—everything from e-mail to online message boards to electronic chat rooms. Used wisely, they can help you strengthen your existing relationships and establish new ones.

I've aggressively put this into practice myself. Just about every day, I wake up to e-mails from far-flung places. I've posted notes to online mail lists, getting literally hundreds of e-mails in response. I've created electronic chat rooms to talk about meaningful workplaces with people from all points on the globe.

Thanks to technology and the Internet, I've even been able to bring other people together. My favorite example has to do with a visitor to my Web site who posted a thought-provoking message on the site's online bulletin board. A couple weeks later, a supervisor thousands of miles away left a particularly frustrating meeting, dropped by my Web site to decompress, and read that message—which happened to deal head-on with his current situation. He sent her an e-mail asking a few questions, and she sent a note in response. Before long, they had developed a coaching relationship that continues to benefit both of them.

Now for the caveat. Although we should take advantage of these wondrous technical powers, we also need to stay keenly aware that technology can keep us apart. Ever send someone an e-mail when you could just as easily pick up the phone? Ever call someone when you knew he or she wasn't there, just so you could leave a message without having to engage in conversation? Ever send the same e-mail to a long distribution list, even though you know that an old-fashioned letter (god forbid, a stamp!) is much more personal? There's an obvious tradeoff that needs to be evaluated every day.

Reality Check: RELATIONSHIP BUILDING

1 = very strongly disagree	5 = agree
2 = strongly disagree	6 = strongly agree
3 = disagree	7 = very strongly agree
4 = neutral; neither disagree nor agree	

_____ People in the workplace understand the need to build strong relationships with each other.

_____ They also see the value of fostering close relationships with suppliers, external customers, and other stakeholders.

_____ Workdays are filled with opportunities to build relationships.

_____ The workspace is designed in a way that allows for constructive mingling and conversation.

_____ People make a point of reaching out to one another.

_____ = Total ÷ 5 = _____ = RELATIONSHIP BUILDING RATING

Getting Results the Right Way

As the publicly elected CEO of Multnomah County (Oregon), Beverly Stein has management responsibility for an organization of forty-nine hundred employees. In Oregon, only the governor leads a larger public-sector organization.

Stein is a results-oriented person who has twice won reelection to her post. In fact, she brought people together to start an ongoing initiative called RESULTS: Reaching Excellent Service Using Leadership and Team Strategies. It's a partnership between labor and management, and it connects measurable goals for the county's day-to-day work with long-term benchmark goals.

Even if you don't like acronyms, you have to like the results. On a recent survey, 93 percent of employees reported doing work they "care deeply about," and 81 percent said that their workplace "is an excellent place to work." Five key measures, ranging from "employees get timely information" to "managers hold no stereotypes about diverse persons," have consistently climbed since tracking began in 1992. As for its service to external customers, the county gets nationwide attention for its stellar performance.

But there's more to this story than a focus on results. Much more.

When she became CEO in 1993, Stein and her 12 colleagues had fairly typical meetings. They'd talk about the business at hand—everything from public-safety incidents to human-services issues to library usage rates. In the process, they immersed themselves in plenty of detail, nearly all of it related to operations.

Six months into it, they started to feel as though they were on a hamster wheel, always dealing with immediate concerns but not getting to the heart of building a more meaningful workplace for themselves and their thousands of colleagues throughout the county. That's when they began to open up, engaging in conversations about workplace relationship building, trust, and partnership. Yes, in addition to operational concerns, these so-called soft issues became very much a part of their regular agenda.

They've been doing it ever since, and they've taken the message to every corner of the county. (See Stein's letter to county employees on the facing page.) People throughout the county are starting to follow suit, talking about and acting on these values in their workplace conversations. And interestingly enough, this "soft" stuff is being cited as a big reason for all those positive measurable results.

What's Love Got to Do with It?

In a newsletter sent to all Multnomah County employees, the results-oriented county CEO shared her views on a topic you don't hear much about in workplace conversations: love. The letter drew a record amount of feedback—all of it positive.

✦ ✦ ✦

To the Employees of Multnomah County Government
From Beverly Stein

Recently I attended a conference featuring Michael Lerner, a rabbi and a workplace psychologist, who has advanced the need for creating a "politics of meaning." By this he means linking our work back to the basic values which give meaning to our work and acknowledging that we don't operate only out of self-interest.

Lerner suggests that a value which should underlie our work in the workplace, community and family is to "maximize our capacities to sustain loving and caring relationships and to be ethically, spiritually and ecologically sensitive." This resonates with me, and when I thought about it I realized it was the basis for my passion for RESULTS. (RESULTS is a countywide initiative calling for widespread employee participation in addressing service improvement, data-based evaluation and decision making, and customer-focused performance measures.)

At its core, RESULTS is about valuing every person as a unique, precious person who deserves recognition and respect. RESULTS is not just facilitation skills, focusing on outcomes and customers. It is not just Pareto charts and fishbone diagrams.

RESULTS also means being open to hearing each other's pain and being compassionate about our defects. It means creating caring relationships at work with each other and with our customers, in the community, in our families and among friends. It means caring enough to be honest, caring enough to take risks, and caring enough to listen to each other with complete attention, valuing our diversity.

Dare I say it? It means trying to love each other in the broadest sense of the word.

Chapter 18

Service

Jennifer calls it the tale of two companies. Years ago, she worked at a manufacturing plant where "service" seemed to be a dirty word. Employees simply didn't want to help one another. It was ingrained in the culture, and one day it hit home for her when she went around looking for someone to show her the ins and outs of new design software. "It was as if no one wanted me to improve my skills." Fed up, Jennifer went to work for a company just down the street—yet worlds apart when it comes to service. As she puts it: "Everyone wants to help everyone. It's incredible." The service ethic is good for employees, suppliers, customers. Even the community benefits from the company's service ways. Jennifer now leads employees on quarterly clean-ups of a local park.

The cynics will tell you that people always want to get— and rarely give. An entire decade's worth of people have been labeled the "me" generation, and social observers are always reminding us of our "commercial culture."

> "Everyone wants to help everyone. It's incredible."

Then there's Jennifer. Her eyes positively lit up when she shared that memorable description of her company: "Everyone wants to help everyone." It was the same kind of look I saw from many other people as they talked about service in their workplaces. The bottom line is, people aren't just willing to help out and to serve. They're eager. In fact, for some, service is among their most essential ingredients of a meaningful workplace.

You're probably starting to see some connections between the meaning keys. Dialogue can lead to relationship building, and both can lead to service.

In a healthy workplace community, people actively reach out to help each other, and they willingly seek help when they need it. The organization makes it easy to do this, providing plenty of formal opportunities (mentoring programs, for example) to serve one another—and the freedom people need to seize informal service opportunities (such as providing a half hour of on-the-spot training to a colleague).

> It is one of the most beautiful compensations of life, that no man can sincerely try to help another without helping himself.
> —RALPH WALDO EMERSON

Someone out There Needs *Your* Help

Service works in a wonderfully reciprocal way. When you get service, you want to give it—and when you give service, people want to return the favor. Jennifer brought this up as she provided more details about her tale of two companies. Recalling her previous workplace, she wondered aloud whether she could have broken the nonservice cycle in a small way by taking the initiative and doing something—anything—to help someone in the workplace. "Here's a confession," she said. "I didn't want to step forward and be of service mainly because no one seemed interested in helping me."

Whatever your workplace situation, the best way to begin building a service culture is by taking action yourself. That's right, instead of dwelling on how unhelpful everyone is, show them how it can work. Look around your workplace to see whether there's a colleague who would benefit from, say, coaching or mentoring. Now ask yourself how you can help—and take action immediately. Perhaps it's a new supervisor who needs guidance on how to stay out of the day-to-day details. Maybe it's an employee who wants to sharpen her database programming skills—and it just so happens that you're the one with the latest know-how.

Or it could be that someone in your midst needs a person who will simply listen—a sounding board of sorts who's willing to keep ears open and mouth diplomatically shut except when advice is directly solicited. This isn't mentoring or coaching, really. It's more like being, well, like being a friend. There are so many formal and informal opportunities to serve each other in the workplace. And who cares whether you call it "coaching" or "mentoring" or some other made-up term? The point is, it's all about service to those around you. And the sooner you can do it, the better.

Open Your Ears to Your Customers

While you're taking action on the inside, it's also essential to be service-minded on the outside. And that means reaching out to your external customers and starting to talk with them. Better yet, ask a few choice questions and have *them* talk to *you*. This can be as informal or formal as you want it to be—anything from a few well-placed phone calls to a stroll through the customer area to a series of focus groups. A lot of this will depend on your type of business.

Your aim, of course, is to engage customers in a conversation regarding service. Do they feel like the organization truly serves them, or does it just plop a product in their hands? If you're in the service business, do they feel that there's passion behind what the company does, or is the feeling conveyed that employees are only going through the motions? What would reflect a greater commitment to service?

Answers to these questions won't be found on the walls of your office or cube or manufacturing plant. The only way to find them out is by posing the questions to real customers. By the way, make a habit of doing this. An annual earful from three customers is better than nothing, but it's hardly the way to move yourself (not to mention your organization) toward a service mindset.

Are You Speaking the Language of Service?

A favorite saying nowadays is that people need to walk the talk. That's fine—as long as the talk makes sense. The way in which you and your colleagues talk about service is guaranteed to reflect and affect your actions. So it's important to watch your language on an ongoing basis.

> The way in which you and your colleagues talk about service is guaranteed to reflect and affect your actions.

For instance, what is your organization's overall mission? You might be inclined to say that "we produce _____," filling in the blank with some sort of service or product. It's an accurate statement, but it raises a question. If service is at the heart of your way of doing business, shouldn't that come across loud and clear in the mission? Here are several other ways to frame your mission. Notice how a few word changes make all the difference.

Our organization serves its customers by _____.

We help our stakeholders to be successful by _____.

Our work unit makes life easier for our direct customers by _____.

Okay, these are just words. But don't you agree that what we say is both a cause and effect of what we think? And don't you agree that what we think affects what we do? If your concept of mission seems a bit disconnected from the notion of service—if the focus is on what you produce as opposed to whom you serve—it's time to start editing so you can walk the right talk.

Making Service a Group Pursuit

Jennifer made it clear that she and her colleagues talk the service talk *and* walk it every day. But she insisted that none of this occurs by chance or by natural do-good inclinations. People in her workplace make a point of routinely getting together for informal conversations about service. It's working well for them—and it can work for you and *your* workplace.

Consider assembling some of your colleagues for a free-flowing conversation about service. If everyone's too busy, invest in a couple of pizzas and do it at lunch. Here are some questions that can get everyone talking—and thinking—about service.

> We must not . . . ignore the small daily differences we can make which, over time, add up to big differences that we often cannot foresee.
> —Marian Wright Edelman

How does service to others factor into the daily routine?

Is it a core part of your overall purpose as a work unit, or functional area, or division, or whole organization? (It ought to be in there somewhere.)

Does it drive what you do and how you do it?

What are some recent examples of service in action, and what can we learn from these?

Questions like these will provoke either a deep sense of satisfaction or the feeling that things could be a whole lot better. If it's the latter, move the conversation to a vision session in which people describe what great service would look like—service to external customers, of course, but also among people within the organization. If you need a series of conversations for this, fine, do it. If you need to invest in more pizzas, fine again. Once people can envision a better situation, they can take their dialogue one huge step further by developing several down-to-earth action ideas.

S-t-r-e-t-c-h Those Roles and Perspectives

All these ideas can make a tremendous difference, but for some people, it's not enough. They're trapped in narrowly defined jobs that make them feel like parts of a big machine. "I don't really serve anyone. My job is to assemble the blah blah blah and the blah blah blah." You'll also hear it phrased this way: "I don't really help anyone. I work in the back office, where we sit in front of terminals all day and . . . . " Some people have a ball-and-chain image of their work. "I do the same thing with the same equipment and the same people in the same place every day. It's all about getting a paycheck."

These are good people who are willing, even eager, to help others. Many are deeply involved in their communities through service-centered groups like the Scouts, Rotary, Red Cross, you name it. Yet the way their jobs are designed, they're sealed off from 99 percent of the people in the organization. Serve others? Help others? They would if they could.

So what to do? Go on the prowl for narrowly defined jobs, and work to expand the roles as much as possible—starting with your own. If you can't help others because you feel terribly cubby-holed, try everything you can to widen your reach. Spend time in other areas, offer help beyond your usual work unit, perhaps try to get on a project team that's forming somewhere else in the organization. If you can do this only with involvement from your colleagues, including your "boss," all the better. Engage them in dialogue, and watch how fast your job *and theirs* begin to touch more people—though expect to get some strange looks when you say you want more opportunities to be helpful!

> ## TIM'S STORY
>
> Things sometimes get out of hand, Tim admits. He can receive as many as three calls a week from different offices within the organization, all asking him to facilitate their most important meetings. He's a great facilitator, and they know it. He's also very willing to help out, as long as he can give enough attention to his regular work.
>
> "Some of my co-workers just don't understand why I want to cram more work into my already full schedule," Tim says with a laugh. "I don't understand it either. All I can say is that I get a great feeling whenever I'm providing help."

As for those around you, if you're in a position to help people expand their reach and contacts, go for it—with caution. Your good intentions could be interpreted as an effort to heap on more work. (Shell-shocked do-good manager: "But I thought you'd appreciate working on the new team. You'll finally get to work with folks from marketing, and your talents will be a big help.") Start a conversation with employees, point out some opportunities, and let people make their own decisions.

The Local Community Awaits

Without a sense of caring, there can be no sense of community.
—Anthony J. D'Angelo

If you're still looking for ways to strengthen service in the workplace, check around in your community. There's surely a project ready and waiting for you—much like the adopt-a-park program that Jennifer coordinates.

Perhaps your organization can gather school supplies for a nearby school or provide tutoring services. Maybe the local senior center needs your help leading social activities for residents or sprucing up the place with a fresh coat of paint. Not everyone at your company will want to get involved, and that's fine. Those who do, however, will be throttling up their service ethic each time they do their community work. And they'll be taking this service spirit back to the workplace, where it can positively affect those around them.

When this service work is done on an individual basis, that's great. But it's all the better when a group gets involved—a whole work unit, for instance—and participants spend some time afterward talking about what happened. Let's say the eight people from the assembly unit devote a day to doing repair work at a local homeless shelter. It's above and beyond the call of duty, and they feel great about themselves by the time evening rolls around. An informal conversation over pizza becomes a recap of the day's hard work—and people begin to share their "lessons learned" and how these can be applied back at the workplace. Their day has been all about helping others, and it's guaranteed to carry over when they go back to work.

Reality Check: SERVICE

1 = very strongly disagree	5 = agree
2 = strongly disagree	6 = strongly agree
3 = disagree	7 = very strongly agree
4 = neutral; neither disagree nor agree	

_____ There's an organizational obsession with helping others to be successful. "Others" is broadly defined: colleagues, customers, the community.

_____ People create all sorts of opportunities to help one another. These can be formal (mentoring programs, training, apprenticeships, and the like) and informal (on-the-spot coaching, explaining a process, walking a colleague through a new computer program, pitching in to help with a task, and so on).

_____ When someone needs help—whether a person, a work unit, or an entire office—people from other areas are ready and willing.

_____ People sometimes serve as "matchmakers," bringing together individuals and groups from different work areas to promote learning, relationship building, and systemic thinking.

_____ Each and every individual can name the customers (internal or external) they serve.

_____ = Total ÷ 5 = _____ = SERVICE RATING

Acknowledgment

"No, no, not that! Anything but that!" It was Eric, and his face was beet red. The news was supposed to be a surprise, and was it ever. Laid off? No. Demoted? Not at all. Shipped off to the Aleutian Islands field office? No such luck. Eric had just been named employee of the month. I'll never forget his anguish. "This is what I get for being a good employee?!" The honor (sorry for abusing the word, Eric) included a country-club lunch with the boss's boss's boss, a canned letter of thanks from the CEO, 30 days of having his framed picture hanging in the lobby, and a front-row parking space among the spots reserved for senior management. He actually gave the parking perk to a pregnant colleague who was sick and tired of walking the quarter mile from her usual space.

Eric's story is a jolting reminder that meaningful acknowledgment is tricky business. It should be simple, right? It's one of our first lessons in life: Say thank you. Yet we continue to turn acknowledgment into an event, distort it with extrinsic motivators, and taint it with an undercurrent of internal competition. And when we do, we end up with lots and lots of Erics.

> "This is what I get for being a good employee?!"

What's the alternative? How does acknowledgment look and feel in a meaningful workplace? For one, it's routine and widely inclusive—in sharp contrast to organizations that wait for the monthly employee-of-the-month award or the annual awards dinner or that other yearly ritual known as the performance evaluation. Sure, it can be prompted each time a group achieves a major milestone or chalks up a new round of impressive results. But people also make a point of acknowledging the small victories and of honoring all those inputs, such as hard work, creativity, commitment, and failure. That's right, failure—when it's transformed into learning and applied in some positive way.

There's also plenty of old-fashioned appreciation. In fact, in a meaningful workplace, it's heard over and over again: "Thank you so much. We couldn't have done it without you." We're talking about genuine, look-you-in-the-eye gratitude—not gratitude in the form of a gift certificate.

Although it sounds simple, it's anything but, in part because we've done such a thorough job of throwing together programs (read: gimmicks) to "incent" people. Fortunately, there are actions you can take, as an individual and with colleagues, to make true acknowledgment a thriving force in your workplace.

> There's something to be said for a genuine thank you that has no strings attached, don't you think?

You Can Acknowledge Anyone, Anytime

It might not be an "action" in the traditional sense, but your first challenge is to shake yourself free of these two mistaken notions: that there needs to be some kind of big success to acknowledge people's work, and that you need to be "upper management" to recognize people and show your appreciation. You don't have to be chair of the Employee of the Month Committee to let folks know how much you appreciate their contribution. And if you don't believe me, I'll be happy to pass along Eric's phone number and let him tell you directly.

There's something to be said for a genuine thank you that has no strings attached, don't you think? "Sarah, I just want you to know how great it is to work with you. I've learned so much from our two years together." Sounds pretty good, don't you think? Here's another: "Frank, will you be on our project team? You're awesome when it comes to helping groups stay focused on their goals. People are still talking about your great work with the down-time-reduction team several years ago." There's a lot wrapped into that last statement. This is powerful acknowledgment, and comments like these should be echoing in workplaces everywhere.

Make up for All Those Missed Opportunities

Think back to the past six to 12 months. What major workplace milestones came and went without acknowledgment? Perhaps it's the analyst whose all-nighter helped you meet that ungodly deadline. Maybe it's the clerical specialist who transformed your ordinary report into a masterpiece or the technician who fixed the conveyor system.

Beyond those easy-to-remember milestones, what about the folks who constantly do small things that add up to big things? Who among you makes a difference day in and day out? If their efforts have gone without acknowledgment, you've got some work to do. As the next two weeks unfold, make a point of thanking them. Even if you feel awkward doing this at first, stick to it. Before you know it, acknowledgment will come naturally. And it won't take long for the thank-you comments to start coming *your* way.

While you're at it, remember to be as inclusive as possible. If you dig deep enough, you'll find that the sleepless analyst crunching the numbers had two people helping behind the scenes to gather data from two other locations. The clerical specialist who jazzed up that report had called on the skills of a desktop publishing whiz. And that technician who saved the day? She got emergency help from someone in the supply room. Yes, this will take some detective work. But people will deeply appreciate your appreciation.

> **MARY'S STORY**
>
> Mary works as a first-grade teacher in an elementary school, and when asked to explain why she finds her workplace so meaningful, she always comes back to the principal.
>
> "Whenever I see him at the end of the day, he always thanks me for my service," she says. "And the way he says it, you know he really means it. I'd climb mountains for him."

The Power of Appreciation

This book has just given you a gentle nudge to start acknowledging people, but you should work to make it a routine part of your everyday life. The best way to do this is by becoming an obsessive observer. Notice what other people are doing, and respond on the spot by recognizing their efforts and celebrating their achievements. You don't need a Harvard MBA to do this, and in fact, you don't need any special skills or funds or equipment. A simple "thank you" or "awesome job"—sincerely conveyed, of course—can transform a relationship.

Your goal here is to do your part in creating a culture of appreciation. Regardless of what you do or where you are in the organization, make yourself a model of down-to-earth acknowledgment. It has to start with you! In this era of teams, people are always working hand in hand, so you should have plenty of opportunities to show your appreciation.

KIMBERLY'S STORY

When she was hired by a Fortune 500 manufacturing company, Kimberly led a team that developed an advanced quality-improvement training program. It was the first of its kind in her industry, and soon after, a national group selected the program for special acknowledgment at its annual conference.

Kimberly assumed that her team—or at least a few of the members, including herself— would be making the trip to receive the award. Wrong assumption. Her boss went alone and brought home the award, even though he had no direct role in developing the workshop. What should have been a time of celebration turned into a tempest of hard feelings.

Put Success Stories in the Spotlight

There's a time for quiet acknowledgment, but there's also a time to pull out the proverbial megaphone and promote the heck out of success stories, even the "small" ones. There are so many ways to broadcast the good news: newsletters, traditional bulletin boards, online bulletin boards, e-mail, intranets, Web sites. All these offer opportunities to acknowledge people and spread innovations throughout the organization.

Let's say the engineers at Location A develop a solution to that chronic problem with the threading process. By telling their success story, and including an explanation of their bright idea, Locations B, C, and D can go forth and copy. They may even decide to get together with the engineering team from Location A and work to make a good idea better. Will the Location A engineers appreciate the acknowledgment? You bet. And the company and its customers stand to gain as well.

All this can be done online if your company has an intranet. In fact, you can use an online bulletin board so anyone can share information with the rest of the organization. There can even be a special thank-you section to go public with your appreciation. If a traditional newsletter is the likely approach, you still have a great way to acknowledge people and to provide reports on success stories. That same story about the threader innovation will communicate just as well on a printed page—though newsletters might take longer to make their way to each employee, and copies might end up in the vertical file more quickly.

Thoughts on Intrinsic vs. Extrinsic

Now that we've just talked about putting success in the spotlight, Eric comes to mind again. His anguish over the employee of the month award reminds us that there's a world of difference between acknowledgment and rewards. The latter, with its gold stars and grade-school roots, is largely extrinsic. The model is straightforward: Do a good deed, get something (gold star, trophy, gift certificate, mug, planter, and on and on) in return. It's a model used by so many organizations throughout the world, yet my research—and a wealth of research by others—shows that it does more harm than good. *Much* more.

For one thing, rewards create a divide between two groups of people: the rewarders and the rewarded. It's a lot like the parent and child—or, if you want to stretch the metaphor, like owner and pet. This is *not* the way to create a mission-driven organization where everyone is working together. What's more, pride and motivation and self-esteem are inside-out propositions. When you toss an extrinsic motivator into the mix, even with the best of intentions, things can go haywire.

Example: "I worked just as hard on this project as I did on the last, but I didn't get a bonus. If they think I'm going to bust my butt on the next round of work, they're crazy!" Another example: "This was a team effort, not a solo effort. Why did *she* get the award?" Yet another: "I felt great about all of my work on this until they gave me that mug. Talk about patronizing! A simple thank you would have been so much better."

Genuine acknowledgment is grounded in respect and gratitude. It knows that people do great work because of deep interests, passions, commitment—stuff that comes from within. And it's remarkably simple: Try a sincere thank you. We're not talking about a hit-and-run thanks, but a sit-down conversation where you let someone know that you truly understand how much time and effort and expertise and brilliance they've put into something. And let them brag about their work. Ask questions and watch their pride come to life.

If the occasion warrants, think about having a celebration involving *everyone* who had a role (even a bit part) in making it happen. There's no need to hand out slogan-bearing mugs or flashy lapel pins. Simply get together and savor the moment.

Intrinsic vs. Extrinsic: Can We Talk?

But what do *you* think about the difference between intrinsic and extrinsic motivation—and what do your colleagues think? Get them together, and use these questions to seed the conversation:

BELIEVE IT OR NOT

Dishing Out Disrespect

An insurance company executive got an idea. Why not inspire the support staff to greater heights by offering an extrinsic motivator?

He created a poster-sized chart to track progress and stationed it in a high-traffic location. Each week, his assistant plotted a new point to show cumulative sales dollars, connecting the points with a line to show the trend.

The big prize was found at the top-right of the chart—the place where the executive wanted that line to reach. He had cut and pasted a picture of a ham. That's right, if the support staff helped the sales force achieve millions in new income, each person would be rewarded with a canned ham.

CARL'S STORY

In his work at an interior-design firm, Carl worked on project after project after project. In fact, after a while it seemed as if all the projects were going past in a nonstop blur. "My boss (the owner of the company) saw it as a sprint, and he had us going flat-out all the time," Carl says.

"It should have been thought of as a cross-country run—one where you have time to pause, celebrate your accomplishments, and refresh."

What kinds of extrinsic motivators are used in your workplace?

What are the positive outcomes?

What are the negative outcomes? In answering this question, you might have to dig deep—not because the downsides are so hard to find, but because those extrinsic motivators might have some stalwart champions who don't want to face up to those unintended effects of their well-intended efforts.

What are some other ways to acknowledge people— ways that would be unlikely to produce those negative outcomes?

And last but not least, a question to be answered individually: How would you like to be acknowledged for your efforts and successes?

Prediction: This will be a mind-opening, myth-crushing conversation. Warning: Don't pose these questions unless you and others are willing to undertake some measure of positive change—if not in the organization as a whole, then in your immediate work area.

Don't Mandate What Should Unfold Naturally

Given everything we've covered about acknowledgment, should there be any hard-and-fast rules? Just one: Avoid creating rules that require awards or award programs. If rules are in place, people will view acknowledgment through the lens of compliance. They'll see it as just another task to be checked off the to-do list instead of approaching it as the right thing to do.

Perhaps you've seen organizations (or maybe worked at one) where the Employee of the Month (EOM) Program has turned into a three-headed monster. Here's how it often works: The EOM Steering Committee gets together once a month to review the nominations. ("We only got nominations from three of the six divisions." "I really think Carol should have been nominated." "Jack is gonna go ballistic if Bill gets next month's award. They could be poster boys for passive-aggressive behavior." "Couldn't we make this the Employee of the Quarter Program?")

Then there's the announcement and (all too often) the hard feelings. If there's a cash award or gift certificate or something else that's blatantly extrinsic, internal competition is almost inevitable. Even the recipient might be miffed—as in Eric's case. It always begins with good intentions. Perhaps it's time to go back to those good intentions and reinvent the approach.

Reality Check: ACKNOWLEDGMENT

1 = very strongly disagree	5 = agree
2 = strongly disagree	6 = strongly agree
3 = disagree	7 = very strongly agree
4 = neutral; neither disagree nor agree	

_____ Genuine appreciation is at the heart of all acknowledgment in the workplace.

_____ People are routinely acknowledged for a job well done.

_____ They're also acknowledged for the hard work, creativity, and commitment that go into those successes—and into the many other activities still under way.

_____ Everyone helps bring acknowledgment to the workplace, and it happens naturally. It is not seen as something periodically "given" to people by management.

_____ Acknowledgment is widely inclusive. When efforts and achievements are celebrated, thanks and recognition go to *all* who made it happen.

_____ = Total ÷ 5 = _____ = ACKNOWLEDGMENT RATING

Chapter 20

Oneness

The government agency where Amy works has eight divisions. And listening to her talk, it's clear that the term "division" is dead-on accurate. She describes a place that's rife with internal rivalries, where people aggressively compete to get the most resources, produce the best results, and accumulate the most praise by year's end. The cold war turned hot just recently, after one of the divisions spent several months quietly conducting original research into certain health trends. The data would have been useful to everyone in the agency, but the division kept it under wraps—because it gave them an edge over the other divisions, Amy says. Word soon got out, and the other division chiefs complained loudly enough that the agency director intervened. Now everyone has the data, but everyone seems bitter. As Amy puts it, "Our workplace is in pieces."

Wherever you turn these days, people are talking about teams. Run an Internet search on "teamwork" and you'll get two hundred and fifty thousand hits. Go to the library and you'll find hundreds of team handbooks. Join a business asso-

> "Our workplace is in pieces."

ciation and watch your mailbox fill with flyers on workshops, seminars, and institutes that will "help you turn teamwork into the ultimate competitive advantage." Most of this stuff promises to help us become better team members, team champions, team facilitators, team players—and to help others do the same. All we need to do is follow the "three principles," or the "five steps," or the "one proven formula."

But if it's so easy, how can we explain Amy's workplace?

Of course, genuine teamwork isn't easy at all. Sure, there are team-related skills that people can learn in a one- or two-day workshop, and it's fairly straightforward to set up some process-improvement teams. But achieving true *oneness* in the workplace is a complex, ongoing proposition. Note the distinction: There's "teamwork" as a set of skills or as an occasional activity; and there's "teamwork" as a state of mind, as a defining part of the workplace culture. The latter definition is what oneness is all about.

In a meaningful workplace, people think systemically. They see the parts, but they operate in ways that benefit the whole. They understand that the organization is full of delicate interdependencies—that their actions over here might affect folks over there and there and there. Collaboration and co-anything (co-development, co-creation, coordination) are the norm, with a unifying mission pulling together even the most far-flung work units.

What's Really Going On?

Amy went on to say that none of the eight division managers had any real problems relating to people. They all had their own styles, she said, but the rivalries seemed to transcend people and personalities. She also noted that the current tensions had very little to do with the release of that data—and a lot to do with deeper issues that people seemed unable or unwilling to pinpoint and address.

Perhaps you feel the same way about situations in your own workplace. The fact is, many of us have been living for years with certain paradigms and approaches that all but guarantee a lack of oneness in our workplaces. They're so much a part of the culture and so readily accepted by everyone, it can be difficult to see them, and even more difficult to come up with alternative approaches. But let's start this challenging work right now by pulling the wraps off the three biggest culprits: fragmentation, competition, and avoidance.

FRAGMENTATION

Early in life, we're taught to take on complex problems and projects by breaking them into smaller parts. It's a logical, rational approach that allows us to focus our attention and effort on one thing at a time. It sounds so efficient, so tidy. It even sounds like a winner: "Divide and conquer!"

Because organizations are inherently complex, many are set up and managed based on this approach. That's why there are separate divisions, work units, and functions. They're a way to organize the people, equipment, space, and everything else that makes up the workplace. But all too often, those manageable pieces become the worst contradiction in terms. People working for the same company or agency—producing the same set of products or services—go about their work as a loose confederacy of many different organizations. Their focus on a single part of the whole becomes a sort of tunnel vision. Communication breaks down, and people start working at cross-purposes.

COMPETITION

The situation goes from bad to worse when internal competition enters the mix. This too is drummed into us during our early years, as soon as we start getting report cards and competing in grade-school sports. There's even an expression that seems to make the win–lose paradigm one of our national values: "Competition is what made America great!"

> The very nature of competition guarantees division—a division between winners and losers.

The fact is, the very nature of competition guarantees division—a division between winners and losers. When it occurs within an organization, it promotes the very opposite of oneness. And over time, it can stoke the kind of intense rivalries that seem to afflict Amy's workplace.

AVOIDANCE

There's nothing all-powerful about fragmentation and internal competition. They aren't forces of nature. They were created by people, they're perpetuated by people, and they can be eliminated by people. But let's be honest: It's a Herculean change-management challenge.

It requires nothing less than stepping back and engaging in honest dialogue about what they are, why the exist, what they inflict on the workplace, and how they can be replaced with approaches that foster oneness. In other words, people have to challenge their assumptions, admit that some of their long-held beliefs may no longer make sense (or never did), go against the grain of mainstream thought, and exert their creativity to come up with new structures and systems that bring out the best in everyone in the workplace.

Amy touched on this when she said that her colleagues didn't seem to be delving into the deeper issues at work in her agency. They were good people caught up in a terribly flawed system. The place had a culture of avoidance, she explained. Rarely did folks sit down and openly talk about *how* they went about their work—and *why*. All of their conversations focused on *what* they were doing in their individual divisions.

Building Awareness Through Conversation

Your first challenge involves coming to terms with these powerful forces. Awareness is the essential starting point. Only by understanding what's happening and why can you ever hope to change the situation.

One way to stay alert while also stirring awareness among your colleagues is to have regular conversations about these topics. If there are periodic meetings, set aside some time. If you and your colleagues don't regularly get together, it might be time to start. Ideally, involve people from a wide cross-section of work areas. Opening the door to those *other* people in the *other* units or divisions just might be your first step toward oneness.

But be prepared. These are likely to be vigorous exchanges, especially at first, when people stake out their positions. Things might look more like a debate than healthy conversation. Don't try to control these sessions, and certainly don't try to impose your thinking onto everyone else. Rather, start with some thought-provoking questions that can get people thinking anew and seeing those paradigms for what they are. Here are some possibilities:

Which of our processes involve multiple work areas (units, divisions, offices, whatever)? How effective are the transitions from one area to another? What can we do to make things run more smoothly?

What is our overall purpose as an organization, and how can we best achieve it?

How are we organized as a workplace? On a day-to-day basis, how does this organizational design help us or hurt us in carrying out our mission, and why? What is the long-term effect?

Why are we organized this way? What factors and assumptions originally came into play? Do they still make sense? Do they still feel right?

If not, why not—and what improvements can be made?

What do we want to value as a workplace in terms of how we work together, communicate, and make decisions? How do these values, these aspirations, compare to the current reality? And what can we do to bring our desired values to life?

You might not be in a position to call meetings in the traditional sense. No problem—slip one of these questions into a lunchtime conversation with colleagues and see what happens. Keep the topic alive during the next get-together, and the next. Awareness building is a nonstop endeavor. Do it whenever and wherever you can.

Stamp out Competition— Or Everyone Will Lose

Competition so thoroughly saturates our national culture that it can seep into just about every area of the workplace. In fact, it can be so present that it becomes a natural part of the organizational landscape—and we lose sight of it entirely.

> Do certain leaders in the organization keep a naughty and nice list comparing work units on key indicators in order to "motivate" those who are low on the list to "work harder"?

What's happening in *your* organization? Do team rivalries pit people against one another? Do divisions go head to head each year to divvy up what everyone sees as scarce resources? Do certain leaders in the organization keep a naughty and nice list comparing work units on key indicators in order to "motivate" those who are low on the list to "work harder"? Do salespeople compete for a scarce supply of year-end rewards? If you're trying to create a true sense of unity, all these I-win-you-lose approaches are leaps in the wrong direction.

Many other forms of internal competition are more subtle. Perhaps it's that daily tussle to see who gets access to the new computer. Or division managers might be assuming their best battle postures for the upcoming year-in-review session. You might be familiar with these get-togethers, which appear as cordial as an afternoon tea yet have the deep-down feel of an Olympic trials track meet.

Again, the solution starts with awareness, and awareness happens with dialogue. Spend some time with colleagues simply talking about internal competition, then turn your eye to the immediate work area. Where are win–lose arrangements causing problems, and what can you do about it? Resolve to take action—some kind of action—immediately as a way of generating momentum in the right direction. Consider focusing your change locally, where you and your colleagues can indeed control things.

But what about the rest of the organization? What about those organization-wide systems and structures that essentially guarantee internal competition? Traditional reward and recognition systems are one chronic culprit. So are many of the traditional methods for internal promotions and raises.

If you're in a position to do so, build a team to start finding these unity-killers. A series of focus groups with employees might be necessary, perhaps coupled with a thoughtful survey. Also important is that you bring in the right help once the reinvention process begins. You surely don't want to trade in one lousy system for another. Finally, start small. Lock your laser onto one process, system, or tradition that has high visibility and can be easily redesigned. A small success can send a big message that the competition culture has met its match.

Planning as a Whole Organization

Fragmentation and competition often get recharged whenever work units undertake some kind of planning. Does this happen in *your* workplace?

Do divisions, regions, work units, and other entities operate in a vacuum when envisioning the future, developing goals, and setting objectives, or do they involve people and ideas from other parts of the system? Do they focus just on their own purpose as a subset of the organization, or do they shape everything with the larger purpose in mind? Do they restrict their view to what

> Strip away all the assumptions about what competition is supposed to do, all the claims in its behalf that we accept and repeat reflexively. What you have left is the essence of the concept: mutually exclusive goal attainment. One person succeeds only if another does not. From this uncluttered perspective, it seems clear right away that something is drastically wrong with such an arrangement. How can we do our best when we are spending our energies trying to make others lose—and fearing that they will make us lose?
> —ALFIE KOHN,
> *NO CONTEST: THE CASE AGAINST COMPETITION*

is generally believed by people in the immediate work area, or do they look at the world in which they operate in a more holistic way?

Amy reported that her agency seemed downright obsessive with planning. Each of the eight divisions held its own planning retreat once every six months, with attendance restricted to the "top people" from the separate divisions. In other words, each retreat involved a select group of people from just one division. They took this work seriously, she said, and kept it close to the vest upon their return. This is the "planning in a bubble" approach. It inevitably leads to different visions of the future, different beliefs regarding purpose, different directions—and a tumultuous workplace. Just ask Amy.

Planning is often a missed opportunity to begin with—an organizational ritual in which a chosen few go to a retreat site for a day or two and dutifully come up with three to five goals, most of which are more about tweaking the old way of doing things than about creating the future. Chapter 4, Direction, went into this in detail.

The challenge is to shatter the bubble and involve more people in what should be thought of as a visioning process. Make a point of including not only those who have their hands directly on the work, but also people whose roles are largely beyond the immediate work area. If Division A is going to have its own retreat, they should include people from Divisions B, C, D, and so on. Better yet, they could scrap the twice-a-year retreat process and organize ongoing planning conversations with people from all the divisions. This isn't easy or efficient. (Chapter 16 can help.) But it's the surest way to think like a whole organization as you think about the future.

More Ways to Turn Oneness into Action

There are many more ways to nurture oneness in the workplace, and some of them are relatively simple. Here are some down-to-earth possibilities:

> The "planning in a bubble" approach leads to different visions of the future, different beliefs regarding purpose, different directions—and a tumultuous workplace.

REACH OUT TO OTHER AREAS

Make an effort to connect with people who work in other work areas. If you've been meaning to get in touch with folks from the supply warehouse, for instance, dispense with the call and drop by for a visit. You're guaranteed to have a richer conversation face to face, and who knows, you

CARLA'S STORY

In her role as a computer help-desk specialist, Carla has seen all too often what it's like to work in a fractured system.

"You've got the help desk, LAN support, PC support, programming—and everyone speaks a slightly different language with their little idioms and dialects. Do you understand LAN-speak? Maybe you do, and maybe you don't."

For customers, the search for help can be terribly frustrating.

"If I don't understand some of the stuff that goes on within information systems, imagine what it must be like for the poor sucker from accounting or HR who gets in touch with us for some quick answers. They must feel like they're dealing with a foreign country!"

might learn a thing or two about the supply business. They might learn a thing or two about your role as well.

If you don't have a grand purpose for the contact—if you simply want to meet other folks and learn more about another part of the organization—go for it. Maybe you've always wondered what goes on in the maintenance area, or accounting, or the design shop. Visit there and check it out. You might have to call ahead, and your request might raise a few eyebrows, but so what? In the end, you'll all be better off for having gotten together.

THINK CROSS-FUNCTIONAL

Involve people from multiple functional areas when developing projects, teams, workshops, internal focus groups, whatever. In fact, right now, pinpoint at least one cross-functional opportunity.

What about workshops? Invite people from all corners of the workplace. If you're concerned about the expense of bringing together people from distant locations, think of it as an investment—because that's what it is.

What about orientation sessions for new employees? Are they conducted by one or two people from the human resources department? Even if they're the best HR people in the world, imagine how much better this first impression would be if new employees met with a group of people who work in wide-ranging areas of the organization. Even internal focus groups or informal dialogue sessions should have a cross-functional flavor.

BUILD ACTIVE LINKS BETWEEN TEAMS

If a work unit or division has multiple teams, conduct a quick assessment to see how well they're communicating with each other. Just like units or offices or divisions, separate teams should be working as a single system, with regular communication flowing back and forth. Even an online system of periodic team reports is better than nothing.

Ideally, each team should have a spokesperson, all of whom get together on a regular basis to provide updates, ask questions, and ensure that all activities remain aligned with the overall vision, mission, and goals. These get-togethers can include the team sponsors, whose involvement can allow for on-the-spot removal of roadblocks.

Just don't let this turn into a bureaucratic drain on everyone's time. And whatever you do, don't let the quest for alignment become a slippery slope to conformity. The organization should give plenty of room to renegade teams that seem to be breeding crazy ideas—no, it should be encouraging them, since this very craziness is the high-octane fuel for innovation.

DEDICATE A DAY TO ONENESS

Hold an open house just for employees. Done right, it can be the ultimate bonding event. Picture a workplace full of creative information booths put together by employees to tell the purpose, goals, and activities of each division, functional area, and unit. There can even be display areas for specific teams, giving them a chance to brag about their success stories to all walk-up visitors. And if the organization is really ambitious, the day can include a series of concurrent workshops and facilitated dialogue sessions, giving everyone a chance to learn along the way.

What about inviting suppliers or customers or both? What about making this a two-day gathering, with one day devoted to an open-space conference? What about having a separate open house for each location, with everyone invited to all of them? If this doesn't seem realistic, is there a way to use conferencing technology to close the gap between locations?

MAKE THE MOST OF TECHNOLOGY

If your organization is all over the map, literally, you face special challenges when it comes to fostering a genuine spirit of oneness. Reaching out

CARRIE'S STORY

As a counselor at a residential treatment center for teens with severe behavioral problems, Carrie knows what it's like to face stressful situations. Yet she reports an impressive ability to switch off the stress the moment she leaves her workplace.

The key? Genuine teamwork.

"I'm able to leave it (the stress) at the door because I know my fellow workers will take care of the kids and follow up with whatever needs to be done."

and staying in touch with those other offices or plants can take real effort, and early on, it can be hard to see the benefits.

It's a lot easier if you have the right technical know-how. A best-practices database accessible on a company intranet can make it so easy to share great ideas. E-mail can give everyone the ability to reach out to everyone. And with a few minor technical flourishes, the company can have its own employee-only online mail lists and message boards. For big get-togethers that bridge the miles, videoconferencing can be the next best thing to being there. Even if you don't have any high-tech wizards internally who can pull this off, there are plenty of outsiders who can do it for you, and they're just a phone call away.

Reality Check: ONENESS

1 = very strongly disagree
2 = strongly disagree
3 = disagree
4 = neutral; neither disagree nor agree

5 = agree
6 = strongly agree
7 = very strongly agree

_____ There's a prevailing sense that "we're all in this together."
_____ People are united by a common purpose, direction, and set of values.
_____ Working relationships are best described as collaborative, not competitive.
_____ People understand how their colleagues fit into the system—what they do, where they excel, how they add value.
_____ Although work units, offices, regions, and other entities might have their own goals, they remain united by a single, overarching organizational mission.

_____ = Total ÷ 5 = _____ = ONENESS RATING

Imagine a Home with 50,000 Visitors

The Wustum Museum of Fine Arts didn't start out as a museum at all. For its first 85 years, the Italianate farmhouse in Racine, Wisconsin, served as a private home. It wasn't until 1941 that the house was converted into gallery space.

Yet even now, there's a family feel among the people who work there. The kitchen serves as the nerve center, bring-your-dog-to-work-day happens *much* more often than once a year, and every birthday prompts a celebration. The eight people who work there have even been known to call it "home."

The fact is they just don't have time for formality and rules and protocol. The museum has six to eight exhibitions each year, a permanent collection, and active education programs for children and adults. Nearly 50,000 people pass through each year.

The flexibility has allowed each staffer to find a niche. For Pat Kardas, it's marketing and communications. But she's quick to point out that she and her colleagues are constantly stepping back to look at the big picture. Weekly meetings help. They use the time to evaluate exhibits and sessions, to plan new ones, to figure out who does what as the week unfolds, and simply to touch base. It's a lot like a healthy conversation around the dining room table.

With such a workload, what keeps them going? For Kardas, it's all about reaching people. "We'll have visitors who come in and say, 'Wow, this exhibit is incredible!' Or we'll be working with children, watching them get so excited about creativity. We can see the joy on their faces." Wustum Museum's small group of staffers has 50,000 opportunities to see that their work makes a difference.

According to museum director Bruce Pepich, the family of employees is now facing a tough question: How can their workplace remain flexible if the number of exhibits, visitors, and program participants continues its upward trend? They're taking a few measured steps, evaluating each as they go—simple stuff like using written agendas at their meetings. What's clear is that this family won't let bureaucracy move in anytime soon.

PART SIX

THE ME KEYS

We value the individual.

The Me Keys

- Self-Identity
- Fit
- Balance
- Worth

Self-Identity

Where he used to work, John had a reputation as an out-of-the-box thinker who could see old problems in entirely new ways. People marveled at his ability to ask just the right questions—ones that brought out their own creativity. Then he moved on to another company, and suddenly, it seemed as if his brainpower lost all its value. At one meeting three weeks into his job, he and his colleagues in equipment maintenance were trying to figure out why a certain machine kept breaking down. John started to describe a new analysis technique that could help them uncover the root cause, but a minute into it, people started rolling their eyes and looking at their watches. The same thing happened a week later, when he tried to facilitate a simple brainstorming session. Fed up with the cold reception, John decided that from then on, he'd keep his creativity to himself. He hasn't spoken up since.

So many workplaces put pressure on people to be the same and to do what has always been done. Even our language is filled with cautionary expressions: toe the line, don't make waves, don't rock the boat, don't upset the apple cart, when in Rome . . . . For John, these aren't just empty clichés. No one seems to recognize the value of his creativity, no one's encouraging him, and no one's even defending him. Worst of all, it appears that John has lost his most important champion: himself.

Perhaps you've been in a similar situation, where your unique know-how, skills, talents, style, and interests have been forced underground. Maybe that's your *current* situation. If so, you probably feel a lot like John—angry at the people around you because they seem so closed-minded to differences and so eager to embrace conformity.

> Our language is filled with cautionary expressions: toe the line, don't make waves, don't rock the boat, don't upset the apple cart, when in Rome . . .

You should be *worried*, too. Being able to use your unique knowledge and skills, and to flex your one-of-a-kind style, isn't just important to your self-esteem. It's also essential for short-term improvement and big-time innovation. In that sense, it can affect an organization's bottom line. Look at John's case: His process for root-cause analysis, if it had seen the light of day, might have solved the breakdown problem once and for all. He and his colleagues will never know.

Compare this to a workplace where self-identity is thriving. There, people feel a genuine freedom to be themselves. Perhaps they want to express an idea that goes against the grain. Maybe they want to use their knowledge of a process or tool, as in John's case, or to try out a skill that's rarely used in the workplace. Maybe it's not so much what they want to express but how they want to express it. It could even be that they want to tap a deep interest that has long remained dormant.

In a meaningful workplace, this expression of individuality is possible, no matter how strong the sense of community. That's because self-identity isn't simply *allowed*; it is *valued*.

Finding the Real You

The silver lining in John's situation is that he knows at least some of what makes him unique—his creativity and his ability to stir creative thinking in others. He can leverage this self-knowledge to improve his situation, which we'll get to in just a minute.

> You better not compromise yourself . . . it's all you got.
>
> —Janis Joplin

But for now, let's turn the spotlight on you. What makes you unique? This isn't a rhetorical question. Pull out a pen and paper, or pull up to a keyboard, and jot down some answers to the following questions:

What unique __knowledge__ do you bring to the workplace? There are certain things you and only you know—areas of expertise that apply directly or indirectly to your work. Perhaps it's a certain type of software. Maybe it's your knowledge of a market segment or a customer or an internal process. There are so many possibilities, so don't sell yourself short. Narrow your list down to the top three or four sources of what we'll call your "unique know-how."

What special <u>skills</u> do you bring to the workplace? This one is pretty straightforward. But instead of creating a laundry list of 10 or 20 skills, try to pick the three or so that distinguish you from the crowd.

How does your <u>experience</u> make you uniquely qualified? You've followed your own path to your current workplace. It's a path unlike the one taken by any of your colleagues. What did you learn along the way that makes your perspective or know-how especially rich? Again, now's not the time for humility. List the several leading benefits of your experience.

> What did you learn along the way that makes your perspective or know-how especially rich? Now's not the time for humility.

How is your <u>style</u> different? We all have our own ways of communicating, making decisions, interacting with others, and generally going about our work. What is yours? Specifically, how is your style unique from the ones around you? If you work in a culture of conformity, it might be hard to tell. Take the time to get back in touch with the real you.

What deeply <u>interests</u> you? There's so much talk these days about "equipping" people with "competencies." The idea seems to be that the only stuff worth learning is tangible, observable, and grounded in specific skills. This way of thinking completely ignores the deep interests that people bring to their workplace—passions, hobbies, and lifelong pursuits that they hold deep within themselves. What are *your* deep interests? List a couple of them, and start to think about how you can integrate them into what you do in the workplace.

If you're having trouble coming up with answers, reflect on some of your recent achievements inside or outside the workplace. How did you make it happen? What skills and knowledge did you use? How did your experience help out? Where did your style or deep interests come into play? Consider talking with a close friend or significant other to get their input. If you feel comfortable doing so, you may even want to have a chat with a colleague or two to see what *they* think.

There is a great deal of
unmapped country
within us.
—George Eliot

Uncovering Your Own Value

Now it's time to synthesize this information into a statement
of what makes you unique. Think of it as a one-pager on your
self-identity—a brief yet revealing summary of the best you
have to offer.

First, prioritize. Look at everything you've put to paper—
your know-how, skills, experience, style, and interests. Select the four or so
unique strengths that seem to stand above all others. Then pose the "so what"
questions. How does this good stuff make a difference? How does it benefit
your colleagues and external customers? Or how *could* it benefit them in the
future? These examples are designed to stir your thinking:

- You have a rare ability to take arcane statistical information and make
  it understandable to the most math-resistant people in your workplace. Without you, a lot of the data would go unused—or worse, it
  would be misinterpreted and foul up the decision-making process.
- Your 20 years of in-the-field sales experience is golden. You know what
  it feels like to be on the front line each day selling the product. Your
  unique insights can be used to improve communications and day-to-
  day support.
- You used to work for one of your company's biggest clients. So when
  it comes to listening to customers, you have an especially keen ear.
- It seems as if you were born to facilitate groups. You have just the right
  touch when it comes to bringing together divergent views.
- You have a certain intuitive feel, a curious mind, and a plain old love
  for the technology that has made you the go-to person whenever
  people need help solving problems or upgrading their systems.
- You're deeply interested in group dynamics. You've attended college
  classes in psychology and sociology, and you've read some of the latest
  books on natural systems and their implications for reinventing the
  workplace.

If you work for an organization that seems to value sameness and conformity, or if that's the culture in your immediate work area, this can be an
extremely difficult exercise. You might even be falling into the trap that snared
John just weeks into his new job. It goes something like this: "If the workplace
doesn't value my unique strengths, they must not be strengths after all."

Rarely is this the correct assumption. Push it aside, and turn your attention to benefits. Figure out how your unique strengths benefit people, or how they *can* benefit people, and you'll be well on your way to making self-identity a thriving part of your workplace.

Putting Your Strengths to Work

The big question at this point, of course, has to do with *how*. How do you leverage your unique knowledge, skills, experience, style, and deep interests? How do you take all that good stuff and turn it into action, so people can actually experience the benefits—and so you can enjoy a workplace that makes the most of your potential?

John didn't seem to give this much thought. His previous workplace valued his creativity, and he automatically figured the same would happen at his new place of employment. During a meeting to discuss frequent breakdowns on a certain machine, John was John. He jumped right in and suggested a new analysis technique to get at the root cause, only to find his colleagues markedly uninterested. The same thing happened at a later session, when he tried to facilitate some impromptu brainstorming.

Part of this has to do with the fact that John is new to the organization. He needs to spend more time building relationships and learning about the strengths that other people bring to the workplace. He also needs to get a better handle on the workplace culture. That doesn't mean he should submit to it. It simply means that he should get the lay of the land before rushing ahead and taking action.

You too need to be thoughtful about how you plan to work your unique strengths into your workplace situation. Think of yourself as a marketer who has something special to provide. How are you going to get people to buy—and ideally, to see you as the one person who's best qualified to give them what they need and want?

There are four basic strategies: direct, invitational, one on one, and guerilla style.

> Regardless of age, regardless of position, regardless of the business we happen to be in, all of us need to understand the importance of branding. We are CEOs of our own companies: Me Inc. To be in business today, our most important job is to be head marketer for the brand called You.
> —Tom Peters
> From his article on "The Brand Called You," *Fast Company*, August/September 1997 (www.brandyou.com)

DIRECT STRATEGY

The direct approach is what John tried. He saw a need in a meeting with his colleagues, and he unleashed his unique know-how and skills.

This works well if you've been among folks long enough to know that they won't take offense at your assuming the role of coach. After all, that's what John would have become, at least briefly, by showing his colleagues the cause-analysis technique. Being direct can also be successful when people feel there's a definite problem that can no longer be tolerated—or an opportunity that absolutely must be seized—and you're the only one who has the expertise, skills, or whatever else is needed to make it happen.

INVITATIONAL STRATEGY

A much different way to offer up your knowledge and skills is to frame them as an invitation. Instead of imposing his creative technique, no matter how good it might be, John could have mentioned it and very briefly explained how it might help the situation. There would be no long coaching at the white board, no strong appeals as to why this must be done, no exhaustive storytelling on how this technique worked wonders at another company.

This approach is all about letting the people around you take some small yet significant ownership over what you have to offer. They might do so immediately, with several people asking for more information. Or the request might come one or two meetings later, when the problem shows no sign of being solved. Or more seed-planting might be necessary before anyone shows interest.

ONE-ON-ONE STRATEGY

The strategies just described apply to groups, but when it comes to using your unique knowledge, skills, experience, and style, you might find more success working directly with individuals. Get clear on the strengths you'd like to use more in the workplace, then try to identify people and situations that can benefit.

- Perhaps you're like John and feel the most fulfilled when you're being creative. Is there a colleague who's always commenting about her left-brain tendencies and would welcome some input from a wildly creative mind? If so, keep an eye out for opportunities to work with her.

> Remember always that you have not only the right to be an individual, you have an obligation to be one.
> —ELEANOR ROOSEVELT

- Maybe you have programming experience from a previous job—the same kind that's needed by someone in another work area. Cross the invisible barrier between work units and offer to share your know-how, even if it rocks the boat a bit.
- Or it could be that a colleague is wrestling with some data. You figure you're the only person in a 100-mile radius who loves statistics, and you know your stats skills would save the day. But you're hesitant to make waves because this kind of work isn't in your job description. Well, at least consider offering to help. This is too good of an opportunity to pass up.

GUERILLA-STYLE STRATEGY

If you want to be yourself and exert your unique strengths day after day, you need to have the commitment, passion, and eye for opportunity that's the hallmark of every good guerilla fighter. Sometimes you'll want to pounce. Say there's an upcoming project that calls for your strengths—offer your services immediately. Other times it'll pay to do some intelligence work. Perhaps you're out of the loop and don't know a thing about what projects are nearing launch—try to find out more from colleagues who are more connected.

When you achieve something big, leverage it. Let's say you get to use your sharp facilitation skills, and you end up turning a nightmare improvement team into a stunning success. Before the team members go their separate ways, subtly ask them to put your name in the hat for future facilitations. And when the team documents its story, make sure you get copies, and don't hesitate to send them to would-be internal customers who might want you to facilitate their teams.

Build on your small successes, too. Let's say John ends up facilitating a 15 minute brainstorming session with his colleagues in equipment maintenance. It's a bit awkward at first, but things turn out fine, with people amazed by all the good ideas they've generated. The next time around, John can try something a bit more ambitious. Don't diminish the value of tiny victories, especially when they occur in an environment where sameness rules.

Perhaps you learn of an opening in a completely different work area. It sounds like a dream job—a perfect fit with one of your deep interests. In fact, as far as you're concerned, the job would hardly be "work." Don't waste time—go for it.

Valuing the Differences Around You

So far in this chapter, we've been talking about what you can do for yourself. But what about your colleagues? What can you do to provide *them* with opportunities to use *their* unique know-how, skills, experience, style, and interests? Our reasons for doing this aren't entirely selfless. By creating an environment where self-identity can freely emerge, we'll get more opportunities to use our own unique strengths.

> Two thirds of help is to give courage.
> —Irish Proverb

Apply a critical eye and ear to everything around you. To what degree can you see signs of thriving individuality? Have people personalized their workspaces? Do differences come out in how people dress? Are conversations marked by streaks of independent thinking, or is there a stifling degree of sameness? Do people act and sound like they've been cloned? In many respects, your challenge is to be on the alert for people like John—the ones who seem to have gone underground with the things that make them unique.

Once you get a fix on all this, decide on several simple ways to take action. There are all sorts of possibilities. You might know that Joan is especially effective as a devil's advocate—a skill she has let atrophy because the organization favors people who are chronically agreeable. Do what you can to let Joan be Joan. At an upcoming meeting, make a point of asking her for a thorough critique of that project, idea, activity, whatever. If you think a group setting wouldn't be the best place for this, get her input in a one-on-one conversation.

Perhaps another colleague is an avid artist, and even though he works in the accounting area, you think his creative side would help you and your team members work through some design issues. Simple enough: Call him over.

Uncovering Strengths Together

We spend a lot of time thinking about the unique attributes and hidden strengths we bring to the workplace, but rarely do

> That discomfort is a sign that you're entering uncharted territory, which is *exactly* where you need to go if you and others want to enrich your workplace.

we talk about it. There might be some discussion among "boss" and "direct reports"—terms that caught my wrath in the chapter on equality, as you might recall. But seldom is there an open, constructive exchange among colleagues.

So why not organize one? Get a group together—perhaps five or so folks from your immediate work area—and pose some questions:

What knowledge do you bring that hasn't been sufficiently tapped?

What are your unrecognized talents and skills?

How can we make better use of your experience?

And what about deep interests? What really stirs you, and how could this reshape what you do and how you do it?

This conversation is bound to be like many of the ones related to creating a meaningful workplace. It will initially seem a bit unusual and uncomfortable. No surprise here—these dialogues are a first for most people. But that same discomfort is a sign that you're entering uncharted territory, which is *exactly* where you need to go if you and others want to enrich your workplace. Stick with it, and if you need to set a precedent by being the first person to open up, take a deep breath and do it.

Reality Check: SELF-IDENTITY

1 = very strongly disagree
2 = strongly disagree
3 = disagree
4 = neutral; neither disagree nor agree

5 = agree
6 = strongly agree
7 = very strongly agree

_____ Differences are viewed as something that people can learn and benefit from, rather than something that must be "dealt with."

_____ The workplace makes the most of people's unique know-how and skills.

_____ Individuals are comfortable letting their unique styles shine through.

_____ People can spend at least part of their time on activities that match their deepest interests.

_____ There's respect for the fact that even in this era of teams, people sometimes need their own space.

_____ = Total ÷ 5 = _____ = SELF-IDENTITY RATING

Chapter 22

Fit

Jane calls them the good old days. Fifteen years ago, when she started working on the production line at a furniture plant, the company was relatively small. She knew exactly how her job fit into the greater scheme of things, and she liked that; it gave her a sense of belonging. But the company got bigger, doubling in size over 10 years, and doubling again in the past five years. Jane was moved around a few times to new jobs, and she now describes her current role as "somewhere in the middle of production. I'm not sure where I fit in, to tell the truth." The personality of the company also has changed. It used to have more of a family feel, she says, but now it's all business.

Having experienced so much growth over the years, the company where Jane works seems to be in sturdy financial shape. But the story reminds us that there's more to work than job security—much more. For Jane, what's important is fit, and it's seriously lacking in her work life.

> "I'm not sure where I fit in, to tell the truth."

Fit sounds simple enough. It's where the individual and the organization come together. But there's more to it than meets the eye because fit means such different things to different people. Some people are most concerned with how they fit into the overall workplace system that produces goods and services. Others go beyond the system and think in terms of mission; they want to be clear on how they fit into the workplace's overall purpose and direction. Still others need to feel that their individual values go hand in hand with the collective values of the organization. That's why fit is included as one of the me keys—it's such a personal proposition.

Jane's situation is a fairly classic example. It illustrates the "I'm just a number" phenomenon, in which she feels lost in a big production system. But even in a small organization, people can be confused over their fit. Or if they understand how they fit in the bigger picture, they might not like it. They might have ideas on how they could contribute more by being somewhere else in the workplace.

Because fit is so individualized and so inherently complex, it's not something most organizations pay much attention to—or even consider. But in a meaningful workplace, all three types of fit are carefully nurtured. It happens through ongoing dialogue and a willingness to take action, so people like Jane can find and maintain their own vision of a good fit without compromising workplace oneness.

MOLLY'S STORY

When Molly went to work for a research lab, it was somewhat unclear what she would be doing. There were several possibilities, and all of them sounded exciting.

Well, things couldn't have gone better. Her colleagues came to appreciate her command of the Russian language, and they asked her to translate a series of Russian research articles. She loved the work and even began taking articles home.

"My productivity was awesome," she recalls.

The Different Shapes and Sizes of Fit

The best way to understand the three types of fit is to hear about them from everyday people. The following statements have been lifted directly from the interviews and focus groups that made up the field research for this book.

SYSTEM FIT

Many people think of fit in an operational context. They want to see where they fit into the larger process or system. They want to know how their work contributes to whatever goods and services ultimately get produced. Here's what some had to say:

I feel like an insignificant part of a big machine.

I have no idea how my job helps to create the end product.

If I suddenly disappeared, the workplace would go on just fine without me.

Don't ask me to tell you how the whole system comes together.

The job I'm in doesn't make the most of my know-how and skills. I could contribute a lot more somewhere else in the system.

MISSION FIT

Others think of fit in terms of mission. They want to understand how what they do contributes to something bigger than the work itself, and how they're helping to create the future. Here are some direct quotes:

> How does that output end up making a difference in people's lives?

> *My job keeps me busy, but it just seems like a lot of motion—without a lot of purpose. There has to be more to work than just being busy.*

> *I understand how my daily work helps us to produce the final output, but what about outcomes? How does that output end up making a difference in people's lives?*

> *I could have a bigger impact if I worked elsewhere in the organization.*

> *We have goals, and I understand them. But I don't see how my everyday work helps us achieve them.*

VALUES FIT

People often sense a good fit when their own values go hand in hand with an organization's collective values. Jane brought this up when mentioning that her workplace had lost some of its "family feel." Informality, relationship building, and oneness are important to her—things that may have gotten lost as the company has gotten bigger. Here's what others had to say:

> *When I'm at work, I feel like I can't be myself.*

> *Implicit in our workplace is the notion that you have to "go along to get along." But for me, "going along" can be awfully difficult, and sometimes downright impossible.*

> *I sometimes find myself compromising my values because it just seems too difficult to take a stand when everyone else is doing things a different way.*

> *People here like to rush to decisions, but I'm the type who likes to analyze things and weigh all the options.*

> *I've always prided myself on keeping my promises, but that just doesn't seem to be important where I work. Promises are a dime a dozen.*

Charting Your Fit in the System

The preceding comments may have started you thinking about your own workplace situation, or about the feelings shared by some of your colleagues. It's easy to despair when fit is lacking, but there are practical ways to improve it. Perhaps the easiest and surest first step is to team up with colleagues to study the process or system that links all of you together.

Tape some butcher-block paper to a wall, or grab the nearest whiteboard, and create a flowchart—or if conventional flowcharting seems too formal, simply draw a picture using whatever icons seem to work at the moment. Sketch out your work process from start to finish, showing what happens at each step. Be sure to include your suppliers and your customers somewhere in the drawing. Always keep in mind that the aim is not to create a textbook-quality flowchart, but to deepen your understanding of the big picture.

Next, mark the locations in the process where each of you does your work. You'll recall how Jane mentioned being "somewhere in the middle of production." Now is her chance to get clearer on where she fits in. This is a critically important step, so don't rush it along. If there's a consensus that the big picture is incomplete—that the process or system isn't fully understood—do the necessary homework to fill in the gaps. If you need to consult with people from other areas of the workplace, do so. Consider having them join you in the flow-charting effort.

> If you've ever been in a room filled with first-time flow-charters, you've heard the exclamations: "So that's what happens over there!"

If you've ever been in a room filled with first-time flow-charters, you've heard the exclamations: "So that's what happens over there!" "Now I know where my work goes!" "I knew it had to fit together somehow!" The process, when done thoroughly, can lead to all sorts of discoveries related to operational fit. But that's only the half of it. Take the conversation to the next logical step, and people will start to pinpoint all sorts of improvement opportunities.

For instance, a person might realize that those marginally useful weekly sales summaries he cranks out each week would become golden if he routinely consulted with the people on the receiving end to find out what *they* needed. Another person might discover that her work as a maintenance scheduler really is essential in keeping the equipment up and running, but that she could have an even bigger impact by working with production to establish wiser priorities for maintenance jobs. In this way, the exercise becomes more than just figuring out how people fit in the larger system. It points the way to fit-enhancing changes that people can implement right away.

Analyzing Your Mission Fit

The second kind of fit, having to do with a person's connection to the larger purpose and direction of the organization, calls to mind the mission keys (Chapters 3–6).

No surprise there. In a meaningful workplace, people share a belief that their work is about more than just work. They're connected not only in the operational sense, but also by an underlying purpose that's more about making a difference, and less about making products or services. People also share a well-focused view of the future they want to create, and they're guided along by a set of down-to-earth goals. All this makes it easier for individuals to see how their day-to-day work fits into the bigger mission picture.

As a companion to the operational analysis explained earlier, consider exploring a few mission-related questions. To enrich the process, make this a group conversation. Others may see your role and contribution in ways that are entirely new to you.

Who's on the receiving end of the work you do? In other words, who are your direct customers? This question, lifted directly from Chapter 3, seems pretty fundamental to the notion of purpose. But perhaps because it *is* so fundamental, it often gets neglected. Develop a clear answer, or risk hobbling the rest of the analysis.

How do your customers benefit from your work? There's a big difference between products and services—and the benefits they provide customers. A person who buys a car is really purchasing mobility, convenience, independence, and access to opportunities (among other things). The patient at a hospital isn't there to get injections and other treatments, but to get healthy. What benefits do you and your work provide?

KATHY'S STORY

Kathy was in the business of helping people to help themselves. Working for a government agency, she put unemployed residents in touch with local training opportunities. A number of her clients went on to build their skills and become a part of the workforce.

That was the great part. The awful part had to do with working in a massive system in which she and her colleagues felt like numbers. Everything seemed so . . . homogenous.

When it started to kill her spirit, she bolted. In her new job, Kathy still serves people, but she does it in an entirely entrepreneurial way: She's an independent real-estate agent.

When your customers benefit from your work, who else benefits? It won't take deep reflection to figure out some answers. The car buyer might use those new wheels to drive her children to school, and that just-released patient might be eager to get back to her fledgling business with its new employees. What about your situation? Who are all those potential "secondary customers" who implicitly count on you?

Given your answers, how does the work you do contribute to a larger purpose? This question gets to the heart of fit as it relates to purpose.

How are you and your colleagues trying to shape the future? And what kinds of practical goals have you and others established to pursue this vision on a day-to-day basis? Your answer sets the stage for the next question.

How does the work you do help bring reality closer to your vision? This question gets to the heart of fit as it relates to direction.

What can you do to be more mission-driven? This concluding question might be the most important one of all. Say you discover that three-fourths of your time directly relates to the mission while the remaining quarter is spent going through the motions on meaningless tasks. This might explain why the fit just doesn't seem right—and be the nudge you need to start retooling what you do and how you do it.

> One of the most coura-geous things you can do is identify yourself, know who you are, what you believe in, and where you want to go.
> —Sheila Murray Bethel

What Do You Value?

In the opening story, Jane mentioned the personality of her workplace. It had changed dramatically over the years, apparently in response to all that growth. When she started working there, it was a warm, friendly place—almost like an extended family. Now, it's a business in the most bottom-line sense of the term. What used to be important no longer seems of much concern to people. The wide-open communications, the deep commitment to respect, an appreciation for the individual, a willingness to work at bringing everyone together—all those things have gotten pushed to the wayside in the rush to grow.

For Jane, obviously, there's more to fit than a connection to the operational big picture or even to the underlying purpose and direction. A lot of it has to do with values. Her own values are often at odds with the organization's newly emerging way of doing things. The result is a feeling of unease. In the long term, something or someone has to give.

Webster has some interesting things to say about "value." One meaning states that value is *worth in usefulness or importance to the possessor*. In other words, something can "have value." The other definition describes it as *a principle, standard, or quality regarded as worthwhile or desirable*. This is what we mean when we talk about a "set of values." Inherent in both of these definitions, and the couple of others you'll find in the dictionary, is the notion of worth. When people feel out of step with an organization's collective values, they start questioning the worth of their workplace, their own self-worth, or both. "I don't seem to fit in. Is it me, or is it my workplace?" (Worth is so important to a meaningful workplace that it's one of the 22 meaning keys. You'll read all about it in Chapter 24.)

What about you? When it comes to values, what's important to you above all else? Is it integrity, honesty, openness, respect? There are so many possibilities, many of which are articulated in the various meaning keys. You probably spend 40 hours a week in the workplace. That's 36 percent of your waking hours. What kind of workplace would be worth so much of your valuable time?

Values Assessment

These questions about values aren't meant to be rhetorical. Gather some of your colleagues together, and have them describe in detail the values they think should be guiding people's actions in the workplace. Write these down on the left side of a sheet of paper or whiteboard. As the conversation unfolds, push for specifics. Instead of simply writing "respect," for instance, explain in a sentence or two exactly how people think respect should look and feel in the workplace. This can take plenty of time, but it's guaranteed to deepen everyone's understanding. It can even bring people closer together as the Janes of the world realize that others in the workplace feel the same way they do about certain values.

MARK'S STORY

Mark thought he had found his dream job when he became director of an executive education program at a local college. But things quickly soured as different priorities emerged.

Key leaders at the college had cash-cow visions of the program. Mark had no problem with generating revenue, but as he saw it, the obsession with profit was distorting all decisions. Certain courses were heavily promoted while others were sidelined—not because of their inherent merit, but because of their income potential.

"The money-making never seemed like enough," Mark says. "I decided that these people just wanted all the money they could get." The different perspectives never came together, and Mark eventually resigned.

> The rich dialogue will seem like hard work at times, but it will lead to a much fuller understanding of what's happening in the workplace.

Next, think about the current situation. What do people seem to be holding up each day as their most important "principles, standards, and qualities"? This is a real-world reality check. What collective values are reflected in people's daily actions? Record these on the right side of the paper, and as you go, expect a vigorous sharing of ideas. People are likely to have very different interpretations of the same situation. The rich dialogue will seem like hard work at times, but again, it will lead to a much fuller understanding of what's happening in the workplace—which can provide important clues to why people may or may not feel like they fit in.

Once you have two full sets of information, step back and take a comparative look. If there's a very close match between your ideal and your current reality, bask in the knowledge that yours is a rare workplace indeed. If you find some major left-and-right mismatches, continue the dialogue. Dig deep to understand what's happening beneath the surface. *Why* is there a gap between the values people want and the values that seem to be emerging from their actions? And based on these insights, what can we do about it?

Strictly Personal

If you don't feel comfortable organizing a group conversation, or if you prefer to keep this to yourself for the time being, you can do the preceding analysis on your own. In fact, you can do it right now by grabbing the nearest piece of blank paper. Just remember to act on your insights.

Focus on one value that's important to you and seems to be sorely lacking in the organization. Then determine one or two simple things you can do right away to become a model for the value you hold so high. For example, if we're talking about honesty, reject the old tradition of keeping information away from "competing" divisions within the organization. In fact, instead of waiting for someone to request the info, take the initiative and start sharing it now, tradition be damned. It's that simple—and that difficult.

A SET OF CORE VALUES

Many organizations have developed their own sets of "core values," just as many have committed to paper their mission statements and vision statements. There's nothing wrong with putting ideas on paper, but all too often, the process gets dumbed down into a two-hour exercise in group writing. The list of values then gets enshrined in a wall-hanging somewhere, and people promptly return to their old way of doing business. In this way, the list itself becomes not only the output, but also the outcome.

Core values *can* make a difference, and they *can* enhance fit by enabling people to create the kind of workplace that embodies what is truly important to them—but only if people commit to the values in their hearts and minds first, and then on paper. This requires nothing less than widespread involvement, open and ongoing dialogue, and a willingness to reach a collective understanding that's more meaningful than any one perspective.

Reality Check: FIT

1 = very strongly disagree
2 = strongly disagree
3 = disagree
4 = neutral; neither disagree nor agree

5 = agree
6 = strongly agree
7 = very strongly agree

_____ People understand how their work fits into the larger operational system. They also understand how what they do as an individual, or as a team, helps create something bigger than the work itself.

_____ Individuals feel connected to workplace goals and other direction-setting elements. They feel that some of their work brings the workplace closer to its desired future, even if it's in small ways.

_____ People believe that they're in roles that make the most of their unique knowledge, strengths, experience, styles, and interests.

_____ There seems to be a good fit between the unique values people bring to the workplace and the collective values that come to life each working day.

_____ = Total ÷ 5 = _____ = FIT RATING

Turning Values into Action

In a market crowded with Internet service providers, MindSpring stands out. Surveys routinely put the company at or near the top—like the 1999 J.D. Power and Associates study that ranked MindSpring No. 1 in overall customer satisfaction. The people who work there attribute much of this success to an intense focus on their set of core values and beliefs—208 simple words full of serious commitments to customers, shareholders, and each other.

These values are highlighted at their Web site, featured in brochures, cited in press releases, and mentioned in their recorded phone greeting. The people of MindSpring even issue a values challenge: "If we don't seem to be living up to them, call us on it!"

MindSpring Core Values & Beliefs
- We respect the individual, and believe that individuals who are treated with respect and given responsibility respond by giving their best.
- We require complete honesty and integrity in everything we do.
- We make commitments with care, and then live up to them. In all things, we do what we say we are going to do.
- Work is an important part of life, and it should be fun. Being a good businessperson does not mean being stuffy and boring.
- We are frugal. We guard and conserve the company's resources with at least the same vigilance that we would use to guard and conserve our own personal resources.
- We insist on giving our best effort in everything we undertake. Furthermore, we see a huge difference between "good mistakes" (best effort, bad result) and "bad mistakes" (sloppiness or lack of effort).
- Clarity in understanding our mission, our goals, and what we expect from each other is critical to our success.
- We are believers in the Golden Rule. In all our dealings we will strive to be friendly and courteous, as well as fair and compassionate.
- We feel a sense of urgency on any matters related to our customers. We own problems and we are always responsive. We are customer-driven.

Postscript: In February 2000, MindSpring merged with EarthLink—and the new organization has fully adopted these core values and beliefs.

Chapter 23

Balance

Linda got a degree in biology because of her deep interest in the life sciences. She now works in a research lab "getting paid for doing stuff I love with people I love," as she puts it. But her job is turning into too much of a good thing. The typical workday begins at 7 A.M. and ends 11 hours later. There's weekend work at least twice a month, and when grant applications or other deadlines come due, it's not unusual for folks to be at the lab until midnight. It used to be pure excitement for Linda, especially when she got out of college. But as a mother of a two-year-old, and with a second child on the way, priorities have dramatically changed. "The work I do is so fulfilling, but that in itself is no longer enough," she says.

While "fit" is where the individual and the organization come together, balance goes one step further. It's where our work lives come together with the rest of our lives. This key, like the other me keys, is very personal. All of us have our own ideal balance, and in fact, this ideal changes at different stages in our lives. Linda's situation illustrates this so well. Even though she loves her job, the field, and the lab, she's still not fulfilled. Her new role as a parent has changed the whole equation.

> Her job is turning into too much of a good thing.

Because balance is such a unique proposition, it can be difficult to achieve—especially when a handful of high-level decision makers obsessively pursue efficiency, standardization, and control. Some organizations seem to have a moderate, one-size-fits-all amount of work for everyone. Other places impose an impossible workload that wreaks havoc with activities and relationships outside work. Also common are workplace cultures that seem to honor excessive

> The person who arrives for work each day is not just an "employee"—he or she is also a spouse, a parent, a grandparent, a neighbor, a friend.

work, so even when people are free to take their own actions to rebalance their lives, they feel pressured to do otherwise.

In a meaningful workplace, there's a deep appreciation for balance. Everyone respects the fact that the person who arrives for work each day is not just an "employee"—he or she is also a spouse, a parent, a grandparent, a neighbor, a friend. There's also an understanding that balance means different things to different people. It's seen not so much as a *condition* but as an *activity*. With flexibility (Chapter 10), ownership (Chapter 11), and support (Chapter 14), people are able to create the balance that works best for them—while staying true to the mission of the overall organization and the immediate work area.

Checking the Scales

Perhaps you're thinking about balance from a very personal perspective. You feel as though your own situation is out of kilter, and you're eager to do something about it. Or maybe you're thinking about other people in your workplace. Perhaps it seems as if *their* lives are out of balance, and you'd like to do what you can to help. Or it could be that all these need some major balance adjustments.

Whatever angle you're taking, start with the one person whose balance hits closest to home: you. Even if you feel as though the scales are looking pretty good at this point in your life, a closer look might make things a little better. At the very least, it will sensitize you to some of the concerns and challenges other people might be facing.

You can get started in a remarkably simple way. Sit down with a very close friend or significant other for a conversation about the state of balance in your life. If you have children and they're old enough, involve them as well. Put aside your own perspective for the time being, and ask them what *they* think. A few well-placed questions should do the trick: Are work-related matters getting in the way at home? If so, in what ways? When it comes to work, what kinds of patterns have become a part of your life? Are these good or bad? If they're bad, why—and what can you do about them? Keep your ears and mind wide open to the responses.

There's nothing like a sincere reality check from the people who are closest to you. If there's any imbalance in your life, they're in the best position to let you know. The challenge is to move beyond conversation and figure out what to do about the situation. If the imbalance has been months or even years in the making, it's probably ingrained in your own personal culture—and we all know how easy it is to change the culture!

You certainly won't solve this in an evening. Continue to talk about it, perhaps involve others in the conversations (like a trusted colleague), ponder it, sleep on it, talk some more. But try to do *something* to move toward the kind of balance that's right for you and all the other people in your life. Even a simple promise—"I'll keep my evening work to just one hour at the most"—can be a leap in the right direction.

Making It a Collective Concern

Linda mentioned having these kinds of conversations years earlier with her husband, back when they were talking about starting a family. The simple dialogue made balance an increasing priority for her, and it even prompted her to cut back significantly on the amount of lab paperwork she brought home. But it didn't go far enough. The work hours kept getting out of control, despite her best efforts to cut them back.

Her story underscores the labored artificiality of separating our work life from the rest of our life. Think about it: Where does one end and the other begin? Surely our thoughts of home don't end when we get to work, and we certainly bring work concerns back home. *Where* we are might change, but *who* we are remains constant. All this is to say that engaging in dialogue with a close friend or significant other is a good start—but it's just a start. It's imperative to make balance an ongoing topic for dialogue among your colleagues. They're an integral part of the system in which you live, which means that they're critical to your efforts to pursue balance for yourself and others.

> Surely our thoughts of home don't end when we get to work, and we certainly bring work concerns back home.

If you have to make it an informal chat in the break room, do it. But if it can be something a bit more structured, such as an hour or two of focused conversation, all the better. And if this can be an ongoing dialogue, better still. Remember, balance is an *activity* more than it is a static condition. It calls for constant attention and active pursuit. Surely a workplace conversation—or better yet, a series of conversations—would be a big help to Linda. The process is likely to unfold in three phases:

Disclosure

What about all the other people who work in the lab? Do they too feel that their lives are out of balance, or are they content to log those long hours? Linda needs to nudge open the conversation, using herself as an example to get things going. It would be interesting to know if some of her colleagues have gone through any big life transitions lately, such as the birth of a child, a marriage, a divorce, the purchase of a new home, and so forth. These personal milestones will have a huge impact on their views of balance.

> I still find each day too short for all the thoughts I want to think, all the walks I want to take, all the books I want to read, and all the friends I want to see.
>
> —John Burrough

Help from Colleagues

At a certain point, people will start looking for ways to help each other. Someone might offer to do some of Linda's paperwork for her; another might volunteer to take over the grant-writing responsibilities. And the issue of balance will be squarely on the table.

Collective Improvement

If the conversation is given enough time, or if folks come together again and pick up where they left off, people may start finding ways to achieve greater synergy—to work more closely as a team, and less as a loose confederacy. Instead of just one person offering to take over Linda's paperwork responsibilities, more people will put their heads together. The likely outcome won't be just temporary relief for Linda, but process improvements that lead to long-term benefits for more people.

Keep Talking, Listening, and Learning

Can all this good stuff happen with simple conversation? Well, not just one conversation—but certainly in a series of get-togethers in which people are able to listen with wide-open minds. In fact, rich workplace dialogue is the single most important factor for Linda and anyone else who wants to make balance a true workplace strength, regardless of how individualized it happens to be. Keep in mind that you don't have to be in Linda's exact shoes to initiate things. If you're a manager, company owner, or agency director who values balance, encourage people to get together and start talking.

You also might want to broaden people's thinking, including your own, by organizing a series of learning lunches on work–life issues. In the past few years, more attention has been paid to this notion of balance, and chances are you can find some outstanding speakers within easy driving distance of your workplace. Some may even be willing to share their expertise and facilitate a conversation for free. To start your search, call a chamber of commerce, a library, a speaker's bureau, or a business association.

As for topics, they can vary widely, so the best approach is to ask people what they want to learn about. Consider conducting a brief and informal focus group, or circulating a simple survey, to uncover ideas. Just three possibilities include time management, dealing with stress, and conflict resolution. Even family issues—including heavies like how to deal with the death of a parent or how to plan for your children's college education—can be a big draw and spark plenty of conversation, even though the topics don't relate directly to the workplace.

Role Modeling Gone Awry

Perhaps you can't really relate to Linda's problem. Maybe you work excessive hours just as she does, and you're perfectly happy doing so.

> There's nothing wrong with long hours, but are you setting a workplace standard that other people are struggling to meet?

There's nothing wrong with long hours, especially if you're engaging your deep interests. But here's the question: Are you setting a workplace standard that other people are struggling to meet? Take a fresh look at what happens when the regular quitting time rolls around. If folks are staying behind, it *is* possible that they have your same penchant for long work days, especially when everyone is gripped by an exciting project. But then again, people might be operating under some kind of real or perceived pressure to do exactly what you're doing.

If it's the latter, do something about it. State in unmistakable terms—to individuals and to the group—that there's no expectation for everyone to work those same hours. Explain why it works for you (assuming it does!), and show that you understand why it may not work for others. If you find yourself working late and folks are still around—especially ones whom you know have plenty of responsibilities awaiting them at home—a diplomatic "why don't you worry about that tomorrow" might be in order.

MATTHEW'S STORY
It was a Thursday evening at about 9:30 P.M. when Matthew realized that for four evenings straight he had dug into his briefcase and spent a few hours doing work from the office. Everything else had gotten shoved aside, including his family.

But on that particular Thursday, Matthew resolved to do something different. He packed his briefcase, snapped it shut, and made a promise: In the future, he would spend no more than two evenings per week doing work, and each time, he would spend no more than two hours.

He knew it wouldn't be easy; he had gotten into the habit, and it seemed that he *needed* to work the extra hours. But too many other important—some would even say *more* important—things in his life were getting neglected.

You can even conduct your own experiment to see what it feels like to leave the workplace at the official closing time. And if you still feel a nagging desire to work overtime, perhaps you can do it at a library or home or wherever your colleagues won't be around. Whatever you do, don't promote your long hours as the workplace daily requirement.

Bringing Respect to Balance

Organizations let people take their work home with them, so why not let people bring some of their home to work? It's going to happen anyway: "My father is in the hospital." "I have to call my mortgage company." "The teacher at my child's school wants to talk." "Our babysitter canceled at the last minute." This is life. It's also a golden opportunity to show that a workplace values balance not just in words but in actions.

People should have the time and space they need to address these situations with dignity. Most workplaces can include a separate phone-equipped room or area where anyone can go to take care of personal business. It's a small way to send a clear message that the workplace respects more than just hard work. And it lets people address their pressing concerns in five private minutes instead of worrying about it for eight hours.

This same kind of respect extends to the enforcement of workplace rules when family and other personal issues appear to interfere with someone's work. A rush to judgment is seldom warranted, and worse, it destroys an opportunity to strengthen the work–life balance.

If a prompt employee starts showing up late for work, for instance, open a line of communication to understand what's really going on. The parent who drives his children to school might explain that classes begin a full 30 minutes later this year—so getting to work on time has become darn near impossible. And it just so happens that five other people at the company, all of whom drive their children to school, are facing the same time crunch. This is hardly the time to quote chapter and verse from the policy manual. Perhaps the parents can get together to talk about car-pooling. Maybe it makes sense to flex work schedules so the six parents can get to work a half-hour later.

Some Closing Thoughts

The introduction to this book began with a quote from Henry David Thoreau. He made the point that it isn't enough simply to be busy. *What are we busy about?*

It's a question relevant to work and workplaces in general, but it has a special connection to the meaning key of balance. E-mail, voice mail, cell phones, Palm Pilots—they all conspire to make us busier. Even the nature of today's work—the fact that it's more about knowledge and thinking, which keep going long after we exit the physical workplace—makes balance much more difficult to achieve.

There are many ideas spelled out in this chapter, but don't neglect the small things that just might be the big things. Make a conscious effort every now and then *not* to multitask. Learn how to say no without really saying no. ("I can't help, but I'll be more than happy to find someone who can.") Learn how to say no—period. Finish projects before starting new ones. Honestly evaluate your work habits, and ditch the ones that don't add value. Try to keep things in perspective, and identify what's really important in your life. And finally, set aside time for tending to your own mind and spirit.

Reality Check: BALANCE

1 = very strongly disagree
2 = strongly disagree
3 = disagree
4 = neutral; neither disagree nor agree

5 = agree
6 = strongly agree
7 = very strongly agree

_____ People at all levels of the organization respect the fact that there's life beyond work.

_____ Individuals can reshape their jobs, take on different responsibilities, or make other adjustments aimed at helping them find a good work–life balance.

_____ People can take work home if they want to, but they don't feel guilty if they choose otherwise. There are no impossible tradeoffs between work and family.

_____ It's understood and accepted that being human means bringing life-related issues and problems to the workplace. Colleagues are empathetic and supportive.

_____ People generally feel that there's a good balance between their work lives and the rest of their lives.

_____ = Total ÷ 5 = _____ = BALANCE RATING

Worth

Michael calls it the "cog factor." At the urban transit company where he works, people are like parts to a big machine. They're expected to punch in, do their work, and punch out—and nothing more. Rarely is anyone asked for input. Contact with management is usually over things like work rules, grievances, and problems. At least, that's the way Michael sees it. He freely admits that he has lost all perspective ever since getting a new supervisor. Before, as an operations analyst, he was involved in making decisions regarding route and maintenance schedules. He was interested in the work, it fully tapped his brainpower, and he knew he was making a difference. Now, the new supervisor has no interest in involving anyone in any of the decisions; he makes them all himself. Michael has been relegated to a computer terminal, where he spends nearly all of his day monitoring the on-screen comings and goings of the company's buses.

Not once does he use the word, but it's easy to see that Michael's story is fundamentally about worth. His intelligence has been disregarded, he feels diminished in his importance to the organization, and his self-esteem is in free fall. Complicating things is the absence of a single underlying cause that would lend itself to a relatively quick fix.

> Where Michael works, people are like parts to a big machine.

Nothing is more personal—or important—than an individual's sense of worth. In fact, because worth is held so deep within, it can even be hard to talk about. Sometimes the best way to reach it is by exploring a few admittedly emotion-laden questions: Do you get the sense that your colleagues truly value who you are and what you bring? Do people believe that what you do in the workplace really matters? Do *you* believe it matters? In a meaningful workplace, the answer to all three questions is a resounding yes. Each person knows that he or she is an important part of the whole.

The Link to Other Meaning Keys

In reading the opening story, you may have found yourself thinking about many other meaning keys. A person's sense of worth heavily depends on the presence of certain keys. Here are the ones that have the biggest impact:

Purpose, Validation (Mission Keys)

Respect, Equality, Ownership (People Keys)

Challenge, Invention, Personal Development (Development Keys)

Dialogue, Service, Acknowledgment, Oneness (Community Keys)

Self-Identity (Me Keys)

Want to see for yourself? Let's rewind the tape and take a second look at Michael's situation—this time in the context of those 13 keys.

> To have that sense of one's intrinsic worth which constitutes self-respect is potentially to have everything.
> —JOAN DIDION

Michael calls it the "cog factor." At the urban transit company where he works, people are like parts to a big machine. They're expected to punch in, do their work, and punch out (challenge). Rarely is anyone asked for input (respect, ownership, dialogue, service). Contact with management is usually over things like work rules, grievances, and problems (equality, dialogue, oneness). At least, that's the way Michael sees it. He freely admits that he has lost all perspective ever since getting a new supervisor. Before, as an operations analyst, he was involved in making decisions regarding route and maintenance schedules (ownership). He was interested in the work (self-identity), it fully tapped his brainpower (self-identity, invention), and he knew he was making a difference (purpose, validation, service, acknowledgment). Now, the new supervisor has no interest in involving anyone in any of the decisions; he makes them all himself (respect, equality, ownership). Michael has been relegated to a computer terminal (challenge, oneness), where he spends nearly all of his day monitoring the on-screen comings and goings of the company's buses (personal development).

Worth-Building Possibilities

What this means is that any effort to increase a sense of worth—within yourself or with your colleagues—calls for a deeper understanding of these other meaning keys. So what about it? Of the 13 listed, which one or two have the biggest impact on *your* self-worth? To what degree are the other keys thriving or lacking in your workplace? And what can you do to work on them? Here are some possibilities.

FLEX YOUR STRENGTHS

People will learn what you can contribute only if you tell them or if they see you in action. So unless your colleagues are unusually telepathic, you're going to have to take the initiative. Perhaps your desktop-publishing skills have never been tapped, even though some diplomatic maneuvering on your part could turn up opportunities. Well, start maneuvering, perhaps beginning with a conversation involving some of your colleagues to let them know of your skills and interests. What other skills of yours have gone underground? Zero in on one (for starters) that relates to your current work, and start using it now. Are there any upcoming projects that offer a perfect match for your deep interests? If so, again, start strategizing and making your move.

DO IT BETTER

Think about what you do that no one else can do, and then ask yourself: What steps can you take to do it even better? Perhaps there's a workshop you'd like to attend that's guaranteed to sharpen your skills. Or you know that a new piece of equipment would make all the difference. Or you've heard about a new technique that you've been too busy to try. Set your sights on some kind of improvement, then start to make it happen.

> Ninety percent of the world's woe comes from people not knowing themselves, their abilities, their frailties, and even their real virtues. Most of us go almost all the way through life as complete strangers to ourselves.
> —SYDNEY J. HARRIS

THRILL YOUR CUSTOMERS

What would your internal customers like to get from you in the way of improved quality, response time, courtesy, communication, and so forth? This can be so simple: Perhaps you're a bit sluggish returning calls from colleagues, even when they need critical information from you. An appropriate goal on your part might be to shave the callback time to an absolute max of two hours. Or the challenge could be bigger: The reports you help produce come back at least a third of the time with data errors, and you know all too well that the process needs a major overhaul. If you can't seem to think like one of your internal customers, go and ask them directly.

REACH OUT TO MORE CUSTOMERS

Try to extend your service reach to even more people. In other words, look for ways to have more internal customers. Sure, this might increase your workload, but it doesn't have to. Perhaps your job has you compiling weekly industry summaries that report on the competition. Is there any way to put that useful information into more hands? Maybe you sometimes serve as an in-house trainer on issues relating to teamwork and meeting effectiveness. Are there any work units that would benefit? Consider approaching them and offering to share your know-how.

KEEP SCORE

Make a point of tracking your accomplishments. Consider devoting 15 minutes at the end of each workweek to taking stock of what happened and how you made a positive difference. Get in touch with an internal customer or two for their feedback. If you've received letters, e-mails, phone calls, or survey data from customers during the week, review all of it thoughtfully. The information might trigger an insight or realization that prompts you to reach out to an internal or external customer, or it might be the nudge you need to overhaul some aspect of your work.

GIVE WHAT YOU WANT TO GET

A lot of the keys that feed into worth are of the reciprocal variety. Respect, for example—when you give it, it often comes back to you. It's the same with dialogue, acknowledgment, and self-identity. So making these keys a workplace priority offers a great win–win opportunity, and everyone's sense of worth will ultimately be the better for it. It can be so simple. With acknowledgment, for example, even a five-second comment can make a difference. "Martha, I'd be lost without you. I'm so glad we work together." Don't assume people know you recognize their contribution. Let them know, and do it often.

Working on Worth Together

So far we've been talking about what the individual can do, but worth building can also be a group effort. One approach is to have a very informal process, with conversations held in a lunchroom or break room. Or it can be something a bit more formal. If you're a manager, you're in an especially good position to make this happen—but certain credentials are by no means necessary. What's important is that people bring a willingness to replace their hand-wringing with thorough analysis and positive action.

A good place to start any conversation about worth is by focusing on those 13 worth-impacting meaning keys: purpose, validation, respect, equality, ownership, invention, challenge, personal development, dialogue, service, acknowledgment, oneness, and self-identity. Which of these are most important to people? Are these keys thriving in the workplace, seriously lacking, or somewhere in between? Use the answers to figure out the most targeted thing you and your colleagues can do to enrich people's sense of worth.

Perhaps a group effort won't work for one reason or another, but there's a Michael in your midst, and you want to help out in a one-on-one way. Consider starting an ongoing conversation based on these three questions: What unique know-how, skills, interests, and

---

SALLY'S STORY

In the early 1980s, Sally was working as a claims adjuster for an insurance company. She had been doing the job for years. So when the company started getting serious about integrating computers into the business, she jumped.

"Computers had been just a hobby for me," says Sally, "but I saw a chance to take one of my strengths and make the most of it." She ended up serving on a planning team, then she became the team leader, and today she's deeply involved in the company's information-systems activities.

Her salary has doubled, but the impact on her sense of worth has been even greater. "As soon as I got involved in this, I could feel life coming back into me," she says.

qualities do you bring to the organization? What do you do that no one else can do? And who depends on you in the workplace? You don't have to pose these questions directly, of course; you can simply have the concepts in mind as you gently guide the dialogue. But these questions go straight to the notion of personal value, and they're likely to put at least a temporary wind in someone's sails—perhaps long enough for them to start examining their situation more deeply and figuring out ways to make it better.

Don't Wait for Others to Change

You might be doing some of your own hand-wringing as you read this chapter. Here we are talking about meaning keys, action ideas, group efforts—about everything except Michael's supervisor. What gives? Isn't the supervisor the problem? Doesn't *he* need to change?

The answer is yes, he *does* need to change. But let's give this some context. For years, people in many workplaces have been labeled "resources" and "assets," terms that have a distinctly dehumanizing ring. Emphasis has been on making the best use of hands, on *doing the work*. We've made a habit of dealing with organizational complexity by moving around the parts, and usually, the parts include people. People have been separated into "thinkers" and "doers."

It's tempting to urge Michael's supervisor, and the many people like him, to see the light, to get with it, to get trained, to visit another company, or to do something, anything that might benefit people's sense of worth. But let's be honest with ourselves. This might bring about change on the surface, but only for a while. That old way of thinking and doing is almost certain to return.

So it all comes back to Michael, his colleagues, and those meaning keys that have such a big influence on worth: purpose, validation, respect, equality, ownership, challenge, invention, personal development, dialogue, service, acknowledgment, oneness, and self-identity. What small yet significant things can be done to start creating a workplace where some of these keys are thriving, or at least showing signs of life? Maybe one or two of these keys are near and dear to the supervisor's own heart. What a great place to start.

Reality Check: WORTH

1 = very strongly disagree   5 = agree

2 = strongly disagree   6 = strongly agree

3 = disagree   7 = very strongly agree

4 = neutral; neither disagree nor agree

_____ There's a feeling widely shared that each person, regardless of title or formal position, is important to the organization.

_____ People are paid what they're worth.

_____ There seems to be a workplace understanding that worth isn't just about monetary compensation—that each person has his or her own sense of self-worth that goes deeper than dollars.

_____ There's a genuine appreciation for the creative powers that people bring to their jobs.

_____ People have plenty of opportunities to exert their intelligence as the workday unfolds.

_____ = Total ÷ 5 = _____ = WORTH RATING

What's More Important, People or Profits?

John Neubert could be the poster boy for high energy. He spent one of his teen years painting not one, not two, but six houses. The bucks rolled in, and he figured he could start a painting business. First came college, but after getting an MBA, he put business and paint together and launched Neubert Painting in 1975.

True to his energy level, Neubert operated with one guiding principle: grow, grow, grow. The company racked up sales and received awards for its rapid climb in the Cleveland market. But they started to pay a price.

With the number of work sites increasing, Neubert's micro-management tendencies had him stretched too thin. The lack of basic management systems made things worse. Tempers started to flare. Neubert took a hard look at himself and made some painful discoveries. "I thought I knew it all, but I realized that I was part of the problem," he says.

Determined to turn things around, he invited everyone in the company to a first-ever off-site retreat. With the help of an outside facilitator, they talked about things like mission, vision, and values. And they made some startling discoveries. For years, Neubert and everyone else had been obsessed with growth and profit. Now that they had finally taken the time to step away and really think about it, they became convinced that the *people* making up the company had to be the top priority—followed by customers, and then by profit.

This seismic shifting of priorities has completely redefined Neubert Painting. The company now has a model training program, involves all employees in ongoing conversations regarding their mission, and sets expectations together in the form of consensus-based working agreements. Off-site retreats have become an annual tradition.

The results? Measures of employee satisfaction and fulfillment have shown a significant and steady climb over the past five years. Sales have increased 75 percent. And Neubert himself, once the meddling micro-manager, is spending much less time at work sites. "On the latest survey, 95 percent of my colleagues say I'm approachable. That's quite an increase," he says with a laugh.

His advice? "Know yourself, be honest with yourself, and be willing to change."

PART SEVEN

WORKPLACE TRANSFORMATION

Crafting an Action Plan

Enthusiasm can only be aroused by two things: first, an ideal which takes the imagination by storm—and second, a definite, intelligible plan for carrying that ideal into practice.

—ARNOLD TOYNBEE

You probably knew it the moment you picked up this book, and if you didn't then, you know it now: Creating a meaningful workplace is a full-time challenge.

For one thing, you're dealing with 22 meaning keys—as opposed to five easy steps or one magical formula. You're also trying to effect change, and we all know that the status quo has remarkable inertia. And last but certainly not least, you're dealing with a large system that's made up of many people, processes, structures, and so forth. Even small workplaces are complex systems. Rarely do one or two actions, no matter how positive, bring about profound and lasting change.

That's not to say that a single action here or there won't make a difference. It can make a tremendous difference, especially if positive change has been slow in coming to your workplace. In fact, as you went through the previous 22 chapters, you probably took some of the action ideas and made them happen in your workplace right away. If so, you might already be experiencing the benefits.

> Rarely do one or two actions, no matter how positive, bring about profound and lasting change.

But workplace *transformation* requires a more extensive, coordinated effort. That's where an action plan can prove to be at least useful, and perhaps even vital. The title of this chapter refers to an action plan, and sure enough, you'll learn how to create one as the next few pages unfold. But we're talking about a very expanded definition of the word *plan*. This stuff goes so much deeper than traditional planning. It's all about making promises and commitments about things that relate to your most important principles and values—and *not* about creating yet another to-do list.

Of course, not everyone is a planner. You might even be inclined to skip this chapter altogether. Please don't! In fact, if you tend to do things on the fly, this chapter may be even more important for you than for the avid planner, whose mind automatically sets priorities and timetables. With 22 meaning keys and a multitude of possible action ideas, you could find yourself with an almost overwhelming array of choices. The pages ahead will help you find those "significant few" actions that can make all the difference.

Who Does the Planning?

The planning process can be a solo undertaking, but given the complexity of change and the systemic nature of our organizations, it makes sense to involve some of your colleagues. Perhaps you've already done so, teaming up with them to learn about the keys. If so, stick together, and strive to get more folks working on it as the months unfold.

> When was honey ever made with one bee in a hive?
>
> —Thomas Hood

If you've been reading and learning entirely on your own, now is a good time to consider whom else you can involve. Every situation is unique, and for good reasons, you might prefer to keep doing things on your own, at least for now. But unless your reasons are very persuasive, try to turn this into a collective effort. Even partnering with just one or two other people could be a big step in the right direction.

A collective approach might require a bit of backtracking. Those who are entirely new to this meaningful workplace stuff will want some time to read, learn, and talk about it. Some may even want to conduct their own assessments using the 22 "reality checks" that appear throughout the book. And of course, once you start building the action plan together, it will take more time to reach a consensus on what to do.

The upside, however, can far outweigh any possible negatives. For one— and this is enormously significant—you'll get people envisioning a new kind of workplace. You'll also benefit from the extra brainpower, which can't help but result in a better action plan. And when it comes to ownership, there's no question that a plan developed in genuine partnership with your colleagues is guaranteed to get their active support.

Refocusing on Your Vision

Before we get into the detailed work of building a plan, let's press the pause button and think big. You may have started doing this in Chapter 1, which posed a few probing questions. Here's one of them:

> Within my area of influence, I would like to see the workplace transform from an environment in which _____ into an environment in which _____.

Perhaps you can recall exactly what you were thinking at the start of the book, when you were asked to fill in the blanks. But the second part of the statement—where you describe what your work environment *could* be—has probably taken on a much fuller meaning over the past twenty-three chapters. This is your vision, and the more vivid and compelling it is, the better.

> Live out of your imagination, not your history.
> —STEPHEN COVEY

This next prompt also might have a familiar ring:

> Thinking in very practical terms, here is what would be happening in my workplace if this transformation took place: _____.

Once again, take time to reflect: How *will* your workplace be different? What *will* it look like? With the meaning keys in mind, try to enrich your vision as much as possible. Be specific; make it less of a general direction and more of a particular destination. Take all the time you need, and if it would help you to write things down, by all means do so.

If you're doing this with your colleagues, these prompts should generate an interesting and exciting conversation. Whatever you do, don't rush it. This is an opportunity to co-create a picture of the future. You'll need plenty of time to develop a picture that's clear, compelling, and deeply held in the hearts and minds of its co-creators.

Creating a Scorecard

Now that you've enriched the vision and brought it into clearer focus, it's important to do something similar with the current reality. That way, you'll have the two side by side, and you'll experience the full force of creative tension. This is powerful stuff, capable of informing your planning process and inspiring you along the way.

You'll recall the "reality checks" in the previous chapters—those one-page assessments for the 22 meaning keys. Now, you'll use this information to create a Meaningful Workplace Scorecard. The card and complete instructions are on pages 258-259.

If you're doing this with a group, take your time in looking at each reality check. Talk about the assessment items in detail, and then reach a consensus on the ratings for all 22 meaning keys. A deliberate process will deepen people's understanding of the keys and boost their confidence that the score-card does a good job of portraying the current reality.

Understanding Your Scorecard

When it's first created, the Meaningful Workplace Scorecard can generate some questions. Let me provide some answers. Be sure to talk about this information as a group if the development of the scorecard was a collective undertaking.

> Study without reflection is a waste of time; reflection without study is dangerous.
> —Confucius

The scorecard is divided into three zones. What exactly do they mean?

Going from left to right, the first one is the danger zone. If you have a point that's plotted in this zone—if your rating for a key set (mission, community, and so forth) or for an individual key is below 3 on the rating scale—you're looking at a red warning flag. It indicates that the key (or the entire set of keys) is lacking to such a degree that the situation is actively making the workplace less meaningful.

The opportunity zone on the far right of the scale is just the opposite. The keys plotted here are helping to make the workplace more meaningful.

The middle zone is labeled caution. Here's where you'll find keys and key sets that are neither helping nor hurting, as well as keys that sometimes make the workplace more or less meaningful, depending on the situation. Their impact is less than that of the keys in the other two zones.

What are the implications for action planning?

Generally speaking, you should approach keys in different ways based on where they're plotted on your scorecard.

The keys on the far right of the scale offer a wonderful opportunity to learn. Let's say dialogue, respect, and support are well to the right. *Why* have they become such workplace strengths? *Who* is doing what to make it happen? There's also a leverage opportunity: *How* can we take the lessons learned and apply them to meaning keys that show room for improvement?

Also consider the connections between keys. Dialogue feeds into many other keys—service, direction, invention, and relationship building, to name a few. If invention, say, is sorely lacking, perhaps efforts to strengthen it can begin with dialogue. Don't just celebrate these strong keys. Figure out ways to learn from them and use them to improve other keys.

> The middle zone, oddly enough, might be the riskiest of all. It doesn't make a clear case one way or the other, and because of that, we tend to neglect it.

Keys and key sets in the danger zone are crying out for help, and your action plan needs to address them. But if there's a lot on the far left of your scorecard scale, you'll need to be selective. Do one or two keys seem to be dragging down other keys? If so, focus on these main culprits. Is one of the low-rated keys deeply important to you? If so, you'll have no trouble taking action. Perhaps aim your efforts there.

The middle zone, oddly enough, might be the riskiest of all. It doesn't make a clear case one way or the other, and because of that, we tend to neglect it. This can cause all sorts of problems. We might fail to see that a certain meaning key is lacking just enough to wreak havoc with several other keys. We might miss the fact that one key, which is just slightly to the right on the scale, is actually a growing strength that holds great promise for the entire workplace. From an action standpoint, be sure to spend sufficient time thinking about the keys in this zone. Analyze the situation on a deeper level, and use the insights to shape part of your action plan.

As you look at the scorecard, you might find yourself trying to understand how you came up with certain key ratings. If so, don't hesitate to flip back to the reality checks to reacquaint yourself with all the assessment items used with each key.

My workplace situation is bleak. Nearly all the keys are in the danger zone. What can be done?

If the majority of your meaning keys are in the danger zone, things *are* bleak. Bleak, but not beyond hope. You need to make some progress as soon as possible, so it's especially important for you to identify a handful of actions that are small enough to be doable yet big enough to make a difference.

What's absolutely vital is that you maintain a steady pace. Once you've implemented one or two action ideas, renew your efforts with new initiatives,

Constancy of purpose is important in all efforts, but in this case, it's a make-or-break proposition.

perhaps trying to accomplish a bit more the second time around. Do this again and again, even (and especially) when you run into barriers. Constancy of purpose is important in all efforts, regardless of the situation. But in this case, it's a make-or-break proposition.

It's also essential not to compromise your vision of what can be, to submit to the despondence and frustration that can result when the vision seems so far from the current reality. This can happen gradually, without your even knowing it. Each day your vision gets a bit more out of focus, and eventually, the time comes when you've lost the vision entirely. What you see *is* what you get. If all you can see is the current situation, you're guaranteed to perpetuate it.

I face just the opposite situation. Nearly everything is in the opportunity zone. Can I put my feet up?

Okay, but only for a few minutes. You don't want to get caught in the trap of resting on your organizational laurels. Determine what can be done to ensure that the organization's strengths endure long into the future. Also, look at those key ratings in a comparative way. Is everything equally rosy, or do some keys still show room for improvement? Don't be misled by "good enough." Strive to make a good situation even better.

Finally, if your scorecard reflects ratings for just one work unit, region, or some other subset of the larger organization, perhaps you can diplomatically share your practices and learnings with people who work elsewhere in the system.

The ratings are all in the middle of the rating scale. What does this mean?

True to the name of this zone, be cautious. Take some time for additional reflection, scrutinizing each rating on your scorecard. Deepen your understanding. If necessary, revisit the individual assessment items in each reality check. Key by key, determine if your initial ratings still make sense. Additional analysis just might prompt you to move one or more of the ratings farther to the right or left on the scale.

Also, as with the keys in the opportunity zone, look at things through a comparative lens. You'll definitely find some keys that show room for improvement and others that are full of learning and leverage opportunities. As you do this, be sure to consider the fact that certain keys are "drivers" that greatly influence and help shape other keys. More on this shortly.

This scorecard is just a snapshot of the current reality. Doesn't it get out-dated the moment it's created?

It is, and it does. That's why you need to take another snapshot . . . and another . . . and another. Plan to assess the workplace all over again at regular intervals, maybe once every quarter or six months, using the same reality-check items. View the initial data as your baseline, and use the new ratings to track progress and determine where to focus your new round of activities. There's more on this in Chapter 26.

Setting the Stage for Planning

Here are several more questions, but these are ones that only you can answer. In doing so, you'll uncover important information that feeds right into your action plan.

WHICH KEYS ARE MOST IMPORTANT TO YOU?

Twenty-two is a lot, and surely not all the meaning keys will strike the same chord with you. Reflect on the full set of keys, and select up to five that have the biggest impact on *your* own personal sense of workplace fulfillment. In other words, which five (maximum) keys are your most important ingredients for a meaningful workplace? (In Chapter 2, you were prompted to take an early look at the 22 keys and pick out your top ones. You've read and learned a lot since then, so your feelings may have changed. Take some time at this point for a closer look to make sure you know your highest-priority keys.)

> Not all the meaning keys will strike the same chord with you. Select up to five that have the biggest impact on *your* own personal sense of workplace fulfillment.

If you're building an action plan with others, this part of the process is a great opportunity to learn more about your colleagues. Each person should describe his or her set of several high-priority keys. Ideally, have people explain why their top keys are so important to them. If they can add stories from their own experiences, all the better.

On the scorecard, you'll notice a column labeled "Personal Priorities." Place a checkmark in the appropriate rows to note these top-priority keys. It will be useful to have this information alongside the key ratings once the action-planning process gets under way.

Which Keys "Cause" Other Keys?

Some of the keys can be thought of as "drivers." Dialogue, for instance, can lead to support, service, relationship building, direction, challenge, invention, and more. Another meaning key, respect, can pave the way to service, support, self-identity, balance, equality, and worth. By comparison, worth doesn't feed into any of the other meaning keys. It's the result of many of the keys, but it's definitely not a driver. The same goes for balance.

This has big implications for action planning. If you want to strengthen worth, for example, you need to reflect on which keys feed into it. In fact, you need to do that with all the keys on which you plan to focus. That much is clear. Where it gets hazy is when you start trying to clarify exactly which keys are drivers and which are outcomes. There simply is no clear-cut, absolute answer. In fact, most of the keys are both drivers and outcomes to varying degrees. Equality, for example: respect feeds into equality, and equality feeds into worth. And relationship building: dialogue feeds into it, and service and support can result from it.

> Most of the keys are both drivers and outcomes to varying degrees.

On the scorecard, there's a column for this, and you'll find several checkmarks intended to highlight meaning keys that are arguably the most powerful drivers. But take time to think more about this, and if you're working with others, try to reach a consensus. Identify additional keys that also "cause" other keys, and record your findings with checkmarks. Remember, there's no such thing as a right answer. Simply strive to deepen your understanding of the relationships between keys.

Given Your New Insights, Where Do You Plan to Focus Your Efforts?

With so many keys and so many possibilities, it's tempting to set in motion an extremely wide range of actions. This lack of focus can result when many people are involved in the process, and they haven't reached a true consensus. Make sure that everyone agrees with the analysis and decisions that have been made thus far.

Perhaps you've focused your attention on a handful of specific keys from different sets—for instance, purpose, service, and respect. Or maybe you're zeroing in on one of the sets of keys, such as the community keys or mission keys. Or it could be that you're tightly focused and plan to concentrate all of your attention and effort on a single key. There are many possibilities. As you make these decisions, remain deeply aware of your vision (which you refocused early in this chapter) and the insights derived from the scorecard.

Time to Make Commitments

Now it's time to decide on and commit to a set of action ideas that will do the most to make your workplace more meaningful. This is an important step, to say the least. But you've done so much front-end work that it should be fairly straightforward. In fact, if you've been going through the book chapter by chapter, you probably have plenty of action ideas already in mind.

You can use the Action Plan Template on page 260 as you build your plan. It's intended as a model, and not as the only way to go about this. Photocopy the template and use it as is, or create your own chart, adding any additional fields of information you deem to be important. Groups should use a flipchart.

As you develop your action ideas and write them down, choose your words carefully. Avoid generalities and vague language. Be specific and action-oriented in your thinking, and reflect this in your phrasing. Tailor everything so it's a good fit for your workplace situation.

For instance, "communicate better" does convey action, but it's too broad. *How* do you plan to communicate better? Develop a specific answer and make *that* your intended action. Maybe you want to "show more respect for colleagues." Again, how? What exactly are you going to do to convey greater respect?

> If you don't have the power to change yourself, then nothing will change around you.
> —ANWAR SADAT

Note the column labeled "Keys." After writing down an action idea, use this space to record up to several meaning keys that stand to benefit the most if and when the idea is implemented. Also indicate when this action will be initiated. There are three time frames: immediate, next two weeks, and next four weeks.

SAMPLE ACTION IDEAS

Notice that in the following examples there's a mix of one-time actions (event-type activities) and ongoing actions (some of these are activities in the traditional sense, whereas others have more to do with changes in personal habits and attitudes).

> We must be the change we wish to see in the world.
> —Mahatma Gandhi

From an action plan developed by an individual:

(one time) *Create my own personal worth-building plan.*

(one time) *Involve all seven people in the work unit in our upcoming conversation regarding the purchase of new equipment.*

(ongoing) *Set aside at least one hour each week for nothing but wild thinking and invention.*

(one time) *Talk with colleagues at next Tuesday's meeting about starting weekly brown-bag sessions focused entirely on innovation.*

(ongoing) *Look for opportunities to provide my group-facilitation skills, not just in my own work unit, but in other areas throughout the region.*

From an action plan developed by a group:

(one time) *Redesign the employee directory to include information on people's expertise, skills, and interests.*

(one time) *At next week's work-unit meeting, start a conversation with colleagues regarding our deep interests, and see how we can match these with upcoming projects. Check whether they want to include this as a regular meeting topic.*

(ongoing) *Organize an ongoing series (quarterly?) of learning lunches to focus on work–life balance.*

(ongoing) *Learn several facilitation tools that can be used to foster constructive dialogue. Use them during meetings as a way of getting wider involvement, input, and ownership.*

Apply a Critical Eye to Your Plan

Once you've developed an action plan, step back and take a wide-angle look to see if it's as good as it can be. If there's room for improvement, now's the time to make it.

Is there a mix of one-time and ongoing activities? There should be. Those one-time actions set the stage for quick victories and immediate impact, whereas ongoing efforts ensure constancy of purpose—both of which are vitally important when building a meaningful workplace.

*Are **you** going to implement these actions?* The last thing you want is an action plan that tells *other* people what *they* need to do. Successful change is an inside-out proposition; it has to start with you. Of course, if the plan is developed by a group, not all the ideas will be implemented by everyone.

Is there enough in the plan to challenge you? If not, make additional commitments. If the plan seems overloaded, trim it down. If you're not sure, start implementing and see what happens. This is a work in progress, so you can easily make adjustments as you go.

Does it pass the doability test? We have to be realistic about hierarchy and control. Some people simply don't have the titles or authority that's needed in their workplaces to bring about certain changes. But don't let reality turn into resignation. Most everyone can exert considerable influence regardless of his or her formal position. The worst thing you can do is sell yourself short.

Are these actions going to make a difference? It sounds like a harsh question, but it needs to be asked. Your aim is to move the current reality closer to your vision of a meaningful workplace—and not simply to engage in activity. Take a critical second look at your action plan. If your action commitments seem to fall short in terms of likely impact, get busy throttling them up, or replace one or two of them with something that will have a bigger impact.

The Journey Continues

> The journey is the reward.
> —TAOIST SAYING

Perhaps your action plan is neatly put on paper. Maybe it's scribbled in a notepad, saved in your computer, or simply tucked away in your memory bank. Whatever the case, you've developed several significant ideas. Now it's a matter of making them happen.

The introduction to this book welcomed you to the "journey" of creating a meaningful workplace. You went on to learn, reflect, and discover. With a plan and the 22 keys now in hand, you're well-prepared for the *next* part of your journey.

The Meaningful Workplace Scorecard

This scorecard pulls together all the "reality check" assessment ratings. It provides a snapshot of your workplace in terms of the twenty-two meaning keys.

INSTRUCTIONS:

1. Go back to the reality checks, and gather the average ratings for all twenty-two meaning keys. (If you haven't completed the reality checks, do so now.)
2. The scorecard is essentially a graph. For each meaning key, plot the rating average as a single point on the graph.
3. Compute an overall average for each of the five key sets.
4. Plot all five key-set ratings.

EXAMPLE:

Purpose = 6
Direction = 2
Relevance = 2.5
Validation = 4   Mission Keys Rating* = 3.6

*This is simply an average of the ratings for all the keys in the set.

In the sample scorecard below, notice that the average for this key set is a single point on the first line, to the right of "Mission Keys." Following this are the ratings for each individual key. By plotting points, you can see exactly where they fall within the three "zones"—danger, caution, and opportunity.

Tip: You might want to photocopy the scorecard, so you can have a clean original for future use.

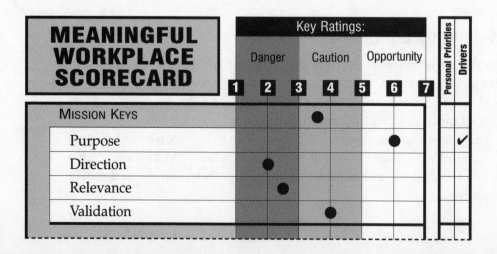

MEANINGFUL WORKPLACE SCORECARD	Key Ratings:							Personal Priorities	Drivers
	Danger			Caution		Opportunity			
	1	2	3	4	5	6	7		
MISSION KEYS				●					
Purpose						●			✓
Direction		●							
Relevance			●						
Validation				●					

| MEANINGFUL WORKPLACE SCORECARD | Key Ratings: | | | | | | | Personal Priorities | Drivers |
| | Danger | | Caution | | Opportunity | | | | |
	1	2	3	4	5	6	7		
MISSION KEYS									
Purpose									✔
Direction									
Relevance									
Validation									
PEOPLE KEYS									
Respect									✔
Equality									
Informality									
Flexibility									
Ownership									
DEVELOPMENT KEYS									
Challenge									✔
Invention									
Support									
Personal Development									
COMMUNITY KEYS									
Dialogue									✔
Relationship-Building									
Service									
Acknowledgment									
Oneness									
ME KEYS									
Self-Identity									✔
Fit									
Balance									
Worth									

ACTION PLAN TEMPLATE	Immediate	Next 2 Weeks	Next 4 Weeks	🔑 KEYS
OTHERS TO INVOLVE:				

Chapter 26

Building on
Your Progress

If we are facing in the right direction, all we have to do is keep on walking.
—ANCIENT BUDDHIST EXPRESSION

Too many initiatives—whether they're solo efforts, group endeavors, or whole-company undertakings—are approached like events. There's a surge of excitement, some serious planning, an earnest effort to make change happen, scattered signs of success, then a gradual decline in interest and action. Pretty soon everyone has moved on to other things, and it's business as usual.

A major change initiative should never, ever be viewed as an event. It's an ongoing process that needs to be nurtured as months and years go by. This clearly holds for all efforts to enrich your work environment. Building a meaningful workplace is the longest of long-term propositions.

That's why this chapter is so important. It provides the know-how you need to keep the process moving forward, whether you're doing it on your own, with a group, or as a whole organization. Take these tips and techniques to heart, and seek every opportunity to put them into practice.

> A major change initiative should never, ever be viewed as an event.

Close This Book and Take Action

My gosh, I didn't know this would be so difficult. After completing the action plan, two weeks went by and I didn't do a thing. My plan just sat there. Come to think of it, I don't even know where I put it.

> Nothing is worth more than this day.
> —JOHANN VON GOETHE

The toughest part of all this is simply getting started, and that's exactly what you need to do. Go back to your plan, decide on one action to implement, and make it happen as soon as possible. If you have to flip back to previous chapters for a quick refresher, go for it. You'll find plenty of things you can do immediately. Keep in mind that this book is just a catalyst for action and not the action itself.

If this approach seems too simplistic, do some cause analysis. Ask yourself *why* so much time has passed without any follow-through. Perhaps there's a project under way that has absorbed everyone's time, including your own. Okay, but can you turn that to an advantage? Is there a way to take one of your action ideas and somehow integrate it into the project? Or maybe it's a simple matter of inertia: You've been so occupied doing the routine stuff that your action plan full of new stuff got pushed to the side. If so, put your schedule under the microscope to find the wasted time—and yes, there *is* wasted time. Replace any worthless activities with time spent implementing one of your action ideas.

Be sure to keep your action plan in a prominent place. Tuck it into your appointment book, or post it on your computer so it pops up when you log on, or give it a visible home on your desk, or tape it to your workstation. You should see your plan each and every workday during the early stages of your effort. Even the most devoted change agents need a reminder every now and then.

> A vision without a task is but a dream; a task without a vision is drudgery; a vision with a task is the hope of the world.

Keep Your Vision in Focus

When I first opened this book, I was so into it. I read the whole thing and developed a fairly extensive action plan, and now I'm doing all I can to turn my action commitments into reality. But it seems like my initial passion and enthusiasm are dwindling. With an action plan in hand, I sometimes feel like this is just extra work. My efforts seem aimed primarily at checking things off my to-do list.

Remember, the plan is a *means* to an end. Each action in your plan is a *means* to an end. They're meant to help you achieve that vision of a meaningful workplace.

If you've gotten into a rut of mechanically checking things off your "meaningful workplace to-do list," you need to get back in touch with your vision. Consider returning to earlier sections of this book to immerse yourself in what a meaningful workplace is all about. Take time to reflect. If you jotted down any notes regarding the kind of workplace you're striving to create, by all means retrieve your writings. If you didn't write anything, perhaps you should do so now. A meaningful vision statement can serve as an inspiring foreword to your action plan.

To enrich this process, consider involving at least one of your colleagues. Ideally, make this a group dialogue. As "your" vision becomes "our" vision, people will begin taking action to create a meaningful workplace, not from the standpoint of compliance, but because of deep personal conviction and commitment. Things will start to happen not because they're part of a plan, but because they align with what is deeply held in hearts and minds throughout the workplace.

> Stay true to your vision while being honest about the current situation.

All this sounds so wonderful, but there's also an inevitable measure of frustration. It comes from the emotional tension we experience when seeing and feeling the distance between the current reality and our vision of what can be. There's an ever-present temptation to relax our vision—to move it closer to the present reality—because doing so gives us some quick relief. If this happens often enough, even a little bit at a time, it doesn't take long for our vision and the current reality to become one and the same. In effect, we surrender our vision, ending up back where we started.

Peter Senge, whose research and writings have developed the powerful concept of the learning organization, talks about this in detail in his book *The Fifth Discipline*. He distinguishes emotional tension (frustration, anxiety, hopelessness) from creative tension. As he explains in the book, creative tension "doesn't feel any particular way. It is the force that comes into play at the moment when we acknowledge a vision that is at odds with current reality . . . . If we fail to distinguish emotional tension from creative tension, we predispose ourselves to lowering our vision."

Your challenge, then, is to stay true to your vision while being honest about the current situation. And remember that none of this will happen by accident. It requires considerable care and feeding: periods of personal reflection, ongoing conversations with colleagues, occasional efforts to update your understanding of the current situation and to renew your vision. As you do this, you'll find that the creative tension becomes an active and very positive force, fueling your creativity and prompting a natural flow of actions aimed at building a meaningful workplace. Your action plan will be ever fresh as you fill it with new commitments to replace those that have been carried out.

Take Time to Celebrate

I've been working hard to turn my action plan into reality. In fact, I might be trying too hard. It's obvious that changing the workplace requires true constancy of purpose. You could call it a marathon, I suppose. I just don't know if I have the energy to keep it going.

You're right to think of this as an ongoing effort, but a marathon? If you attempt to keep going and going and going, this will soon seem more like garden-variety work, and a lot less like a mission. Even the most devoted, mission-focused change zealots take time to savor their successes. And that's what you need to do. When you make progress—say you've hosted the first-ever focus group with internal customers, or you've just taken a bold stand for equality in your workplace—do whatever feels natural to celebrate.

> Even the most devoted, mission-focused change zealots take time to savor their successes.

This can take many different forms, depending not only on your personal style, but also on the actions that are cause for celebration. Maybe you're the kind of person who would most enjoy a walk through the woods, where you can reflect in a very personal way on your achievement. Perhaps several people have been involved, and all of you decide to honor your success with a special lunch together.

Then again, the accomplishment might be of such a proportion that it calls for an out-and-out party. If a team has just redone the policy manual, cutting it from 200 rule-bound pages to a 5-pager that honors people's best judgment, I'd recommend something big. Why not throw a lunchtime party for everyone in the workplace, and use the occasion as your rollout?

Leverage the Heck out of Your Successes

I've been keeping all the promises I made in the action plan, and it's really making a difference. The biggest change has been in our work-unit meetings. Gone are the days when just one person (me!) dominated the conversation. We take turns facilitating, everyone has an equal opportunity to shape the dialogue, and at the end of each meeting we all develop the agenda for the next meeting. These sessions have become so much more productive. What's unfortunate is that all the other work units are still doing things the same old way. If we want to enrich the entire workplace, shouldn't these other work units be following suit?

If you're in a position to tell people what to do, it's so tempting to make this new approach for meetings the standard way of doing things. Write something up in a memo, or declare it at a staff meeting, and *voilà*—change has happened. Or has it?

You'd surely make efficient progress, but it would be progress through compliance, not commitment. And that "progress" would come at a high price. People might resist your efforts to control their meetings. Some might blatantly ignore the new approach while others might lash out in other ways. Even those who adopted the new approach could slip back to their old way of doing things, simply because that's what they "own," regardless of whether it's effective.

If change by decree has problems, so does the opposite approach. Some people figure that their new way of doing things will spread like wildfire, and everyone will eagerly adopt it as their own. "This is such a better approach to our meetings, who's *not* going to follow suit!" It's wishful thinking. A few scattered folks might take notice, but as far as widespread implementation is concerned, forget it.

A wise middle ground is to put the information out there and let people make their own decisions. Perhaps your organization has an intranet that includes a section on best practices. Write something and post it for all to see. Maybe everyone periodically gets together for all-company sessions. If so, get on the agenda to tell your success story. Even e-mail and traditional newsletters can be used to spread the word.

Regardless of how you let folks know, be sure to include plenty of details, so people who want to try your prized approach will have everything they need to get started. Include the names, phone numbers, and e-mail addresses of everyone who has helped make it happen. This will have the double benefit of providing recognition while letting others know whom to contact for more information.

Last but not least, provide evidence to indicate why this new approach is so wonderful. Let's say you're telling everyone about a recent series of customer focus groups. You'll capture plenty of attention if you can report, for instance, that customer input helped increase the rate of repeat business by 20 percent.

> ## The Power of Stories
>
> Simple stories can make quite an impression. In fact, their power to influence can outweigh even the best statistical case for change. Keep an eye out for all story opportunities.
>
> For example, if two chronically competitive divisions begin to show signs of true partnership, and the latest get-togethers have been downright fun and productive, put on your best public-relations hat and start spreading the word.

Think Involvement and Co-Creation

A workplace is a system, so it seems almost futile for someone to work alone in trying to make the workplace more meaningful. At least, that's the feeling I've been getting while developing the action plan and turning it into reality.

One person really *can* make a difference. In fact, even the most profound visions and sweeping changes get their start as tiny seeds in someone's mind. These individuals carefully nurture their ideas and help them germinate. But as your comment makes clear, rarely does anything flourish without wide involvement. Wilbur and Orville had a vision, and they were standing alone at Kitty Hawk. But it took many more people after that to work from their monumental start and turn it into today's airline industry.

Whether we're talking about high-flying invention or down-to-earth change in your workplace, the same applies. You need to do whatever you can to get more people involved. And you don't want to engage just their hands. True to the spirit of a meaningful workplace, you want to engage their hearts and minds. People should approach this through commitment and not compliance.

> I may be given credit for having blazed the trail, but when I look at the subsequent developments, I feel the credit is due to others rather than to myself.
> —Alexander Graham Bell

Involvement can be fostered on two levels. One way is to get more people more involved in developing specific action ideas. Rather than being innocent bystanders who have change done *to* them, they should be co-creators. You can also get people directly involved with the 22 meaning keys. The power of these keys lies partly in their tangibility. People can finally get their hands on a concept that has long eluded their grasp. And there's so much that can be done with these keys: learning, dialogue, visioning, assessment, planning, action. Even a simple series of conversations can make an enormous difference.

If you haven't already, why not organize one? Challenge individuals to identify their top several meaning keys, have them informally evaluate their workplace in terms of the keys, then listen as the conversation unfolds. Certain themes are likely to emerge, and through gentle facilitative guidance, a single vision will start coming into focus. Imagine the power of a single vision for a meaningful workplace, all tightly held by everyone in the organization.

The conversation can then move on to action possibilities. The group can even use the action-planning process spelled out in Chapter 25. You may already have a plan that you created on your own. As you carry out your commitments and look for new action ideas, this may be your big opportunity to widen involvement. It's never too late to turn your colleagues into partners, with all of you working together to create a meaningful workplace.

Of course, genuinely wanting to involve people is one thing, but getting involvement is something else entirely. If you're reading this book, you obviously have more than a passing interest in meaningful workplaces and how to create them. On the support scale, you're probably a champion, an advocate, or at least a passive supporter. As for your colleagues in the workplace, who knows how they feel? You probably have some champions, advocates, and passive supporters in your midst—along with a fair number of fence-sitters, skeptics, and active resisters.

Why would people resist the idea of enriching the workplace? The reasons abound. "It's too touchy-feely." "We should focus on the bottom line." "We're too busy." "It's too nebulous of a concept." "It doesn't relate to our real work." The preceding pages give you plenty of high-fiber ways to respond to all these comments. But we both know that a quick response is far from enough to turn skeptics into supporters. So what to do?

Here's what *not* to do. Don't appoint people to a "Meaningful Workplace Committee." Don't set up a meeting with the goal of group-writing a "Meaningful Workplace Vision Statement." Don't require everyone—champions and active resisters and everyone in between—to attend an all-day workshop on developing a meaningful workplace. In fact, don't mandate anything even remotely connected to this concept of meaningful workplaces. Mandates are inherently counter to the freedom and ownership that we've been talking about since page 1.

That leaves you with the simple stuff. Get together with a trusted workplace friend and share a copy of this book. Talk about it. At an upcoming get-together with colleagues, mention the twenty-two meaning keys. Offer to circulate a few photocopied pages from this book. Organize a general conversation around the topic of meaningful workplaces. Keep things loose, letting the dialogue meander wherever people want to take it. Your aim at this point is simply to stir interest.

When the time seems right, nudge things along and foster active involvement. Perhaps there's someone who

> ## A Virtual Community
> At www.22Keys.com, you can post questions, gather more information, and even tell the world about your change-related struggles and successes. This electronic gathering place is open to everyone, but it has been designed especially for readers of *22 Keys to Creating a Meaningful Workplace.*

> Adopt the pace of nature, her secret is patience.
> —RALPH WALDO EMERSON

would like to team up with you to update the action plan. Or someone else might be eager to try something on his or her own. Maybe your loose dialogue group seems to be bonding into a team, and they want to set up a regular schedule for ongoing conversations. These are slow but sure developments, all of them in the right direction.

But what about those fence-sitters, skeptics, and active resisters? Forget about any overnight conversions that turn naysayers into champions. The best you can hope for is a steady evolution, with resisters becoming skeptics, then fence-sitters, then passive supporters, and so forth. It really is that gradual. To hold the vision of a meaningful workplace, a person needs deep understanding, and understanding is partly a function of time. You can't speed up the clock's hands, no matter how noble your intentions.

> The best you can hope for is a steady evolution, with resisters becoming skeptics, then fence-sitters, then passive supporters, and so forth.

What you *can* do is leverage your success stories so everyone can see that these efforts to enrich the workplace really do make a difference. Continue to circulate any useful information—even passing around a copy of this book might pique someone's interest. Keep an open invitation to all dialogue sessions related to meaningful workplaces.

And if you get the right opportunity with people you consider to be skeptics or critics, consider asking them why. They probably have some legitimate issues—perhaps they've just been on a team whose recommendations ended up on the shelf, or maybe they're tired of "programs" that come and go, or they might believe deep down that the status quo is here to stay. By engaging them in a conversation where you do more listening than talking, you'll certainly gain insights—and it just might happen that the skeptic will become a fence-sitter, or the fence-sitter will become a passive supporter. At least you'll have started a dialogue.

Learn from Your Missteps (Real and Perceived)

I tried to organize a dialogue session about purpose, and my colleagues looked at me as though I were crazy. Then I called several customers to start strengthening our communication link, and without exception, each one made it seem like my call was more of an interruption than anything else. Then I got busy trying to create a worth-building plan like you explain in the book, and I just couldn't seem to get in the right frame of mind. Is this supposed to happen?

First of all, you're assuming that something really did go wrong. Maybe it did, and maybe it didn't. Think about it: If you pull folks together for a conversation about purpose, and they've never talked about such a thing, how *should* they respond? Expect the get-together to feel a bit uncomfortable at first. This has nothing to do with you. It's the same with those phone calls to customers. If they seemed surprised by your call, perhaps they're simply not used to hearing from you. Don't overreact by ditching the idea entirely.

Failure is often self-inflicted. It occurs not because of what happens when we try something, but in how we respond when something appears to go wrong. If you toss up your hands and walk away, sure, you've failed. But if you take time to analyze what happened, why it happened, and what that means for your future actions, you've turned things around. You've transformed failure into learning, and you've set the stage for success down the road.

The most important part of all this is deciding what to do next. Perhaps you can take the old idea, reshape it based on your snap analysis of what happened, and try it again. For instance, it might be that your calls to customers were all placed in the morning—their busiest time of the day. So call them in the late afternoon. Say you've tried to create a worth-building plan, but it just doesn't seem to be coming together. Instead of scrapping the whole idea, consider pairing up with someone, with each of you building your own plan and maintaining an ongoing dialogue along the way. Having a partner might make all the difference.

The alternative, not to be taken lightly, is to abandon an action idea altogether. If you believe that's the right choice, be sure you commit to another action that will help you achieve the same intended outcome. And of course, incorporate into your implementation all the lessons you learned from the previous attempt.

Keep an Eye on Key Indicators

Perhaps this is a style thing, but I need to see measurable progress whenever I'm involved in a change effort. And by that I don't mean just a gut feeling that I'm making progress. It would be great to have a set of indicators that are used periodically to assess the overall situation.

> Everyone gets their rough day. No one gets a free ride. Today so far, I had a good day. I got a dial tone.
>
> —RODNEY DANGERFIELD

You *should* have a set of indicators, and in fact you do. The Meaningful Workplace Scorecard is an excellent tool for keeping track of overall progress.

The Meaningful Workplace Scorecard is an excellent tool for keeping track of overall progress.

You've already established a set of baseline readings on all 22 meaning keys. Conduct the same assessment on a regular basis—say, once every quarter or six months.

By doing this, you'll get a quick refresher course on the meaning keys and a gentle reminder of the big picture. You'll see where progress has been made and get hints on where to focus your new round of efforts. No, the assessment tool in this book isn't a statistically complex device that requires hours of computer processing time. The concepts it measures are too qualitative to allow for crisp measurement. But it's excellent for taking a snapshot of the current reality, and that's just what you need.

Look for ways to get more people's eyes on the measures. What about using the scorecard as a survey tool, either with an office, a work unit, a plant, or the organization as a whole? I've used it that way myself, and it works great. But there are three important caveats: Everyone (not just managers) should be able to complete a survey, everyone should see all the results and have an opportunity to engage in dialogue about them, and everyone should have the freedom and tools and support needed to take action based on the findings.

Renew Your Effort with New Actions

Perhaps I'm just not trying hard enough. I've been doing lots of things to make my workplace more meaningful, but nothing seems to change.

It might take weeks and months of effort before anything seems to register. But it registers only because of all that preceding effort. Stick with it.

Of course, there's a difference between sticking with it and banging your head against the wall. You might want to go back to Chapter 25 and re-evaluate your action plan, perhaps with your colleagues. Take a fresh look at the ratings on your scorecard, paying special attention to the keys that are important to others. It could be that the actions you're pursuing simply don't resonate with the folks around you. While you're at the scorecard, revisit this notion of "drivers." Some of the keys are more powerful in that they feed into other keys. Explore ways to focus on these.

Then use your new analysis to make a midcourse adjustment. This book is a rich reference source for determining new action possibilities. Revise your plan, and start making it happen all over again.

Meanwhile, try to incorporate some of the recommendations that have been spelled out in this chapter, especially those on holding fast to your vision, getting others to join you in your efforts, learning from your real and perceived missteps, and using the scorecard on an ongoing basis to pinpoint areas that are ripe for new action.

Make It Your Natural Way of Doing Business

There has been so much talk about action plans. I can appreciate the need for one early on, but am I supposed to maintain an up-to-date plan for the rest of my life?!

The answer is no. As a matter of fact, if you're still crafting action plans two or three years from now, it's a sign that your workplace has become meaningful only on paper. What *should* happen is that you start taking action automatically, naturally, without explicitly thinking about it. You might flip through this book every now and then in search of a new action idea, but for the most part, you and your colleagues will have made this your new way of doing things.

That is part of the vision. For now, you need to maintain an active and up-to-date plan. As you turn your commitments into reality, take on new challenges. Keep an eye on the scorecard for guidance, proactively involve others, learn every step of the way, and celebrate and leverage all of your successes.

But where, you might be asking, will you find the time?

In his wonderful guide to personal excellence, *The 7 Habits of Highly Effective People*, Stephen Covey shares an exquisitely simple and powerful time-management matrix. It's made up of four quadrants, each a function of two factors: importance and urgency. He helps us realize that so much of our time is spent on activities that are important and urgent (Quadrant I) and those that are not important but urgent (Quadrant III). This latter category is especially insidious. Urgency can make things seem important even when they're not—like the report you absolutely must finish in 30 minutes even though no one's going to read it until next week. And of course, activities that are neither important nor urgent add no value whatsoever (Quadrant IV).

> We must use time wisely and forever realize that the time is always ripe to do right.
> —NELSON MANDELA

Covey challenges us to spend more time in Quadrant II, where our actions are important but not urgent. This is where we nurture our vision, build relationships, engage in dialogue, prevent problems, pursue new opportunities, develop plans, restore our energy, celebrate our success, learn from it all—in other words, where we do what it takes to build a meaningful workplace.

Initially, you can get more time for Quadrant II activities by grabbing some minutes or hours from Quadrants III and IV. But it's going to require some real exertion. For starters, you need to scrutinize how you use your time during the typical workday. What exactly are you doing, and is it really important? This can turn up some painful revelations. ("You mean to tell me not a single person reads my reports?") Then there's courage and persistence. You'll need plenty of both if you're going to do things differently. Eventually, your efforts in Quadrant II will reduce the crises and fire-fighting that characterize Quadrant I, so you'll have even more time to enrich your workplace.

Continue to Learn about the Keys

The concepts that are embodied in the meaning keys are extraordinarily rich and complex. A person could spend a lifetime learning about them.

You're right. In fact, now is an excellent time to decide how you plan to continue your own learning. Here are five possibilities:

- Select several keys that interest you the most, then research what's out there on the Internet, in print, at conferences, and elsewhere.
- Organize a series of informal dialogue sessions in your workplace, each focused on a separate meaning key or set of keys.
- Schedule monthly or bimonthly lunch-and-learns.
- Pay a visit to another organization where some of the meaning keys are thriving.
- Start communicating with people throughout the world who are using the 22 meaning keys in their organizations and lives. Turn to the next page for details.

An Invitation
from the Author

Here we are, on the last page, and I find myself wanting to go on and on about the 22 meaning keys. But we both know that there's plenty of work to be done. The journey of a thousand miles really does begin with a single step, and that step is awfully hard to take when your nose is stuck in a book. So I'll be brief.

It seems to me that we can learn a lot from each other during the coming months and years, as we go about putting the meaning keys to work. But we can learn together only if we stick together. So I've created a Web site just for that purpose:

www.22Keys.com

The site is designed to pick up where this book leaves off. It can serve as our virtual meeting place for talking, listening, learning, asking, coaching, and brainstorming. You'll find stories, tools, message boards, and more—all of it relating to the 22 meaning keys. Quite literally, we can use this Web site to create a community of people from all over the world.

It's an exciting prospect, and I hope you'll stop by soon. In the meantime, best wishes for a fulfilling journey as you strive to make your workplace more meaningful!

Tom

E-mail: *TomTerez@aol.com*

Index